10 GOOD MINUTES
IN THE LIBRARY

MARK S. CARLTON

po23coach@yahoo.com

DEDICATION

It's February 25, 2014, and Harold Ramis has just passed away. He was an actor, writer, and director. His fingerprints were on some of the classic films I grew up with, including Caddyshack, Ghostbusters, Groundhog Day, Stripes and the cult film Animal House. As my wife sat on the couch and read about his death last night, an eerie look came over her face. There was even a little liquid in the eyeballs. Ramis died from a disease called autoimmune inflammatory vasculitis, he was 69. To put this in layman's terms, it's when your immune system starts attacking your blood vessels thinking they're the enemy. This is the same condition that my wife has. They bulk you up with a variety of drugs; my wife usually gets the prednisone, which to this point has worked pretty well. She has been in remission for several years now. Enough said.

Besides dedicating this book to my wife (who has probably heard most of these stories at least once), I would like to acknowledge my friend, coworker for years, and the guy who made the worst days a little bit better with his sarcasm, wit, and big Irish smile; Mike "KEGGER" Lawlor. I'm not sure who gave him his nickname or what it symbolized. The fact that he could drink a keg of beer and it looked as if he swallowed one were both on the radar. We worked together for about 15 years as police officers. He was a friend and companion and the funniest guy I've ever known. Don't tell me about comedians who stand in front of a mirror and practice all day and have cue cards with applause signs overhead. Give me the person who can make a joke or tell a story off the cuff that would have you in tears in 30 seconds. That was Kegger. He could find something to laugh about in any situation. He made fun of himself, life, your dog, your cat, everything. You were having a bad day? Not when Kegger was around. Had a fight with your girlfriend or wife? He made fun of it. Somebody said something stupid on the police radio? Kegger was all over it. I still have the last words he ever spoke to me on my voicemail, some things you just can't erase. We used to eat a lot of dinners together and his go-to line was always, "Damn, eating like I got two assholes." He never called the bathroom the bathroom. He was either going to "hit the head" or spend some time "in the library". Kegger was a happy drunk for years, but it soon became a problem that he had to get help for. Partying all night and not being able to make it into work caught up to him like it will for most. He got called one morning when he no showed for a 7:50 a.m. roll call. "Mike, you're late for work." "I know - I'm on the bridge, there's a lot of traffic, must be an accident." "Mike...I'm calling your house phone." Silence. He was on his way home after a bender one night and basically fell asleep behind the wheel while on the highway. He awoke to the radio and the traffic reporter advising of a car that was disabled in the right-hand lane on the Hutchinson River Parkway. As he shook the cobwebs out of his head, he said, "I think that's me." He had an infectious laugh that made my dimples hurt at times. He told me about his checklist that was always on his mind after a night of drinking. First thing you have to do after waking up is go through the five steps: #1.Where is my gun? #2. Are there any bullets missing? #3. Where is my shield and ID card? #4. Where is my car? #5. Are there any dents? After that you would listen to your cell phone and check to see if there was anything else you missed. Kegger should have been a standup comic - he was that funny. We were talking one day as we dressed in the locker room and Mike was putting on his bullet proof vest, "I get a kick out of some of these guys – if it's too hot out, they won't wear the vest? You either wear it every day or ya don't." His wife was a registered nurse at a local hospital and he was home with his two children on a typical afternoon. He could have been watching a Mets game or, like most guys, trying to fix something around the house that the wife had been bugging him about for the last six months. While his kids played and argued over some stupid toy on the floor, Mike leaned back in his favorite chair, looking forward to the bottom of the seventh inning. His kids were really good looking; a little Irish, a little Filipino. He had given up alcohol and was now settled into a good routine. Married, making dinner, and going to Home Depot on the weekends. Somebody had asked him one time if he was going to meetings. "I don't need to go to meetings, I need to give up the booze!" He drifted off to sleep and when he woke up he stared at his kids and realized he could not remember their names. He sat there staring at them.....nothing. He told me, "It was weird. I know they're my kids, they're making a mess of the house and have Cheerios everywhere, but I could not put names on their faces." After a couple of doctor visits the word was not good. There was a tumor that was affecting a portion of his brain. He showed me the scan one afternoon. As he took what looked like an x-ray out of a manila envelope, I stared at the realization of what I was seeing. The film was divided into cross sections of tiny little squares. "See that, section 35 and 36, that's what's fucking me up!" It never got any better, even after surgery. They take away the car keys next and start doing clinical studies in an attempt to prolong your life. In time, his voice became a little slower and softer. He told me how he was going to miss his family, that stupid game called golf, and all the fun we use to have in the locker room at headquarters. Kegger and I drank a lot of coffee together. We would park our cars so that both driver side doors were next to each other. We would bullshit over the last call, talk shop and help each other out with the crossword puzzle in The Daily News. He would sit in his car as we anguished over 27 down and 13 across. "What's the name of that city in India with the Taj Mahal?" "Agra." "What's a six-letter word for friend?" "Kegger."

INTRODUCTION

The door to my parent's room opened and I could hear my father's footsteps as he plodded across the hallway and into the bathroom. The next question was whether he was going to stay awake or make that feeble attempt to fall back asleep. It was midafternoon and the five-hour nap was over. I could hear the faucet running and him splashing cold water on his face, the usual ritual whenever he worked a midnight shift. Then came the snorting and the blowing of the nose. There were a few rules in the house growing up that were never questioned or brought up for a second vote. When your father works from midnight until 8 a.m., the house must be quiet. We weren't even allowed to flush the toilet. Go outside and play and hope the Good Humor man doesn't come early ringing his bell.

Growing up I always felt like there was never enough money. When the rest of the kids were going back to school with new clothes, I was still wearing the high-water pants from last year and shirts that mom had sewn or patched up where the holes had been. Friends got new Pro-Keds and CONS and I got the $2.99 skips. Where did you go on vacation over the summer? Cape Cod, Disney, the Jersey Shore? No, our usual trip was to the Poconos to see my grandmother. Dinner was mom trying to do her best on a limited budget. There were meals like tuna noodle casserole, meatloaf again (even though we just had it a few days ago), well done pork chops (because that's the way Dad liked it), and - my personal favorite - breakfast for dinner. Sometimes mom would go all out and include pancakes, eggs, home fries, and burnt bacon (because that's the way Dad liked it). But there was always food on the table and if you didn't like it you could go hungry.

It was probably those evenings, sitting around the dinner table as a child, when I first thought about becoming a cop. Nobody had better stories than my dad. Today it's no longer a sexy job and I wonder why anybody would even think of putting on the badge. Each evening was different with a new tale and a new character. Before long I could picture the events and had a rolodex in my mind of the guys he worked with. They had tough guy names back then; names like Joe, Charlie, Steve, and even guys called Howie and Bernie that you wouldn't want to mess with. There was no sensitivity training and a class in sexual harassment would have been met with laughter. No cameras, no cell phone videos... if somebody didn't see it, well it just didn't happen. You did what the cop told you to do or you got a size 12 in the ass. It seemed like cops were having more fun than everybody else and getting paid to do it. Why wouldn't you want that job? My father let me use my imagination when it came to certain individuals. Each cop had his own vices and places he liked to frequent; in other words, some guys would hit up the meat market for steaks and others would be loading up the back of a squad car with Entenmanns baked goods. There were even landscaping plants and bushes that went missing from a nursery under a full moon one night. The cop suspected of taking them already had them in the ground around his new deck before the next day's shift. There was never a dull moment.

When the call was received at headquarters, it was just after one o'clock in the morning. A little disturbance in a bar and an officer was dispatched to handle the situation. The police officer walking the beat that night knew the establishment and most of the regulars that frequented it. As Dad told the story, it unfolded very slowly. I took another bite of the dried-out pork and tried to wash it down with some applesauce. I was hanging onto each word he uttered. The officer got the fight under control and headed back out onto the streets to check his post. Within minutes the problem in the bar flared up again, pushing and shoving and a few vulgarities that were not spoken at the dinner table. This cop, like so many others my father worked with, had his own way of doing things. When the cop walked back into the gin mill, he didn't say a word. He slowly walked to the far end of the bar and stepped behind it. He pulled his nightstick out and slammed it down on the oak countertop, immediately getting everyone's attention. The place went silent. He then walked the entire length of the bar, dragging the stick along with him. He knocked over drinks, bottles, and ashtrays, spilling them on the floor and on top of the bar. When he got to the end he calmly addressed the crowd, "The bar is now closed."

My birthday was earlier this week and turning 52 wasn't much different than turning 51. At this age, we all have arthritis and if I wake up and my back doesn't hurt it's a minor miracle. After finishing high school, I could have continued working or gone the safe route and found a college to kill another four years. I knew that would have been a waste of money and time because at 18 I couldn't separate my social life from my academic life. Spending over four years in the Air Force taught me some great life lessons. My first night in basic training, while standing in formation at midnight, I learned how to pick up my luggage. We had been traveling all day and I figured we were going to the barracks to finally get some sleep? The next words that were spoken were, "Put them down." "Pick them up." "Put them down." This went on for over an hour as we stood on the tarmac in 90 degree heat in San Antonio, Texas, listening to a drill sergeant yell at us. He told the group that our sisters were whores and our mothers hated us. "The best part of you ran down your father's leg." Some guys cracked right away, they weren't able to take direction and just deal with what they had signed up for. The service was a good career path, though I did get tired of wearing olive green.

After leaving the service reality hit me pretty hard; what the hell should I do now? I had sent out a good number of resumes to companies like Boeing, Lockheed Martin, and Northrop Grumman. I've got four years of experience fixing radios and communication systems on aircraft and nobody wanted me, not even an interview. I wound up at small regional airport just north of New York City where I became the ramp supervisor shortly after getting hired. How many people can say they parked Air Force One and dumped the lavatories on Pia Zadora's jet? After my second winter there, freezing my nuts off deicing aircraft, it was time to make a change. It was 1986 and not even all the free flights and partying that was going on could keep me around. I decided to start taking tests to become a cop.

You wake up one morning and 20 years have passed. I rolled out of bed and hit the button on the Keurig. The black coffee began dripping into the mug. I reached for the remote control and realized I still had no idea what channel SportsCenter was on. For the first time in 20 years I didn't have to put on a uniform, wear the shield, or carry a sidearm. 45 years old, retired and living on the west coast of Florida. It didn't last long. My next-door neighbor knocked on the door one morning and wanted to know if I was still thinking about getting a part time job at a golf course. I was still unpacking boxes and listening to the wife tell me what kind of area rugs and paint we should get. Some guy just got fired and I had an interview in one hour. Should I take a quick shower? It may sound strange, but whenever I had a shot at a job and could talk to somebody for ten minutes I've been hired. I began working at Palm Aire Country Club in Sarasota, Florida, doing everything from working in the cart barn, the pro shop, and even a couple of years in maintenance repairing greens and taking soil samples.

I've had a lot of nicknames over the course of my life; not sure if that's a good thing or bad thing. Can't remember somebody very well? Give him a nickname. Or maybe it was just that my first name didn't suit me? Whatever the case, if you have red hair in kindergarten you're going be teased and called "Redhead." Later, in junior high, it became "Captain" – I really can't remember why. When I got to the service somebody thought I looked like John McIntyre from M*A*S*H, so the latest label was "Trap." While working at the airport one afternoon, we were slammed with a few aircraft all landing within minutes of each other. They all had to be serviced, loaded with luggage and turned around for departure. We were shorthanded and I gave some quick direction as to what I needed everybody to do. Our usual fueler was standing by and said, "Man, you're like the "Coach" out here." Next thing I know the whole crew is calling me Coach. There have also been other names that my kids have given me, some that hang around longer than others. Kramer and Chucky seem to be their favorites right now.

The whole idea about writing this book came on an early morning with nothing to read while sitting on the throne. My wife had a number of magazines in the rack, stuff that most guys love reading like Women's Day, Cooking Light, and Real Simple. I looked at the Sudoku book and realized my hangover was in no mood to tackle calculus at eight in the morning. She's never afraid to remind me to turn on the fan – or that a courtesy flush would be appreciated. Hope you enjoy it.

CHAPTERS

THE END

CHAPTER 1

FLYING

It was sometime in late February or early March in 1986 and I was working at Westchester County Airport. I had become the evening ramp supervisor after a short six months there and was babysitting about 8-10 guys on each shift. We handled approximately 30 or so flights between 1 p.m. and whenever the last flight came in. Bags on, bags off, cleaning the aircraft on turn-arounds, filling the aircrafts with water, dumping the lavatories, parking aircraft and whatever else they could get a bunch of 20-year-olds to do on the cheap. The operation was fairly mundane, but there was always that one or two irate customers per day that got your attention. If you're going to scream and yell at the counter because of a delayed flight or bad weather, don't check any bags as they may not get there. One day I'm talking with two guys who worked the ticketing and security desks inside and the conversation soon turned to what everybody was doing for St. Patrick's Day. Let's face it, we're all Irish that day. Scott said that there was a party in Ithaca, NY but he didn't want to drive the four plus hours to get there. Scott had a scholarship up at Cornell University the year prior playing football, but didn't make the second year - ugly grades if I remember right. At this point Alan said I can get an airplane and fly us up there. Alan had been taking flying lessons for some time and had recently been VFR qualified. That means as long as it's clear outside he's good to go, he just hadn't been certified to fly with instruments-only yet. We started figuring out the logistics of the trip; how much fuel was going to cost, where we were going to be sleeping, and (most important) where we were drinking. After doing a little math and making sure we could all get a couple of days off, it was set. The three of us would fly from Westchester Airport to Ithaca the morning of St. Patrick's Day, spend the night and return the next day.

We met Alan early that morning as he went over the pre-flight checklist of the Cessna 172. He did the full walk-around; checking the tail section, kicking the tires and taking a fuel sample from the wing to test. The aircraft is a tiny four-seater with a single engine. Alan looked over the paperwork and told us that the weather in Ithaca was iffy at best; rain, fog and the chance of sleet as they predicted the temperature was going to fall throughout the day. We huddled around the aircraft talking about options, but really just trying to convince Alan he could do it. "Look, if it gets too bad we'll turn around and head back." Alan now had to convince himself. We had both seen him fly and felt confident in his abilities. After five minutes of conversation and a few more sips of my coffee, he unlocked the doors to the plane and it was game on. We're going to a party in Ithaca. Scott climbed into the back seat with his backpack and his 6'2" frame and 240 pounds of lean muscle. The plane was now a three-seater. So I'm in the front seat getting settled in and fastening my seat belt as our pilot is calling the tower to get clearance to taxi. It was right about then that I heard that noise coming from the rear.....*pssssst*. Was that a Bud Light? Scott had cracked the first one of the day and we weren't even cleared for takeoff. Alan just shook his head and I reminded him that there wasn't a bathroom on this flight. Our takeoff was smooth and we headed northwest as we climbed in altitude, Alan with his perfect part in his hair and headset on. Due to the lack of space in the aircraft, I got stuck with all the maps and charts on my lap. As we made our way towards the Hudson River I glanced over to my left and observed that Alan's door was closed but not securely latched. "Hey Alan, want to close your door?" We had been in the air for less than five minutes.

15

We joked and laughed for the better part of the next hour or so, going over the plans for the day and party that night. Scott had some friends who were picking us up at the airport so everything was coming together as planned. We were probably about a half hour or so from landing when the weather outside started getting nasty. The fog started rolling in and raindrops and sleet were hitting the windshield, even the wing was starting to accumulate some icy buildup. Not good. The tower at Ithaca radioed Alan about another aircraft off to our left, asking if he could see it. We couldn't see anything. We were flying in the clouds. We got permission to descend from 3000 feet to find some warmer air and get out of the soup. As we broke out around 1400 feet it was the first time I sensed a little panic in Alan. We could see the ground at this point, some farms and fields and an occasional barn. The tower was still squawking numbers and headings at Alan and I could tell that he and tower operations were not on the same page. So there I am with Scott in the rear on his third or fourth beer, looking very relaxed, and Mr. Pilot to my left, looking very tense. The act of finding an airport shouldn't be this hard. "Hey Alan, we're getting more ice on this wing over here." "I know, I know!" We were in a metal tube that's not much bigger than your standard couch. Ithaca tower continued to shout coordinates, numbers and information at us; some of the things I could understand, but I left the driving up to Alan. It was at this point that Alan turned and looked over his right shoulder at his rear passenger, "Scott, you went to school up here - where are we?" That's the laughter that we all needed to break the tension. With the tower now practically yelling at us for the whole world to hear, Alan was able to find runway 32 in Ithaca and make a perfect landing. We taxied towards the terminal and heard the bad news over the radio; Alan was to report directly to flight operations where I'm sure he was going to get grilled like a pig at a luau. After about ten minutes the beatings stopped and he came over to tell us that he was heading back to Westchester. We both looked at him and couldn't understand his reasoning. There was no talking to him at this point, he had made up his mind or somebody had made it up for him. Scott and I met up with two of his old college friends and we headed off to drink some green beer at a bar called The Pines in downtown Ithaca.

Later that night I remember carrying a keg up a flight of stairs to some house party and waking up the next morning to a house full of people and some banging in my head. The girl that was lying next to me was passed out and I didn't say goodbye. Alan had told us before he left that if the weather was good he would come back and pick us up. The skies were clear that morning and we headed home just before noon. There was little talk of what happened the previous day. You never forget that kind of adventure or what could have been. Just a little bit on the scary side when you can't find an airport. I don't know what ever happened to Scott or where he wound up in life; for all I know he may still be working at the airport. Alan continued to fly and got all his accreditations. He now lives in Las Vegas and flies with a major airline. He's the right guy for that job, but no longer has that perfect part in his hair.

I had only been working at Westchester County Airport for a few months when I had met Rob and Mike. They were both pilots flying for different carriers. Mike worked for a small airline and was dating a girl that worked with me. She was a reservationist with that girl next door smile and a killer body. Rob flew for a private company and he would often have a peculiar schedule. Two days on, four days off, six days on - it was always different. Rob had grown up living at Westchester Country Club but never had the cocky attitude like he was getting ready to christen his yacht, The Flying WASP. We had often thought about all three of us getting an apartment together, but we knew that wouldn't work. Three guys living in the same residence never works out. We talked about it at length one afternoon and then decided to take the plunge. I was being promoted to ramp supervisor and it was time to tell Mom and Dad the handyman was leaving their home. It was late summer of 1985 and we found a brand new home in North Tarrytown, NY that was set up as a duplex. The owners were going to be living downstairs and we had the second floor. Three bedrooms, two baths and on-street parking out front that sucked. One day you parked on the north side of the street, the next day the south side. I had started dating a girl from work who had old style family values and attempted to keep me in check at all costs. She had graduated from

Embry Riddle University and was no stranger to danger. She had some great jobs in college; a bikini model selling suntan lotion on Daytona Beach and lighting frost pots in the orange fields during winter so the trees didn't freeze. She had a little bit of a wild side to her also and disclosed how she and a couple of friends used to frequent dentist's offices for nitrous oxide. Getting those tanks into the back of your car at 2 a.m. was a little risky. I think the statute of limitations is over. I think she also had a trust issue when it came to our relationship. I was in the cockpit of a United 737 one night - once the cleaners finished up I would shut down the auxiliary power supply and close up the plane for the night. As the cleaners exited the aircraft, one of her best friends (a ticketing agent) came on board and retracted the stairs so nobody else could board the plane. She wanted to hook up right there in the left seat and I thought to myself *this is too good to be true, she's setting me up*. There was a restaurant at the tiny airport where we all spent our fair share of time and money assaulting our livers. It was a small company I worked for and a lot of us became very close; there was always a Days of Our Lives situation going on.

Rob and I woke up one morning and tried to figure out who was going to make coffee and who was going to take out the empties from the night before. I got the empties. We sat on the couch bullshitting for a while watching something on TV to pass the time. It was going to be a gorgeous day; clear skies and 75 degrees. I had nothing planned. Rob said he had access to an aircraft and thought we should fly over to Pennsylvania. He knew of this tiny remote airport over there with a turf runway. Situated right next to the airport was a driving range where we could hit some golf balls. "Let's go man." We drove over to our workplace and on the far side of the field was a small Cesena that Rob had the keys to. He did a quick preflight inspection and we were off. Golf bags were loaded into the back seat and Rob taxied to runway 11. We crossed over the Hudson River and headed west crossing into New Jersey and then into Pennsylvania. Rob looked at a map once just to get his bearings and before long we were on the ground. We tied the plane down and, just as Rob promised, there was a driving range right across the street. We were in the middle of the Poconos in PA. We grabbed our bags and went to the office to get some balls. It was about noontime when we were informed that the range was closed until the maintenance worker picked up the balls. He was driving a ball picker that had no protection so it was going to be at least an hour. The gentleman suggested we play golf down the street, he said there's a nice nine-hole course and they will even come and get you here at the airport. He made a call and five minutes later an older gentleman pulled up in a Ford Country Squire with the fake wood paneling on the side. What's better than hitting balls on the range? Playing an actual round of golf.

After nine holes we were thinking about playing some more but Rob had different ideas. It was midafternoon and we walked into the office where there was a small golf shop area and a place to get some food and beverages. I was starving. We ordered a couple of sandwiches and grabbed a few beers to take outside where we finished them on a picnic table. "You want another beer?" Rob asked. Twist my arm. He went back inside and after ten minutes he still hadn't returned. Where the hell is this guy? The can? I walked back to the bar area and there's Rob doing shots as he was talking with a pretty hot bartender. Rob did a couple of more shots while I was there and it was beginning to get a little uncomfortable. Look, I'm all up for a party but somebody has to fly us home. I was trying to convince him it was time to go. I found the guy who had brought us over from the airport and asked him if he could take us back. "Sure, no problem." Rob, it's time to leave - that guy is going to give us a ride back to the plane. We thanked the driver as he dropped us off and I was wondering what he was thinking about at that point. I loaded the clubs and waited for Rob to crank the engine over as I fastened my seat belt for the ride home. My friend Kegger would often say, "Buckle up for safety!" Rob looked over at me from the left seat and said, "You're gonna have to fly us back." "Excuse me?" "Yeah, just get me to the Tappan Zee Bridge and I can land it." My experience with flying airplanes is zero. I had worked for the past five years around aircraft and could taxi them, tow them and start them up with no problem - but never had the knowledge to fly one.

The moment of truth. I took the control and taxied along the bumpy grass and dirt turf and checked off to my left as to which way the windsock was blowing. There was no tower at this location, nobody to call for permission to take off. It was just check the skies and go. Looking back later, maybe Rob didn't want anybody to know we had taken off. The area around the airstrip was dense woods with trees on three sides and the driving range filling up the remainder of the perimeter. At the end of the runway stood a cluster of tall pines that looked very tall and ominous. While taxiing out, I got used to the right and left pedals and Rob gave me a few quick pointers. When I released the brakes and started heading down the runway, I thought to myself, *I can do this*. At about 60 knots Rob had told me to pull back on the stick slowly and the fixed wing aircraft rose off the ground without difficulty. Those scary trees at the end of the runway were now just toothpicks underneath the plane. I knew enough about the instruments to feel comfortable as we gained altitude and I headed the aircraft east. Rob was awake for most of the journey, he nodded off once or twice and all I was thinking the whole trip was "Damn, I hope he can land this!!" The hour trip had passed fairly quickly. There's so much in front of you to be observant of that I always felt I should be looking at a different indicator. Speed was good, heading correct, the air outside was calm without any turbulence; what could go wrong? Oh, that voice on the radio asking for something, something. Rob grabbed the mic and threw back some numbers and letters as fast as they were thrown at us. As we flew over the Hudson River and the Tappan Zee Bridge, Rob said, "I'm good, I'll take it from here - thanks."

Two stories about the Tappan Zee Bridge. Rob had told me that there were a handful of pilots that belonged to a kind of underground pilot fraternity. In order to be part of the club there was something you had to do to be indoctrinated; fly a plane between the water and under the bridge. That's 138' in clearance, between you and me. I wasn't quite sure if this was real or just a bunch of guys telling stories. He stated it was usually done around 4 a.m. when the bars closed and before the bread trucks hit the road.

When I asked him if he was a member he replied, "You're living with two members."

The bridge was opened in 1955. There was a ceremony of the 3-mile-long bridge that brought a lot of politicians, builders and hand shakers together. This bridge would link two counties 25 miles north of New York City together. The police chief in my hometown of White Plains, NY was invited along with the mayor and commissioner. The only thing they didn't have was a driver to take them there. In December of that year my father, a rookie police officer, was selected to drive these men over for the formal ceremonies. He told me that after the ribbon cutting ceremony and palm pressing they all went out for lunch and he was treated to a meal on the city.

Rob lined up on the runway as we dropped in altitude and gave me that look. He said, "After we land, you grab the clubs and I'll tie up the plane. Don't talk to anybody." That seemed like good advice. Rob made a perfect landing and ten minutes later we were off in the car making the great escape. McQueen and Bronson were glad to be back on the ground. I've often thought, *What would have happened if I had to land the plane?* Sometimes I tell myself it would have been no problem, maybe I would have bounced a tire or a little scrape on the wing. Then reality sets in and I see the plane cart wheeling down the runway in a ball of flames. Glad I never had to find out!

CHAPTER 2

BEACH BUM

Ok, let's set the stage with the players. There's me and my wife Sue, her two girlfriends Amy and Peg, and their husbands Mike and Pete. We've all known each other since 2007. When we first moved to Florida the girls all met and worked together at a local pain care center. Back then there was a pain care center on every other block in Florida and if you came into the office with severe back pain or a hang nail they would give you a three month supply of Vicodin without batting an eye. The ladies had decided it was time for all the guys in their lives to meet each other. I had the pleasure of meeting Mike and Pete one night at a local liquor store that was having a tasting and promotion party. Talk about a cheap date. We hung out in the parking lot of the liquor store where vendors had portable tents set up to push their products and a cigar roller was nearby cutting up tobacco and rolling ropes for anybody who wanted one. It was our first time together and everybody was still learning about the others' background, family and favorite color. It's now seven plus years later and Mike and Amy (who had moved out of the area) were back for a short visit. We had all decided - well our wives had decided - that we should hit the beach with some sandwiches and cocktails and watch the sunset. It's Florida, that's what we do. There is a barrier island off the coast of Bradenton/Sarasota called Anna Maria Island. It's a great beach that's a popular spot with the tourists as well as the locals; we had been going there since we moved down here and never had any problems. Until now.

We set up the chairs in line on the beach facing west, girls on one side and boys on the other 'cause we don't want to talk about nail polish color or what was on sale last week at Macy's. It's an absolutely perfect evening; tee shirts and shorts and just a couple of clouds to make the evening sky all the more attractive. Pete was throwing back a few Budweisers and Mike, to my right, had just poured himself another rum and Coke. We're eating sandwiches from Subway and having laughs when we all notice a guy about 25 feet in front of us roll over on his blanket. You could tell he's been boozing all day; a six pack of empties around him and a bottle of vodka that's lying next to him about half empty. He's 65 or so and staggered as he rose to his feet off his blanket. He waddled into The Gulf to take a last dip for the day. I looked at Mike and said, "He doesn't look good, better keep an eye on him." A few minutes later he was out of the water, drying off and putting his empties into a plastic bag. He reached down and picked up a bag of Cheese Puffs or Doritos and popped a few in his mouth - that's when it happened. With nothing left in the bag but the crumbs, he proceeded to take the bag and fling it into the air. What did that moron just do? Within seconds every seagull and scavenger bird that hangs out near the beach was dive-bombing the area. Here are a couple of simple rules to live by when you're at the beach: it's okay to pee in the water but it's not okay to feed the birds.

Peg is pissed. She's the first one to confront the guy and tell him that he's crazy and that you don't feed the birds at the beach. The verbal assaults go back and forth, "I'll do whatever I want", he says, "what are you gonna do about it?" Peg is originally from Philadelphia and she will tell you what she is gonna do about it. F bombs are flying out of his mouth and the calm sunset is now turning into the Thrilla in Manila. Well, maybe not that bad. After Peg got off the soapbox, my wife started yelling at this guy. Then Pete joined in. He stood there scratching and rubbing his salt and peppered beard that hadn't seen a razor since the Nixon administration. There's an old saying that you can't argue with drunks or crazy people. There are other families and small children in the area and this guy couldn't have cared less about his behavior. He looked at us and said, "I'll fight all three of you." I wasn't quite sure if he wanted to fight us or our wives. Moments later he's still cursing at us as he walked up the beach, got on his bicycle and pedaled away. The good news is none of us had to start throwing punches or leave our seats during the confrontation; the bad news is I can't remember if we got to see the sunset that night. Sometimes it just happens that way; no autopsy, no foul.

CHAPTER 3

ANDY

Most people I know have a best friend or did; that person who comes into your life that you can call at any time, day or night. That person you would go to jail for, back up in a fight, or lend money to in any situation - and I'm not talking about a wife, husband, or partner. The problem is that it's never forever. Nothing is forever. Arguments, time, and all of life's little nuances cause most of these friendships to break apart and you're left with a void in your life.

I met Andy late in 1980. We had both grown up in the Northeast; he was from a medium size town just west of Boston. We had both gone to basic training together in Texas and were now enrolled in the avionics program in Biloxi, Mississippi. Avionics is a fancy word for all the radio and communications gear on an airplane. We hit it off from the start; liking sports, the same kind of music and we were both there for the same reasons. He and his dad were not on the same page and at 18 years old it was time for a change. It was going along pretty smooth for the better part of five months, until we got our orders for our next base. We were all set to graduate from the United States Air Force Tech School when I found out I was headed to the northern frontier of New York and Andy was going to the Upper Peninsula in Michigan. We had been separated for approximately a year and a half when our paths crossed again. I walked into the communications shop at Kadena Air Force Base in

Japan and there he was. We were both half a world away from our families.

We had great times in Okinawa, Japan. There were a few typhoon parties in the dorm where we lived. We would be locked down for a few days waiting for Mother Nature to finish dropping 15 inches of rain and hurling some 125 mph winds at us. We learned to drive on the left side of the road, always entertaining with the steering wheel on the right side of the car. We had a small dayroom in the dorm with a TV; if pushed to the limit, you could squeeze in about 25 or so. In 1983 there were only three American TV shows that were broadcasted to us. I remember watching Knight Rider with David Hasselhoff and becoming a soap junkie with General Hospital. Andy was always up for anything, relaxed, easy going and reminded me of myself. Maybe that's why we got along so well. We worked on the flight line on the AWACS aircraft. It's your basic 707 Boeing with four engines and has what looks like a Frisbee mounted on the top of the fuselage. It was a year and a half of parties, travel and fun; we even found time to get some work done. Stranded on the island, we had to make do with what we had. There were times when a "Robo" party was necessary. The main ingredient was the cough syrup Robitussin DM. Fill a large punchbowl with six bottles, add your favorite juices and cut up some lemons and limes for decoration. We would hangout by the seawall or party on the roof of the dorm. Then the shit hit the fan. Andy's piss test came back positive. When we talked about it, he admitted that he had been out with a staff sergeant that we all knew from our division. They had both been smoking but Andy believed he was being set up.

I was getting ready to be relocated to Minot, North Dakota when Andy was set to separate from the service. He had agreed on a plea bargain that gave him a general discharge. *You're out, go find your own way home.* It was the mid-80's and Andy's father sold him and his sister the family business; a heating and air conditioning company located in Framingham, Massachusetts. Andy was always fair with his customers and on the few times I went up to see him I could tell he was getting use to the long hours and working in some lousy conditions. Nobody's air conditioning breaks down when it's 65 and sunny, and nobody's heat stops working in July. He crawled around in attics littered with rat droppings and would smile as he got back into his truck for the next call. He didn't miss the Air Force one bit. Our friendship continued over the next 25 years. I was with him at both his weddings and talked him down off the ledge as both fell apart. He was also at my first debacle (aka wedding) on a beach behind the Breakers Hotel in Palm Beach, Florida. Hundreds of phone calls, texts, and the occasional visit couldn't stop the inevitable.

I was leaving work one evening and got a call from Andy who told me he was helping a friend move down to Tampa, Florida. That's about an hour away from where I was living. *Great,* I thought, *when's the move?* It was two days away. I told him I had already made plans for the weekend and couldn't make it up to see him. If you're an hour away, is that considered "in the area"? I was scheduled to work that Thursday through Saturday and had already planned to watch a New York Jets playoff game on Sunday with my brother-in-law and some friends. Let's be serious, how often can you watch a Jets playoff game? I thought it was kind of short notice, I was tired, working a couple of jobs, and didn't have the energy for the two-hour round trip. I invited him down to the party and told him he was welcome to stay overnight. For whatever the reason, this was not what he wanted to hear. We never raised our voices on the phone, we just said goodbye. We haven't talked since. Maybe he was pissed and still holding a grudge because I had slept with his sister once or maybe because I didn't root for the Red Sox when he took me to Fenway Park. I don't expect to ever hear from him again.

CHAPTER 4

CADDYING

Golf has always been a favorite part of my life. I made my first golf club from an old blue mop handle and a small piece of wood I found at my grandparent's farm house. The arduous task was trying to hammer that one nail into the handle without splitting the wood. After about five or six tries - and hitting my thumb just to remind me what pain feels like - it was finished. The perfect golf club. I was probably about 10 years old. That afternoon, with a couple of plastic golf balls and a few apple trees, I turned my grandparent's orchard into the toughest golf course in the Poconos in Pennsylvania. After 20 years as a cop, I told myself that if I could retire and just work a little time at a golf course, I'd be happy. I'm now working at two different tracks so I must be ecstatic. I've had the opportunity to play some incredible golf courses, from Wing Foot and Bethpage Black on the East Coast to Pebble Beach and Spyglass in California. Last year I set foot on Ballybunion and Old Head in Ireland where the wind blew at about 40 mph all day.

I caddied at Century Country Club in Purchase, NY for a few years from 1993-1996. The caddy motto: show up, keep up, and shut up. Dick Siderowf, British Amateur Champion, was a member there. He was easy to caddy for; I never had to give him yardage or read a green. Caddying for Mrs. Tisch, wife of New York Giants CEO, was also amusing. I would hand her a 3-wood on the tee and tell her to keep hitting it till we got about 60 yards from the hole. During a golf outing I was on the bag for Dave Stockton and his wife, Cathy. Stockton had recently captained the US Golf Ryder Cup team and was very full of himself. He may have injured his wrist that day patting himself on the back so often. His wife, on the other hand, couldn't have been nicer. You learn a lot about somebody over the course of 18 holes. There were a lot of big money games being played each weekend and I got the opportunity to walk with some pretty high rollers. It was a steaming August afternoon, about 90 degrees and the heat index was like a pizza oven. We had just made the turn and I thought to myself *I've got just enough energy to make it back to the clubhouse*. As we walked down the 10th fairway, one of the guys I was caddying for said, "Look, I'm gonna give you a little tip - if you've got about 10 grand, put it into Sears and Mobile Oil." I handed him a 6-iron and recapped the situation for him; "It's 90 degrees out and I've got two bags on my shoulders, do you really think I've got an extra 10 large in my vault?"

There's not a cloud in the sky and the forecast doesn't call for any rain, but sure enough there is always that one asshole who feels the need to carry an umbrella. It doesn't seem like a lot of weight until you're dragging it down the 14th hole three hours later. We would always tell people what they could and couldn't carry. Some of the guys felt it necessary to have at least two dozen balls on them at all times. We would walk down the fairways throwing brand new Titleists into the bushes and woods just so the bag was lighter. The betting was obscene on the golf course. They played games like PIG and VEGAS and wouldn't even blink if they just lost 300 dollars on the last hole. There was one guy who always wanted to play progressive golf; one hundred on the first hole, two hundred on the second, etc. - it gets expensive. There were a dollar a yard games also. So if you just lost on a hole that was 410 yards long, you just lost $410. During the tournaments there were always various rules that came into play. I watched a guy one day whose ball was lying in the fringe bend over to fix a ball mark that wasn't on the green. Before I could get the words out of my mouth, he had lost the hole.

Remember that motto! Most players didn't want to talk to the caddies; *you're just there so I can tell my doctor I got some exercise today.*

Two guys I worked with at Century CC were Paul and Justin. Paul would work there a few days a week and had his steady group on the weekends. They were some of the heavy bettors at the club and liked Paul's attitude. If the mood suited him he might catch an afternoon loop riding on the back of a cart, passing out putters and raking traps. One of the guys Paul caddied for had asked him what he was going to do with the rest of his life. I don't think Paul had come up with that plan yet; part time teaching at a school and caddying was good enough for him right now. After much thought, Paul had accepted the offer. "I'm gonna go work for a member from the club," he told me. "He thinks I would be good selling stocks and bonds." Look, you buy a couple of suits and start riding the train back and forth from the city. He told me that if he didn't like it after six months he could quit and still come back to the club to caddy. This was the perfect opportunity for him. He was promised that he would be making six figures after the first year. He turned that offer into a career, working as a trader for Cantor Fitzgerald in the North Tower on the 104th floor of The World Trade Center. When it came to caddying, Paul was never late. He had a good work ethic and was always punctual. He was also on time September 11, 2001. RIP, Paul.

I remember Justin being a little smaller than the rest of the guys there; he walked with a limp but never complained. The caddy master liked him, and if there was work in the bag room or doing other chores Justin was always up for the task. He was a little shy but would always come back with a verbal jab when the situation called for it. Justin is the caddy master at the club now, doing all he can to look after the members and tries to motivate some caddies. It ain't easy.

One year during the annual club championship, I was caddying for a guy who was a major player from Shearson Lehman Brothers. It was Labor Day Weekend and perfect weather for golf. It was a match play event and after the front nine my guy was already down four holes with the back nine to play. I gave him a small pep talk walking down the 10th hole fairway and told him, "You're not out of this yet." He made some good shots and his opponent choked it up a little bit. We had made up the entire deficit - except for one hole - and were trailing going into the 18th. We got to the green knowing we needed a 20 foot uphill putt to force a playoff. I read the putt one way and he saw it staying fairly straight. Just to the rear of the green were all his associates and golfing buddies. The backdrop looked like a page out of a J Crew magazine. There were some 50 or so onlookers with cocktails in hand, most of them betting he wasn't going to make it. I had seen this hole location before and knew that the ball was going to break to the left. I told him he had two choices; if he read it wrong, it would be a long winter. But if I read it wrong, well...you can always blame the caddy. The putt fell in the hole and this guy thought he had just won the US Open. A good size roar came from the crowd and a smile across his face like he just bought Apple as an IPO. Have ya ever seen a grown man dance really badly on the 18th hole? Five minutes later, on the first playoff hole, he pulled his drive dead left into the trees and the day was over. He looked at me like I had just killed his dog. I located the ball and told him to just get it back into the fairway; anything can happen in golf...anything. He hacked it up pretty good after that and, after hitting almost every tree on the hole, it was time to concede the match. It was a long walk back up that first hole to the clubhouse for him. He looked like he could use a hug and a martini.

I played in a golf outing one year at Bonnie Briar Golf Course in Larchmont, NY. There are so many gorgeous golf tracks just north of New York City, you would be hard pressed to find a bad one. That day we got our caddie who looked like he was just pulled out of a crack den. He was wearing a St. Louis Rams jersey with Marshall Faulks number and name on the back. The vivid blue and yellow was an outstanding backdrop against the fall colors. He was the new kid on the block and looked as if he still hadn't earned his stripes yet to get proper attire from the club. He had a sense of humor though, and that went a long way in my assessment of him. I yanked a ball left early in the round off the tee and had the feeling it was either up on a hillside in the trees or lost forever. As we made our way down from the tee box I yelled over to him from the fairway as he stood waist deep in saplings in the tree line, "Any luck up there?" He told me he had it. "Is it playable?" His answer: "It's getting better". A few seconds later it was rolling down the hill past a rock outcropping into the fairway. "A" for effort.

Our cruise ship docked in the Dominican Republic around eight in the morning and we made our way over to the Casa da Campo Golf Course, also known as Teeth of the Dog. It's a $200 bill to play, but what the hell. Situated on the south side of the island, the course plays for several holes right along the Caribbean Sea. Seven holes that I believe are even nicer than Pebble Beach. I really hadn't thought about playing on the trip. I had left my sticks at home and playing with rentals is always scary. After a quick five-minute warm-up on the range we were on the first tee and my caddie tried to explain the hole and where to hit it. After an opening eight I felt like returning to the ship and finding a bar. It could have been the nerves or the different clubs in my hands, but I was blaming it on the bourbon from the previous night. The day got a lot better though as we reached the fifth hole. I looked at the sea to my left and about 157 yards to the par 3. My caddie stepped in to interfere and asked what club I was hitting. The wind was blowing a little into my face and I thought I'd hit an easy 6-iron. He looked at me and suggested a 9-iron. What? He gave me a quick explanation that the wind above was blowing out. Look, I bought a sleeve of balls and had already lost one, but he assured me that if the ball went into the aqua he would jump in and get it. I stuck the shot 14 feet from the hole and, of course, missed the putt. At the turn the caddie asked if I wanted to try some fresh coconut water. Seconds later he's climbing a palm some 25 feet up, knocking down the fruit, then slicing it open with a machete that was conveniently located nearby. I thought he was going to slice his hand off the way he opened it. Definitely not the first time he's done that. At some point on the back nine, I hit one to the right off the tee and my caddie looked at me and shook his head. "That might be in the water." I gave a quick glance at the scorecard and couldn't see where any water came into play on this hole. As we got to the ball, there it was about 20 feet from somebody's swimming pool (which was in the backyard behind another mansion on the course). This caddie was pretty awesome reading putts and had a lot of great stories about the course and people he had caddied for. I can't remember what I tipped him but he looked at the cash then back at me. "You play tomorrow sir, I caddie for you."

CHAPTER 5

4 SYCAMORE

In 1988, after being a cop for only six months, I got called into the lieutenant's office one morning. Now I'm trying to think of what I had done wrong or who had made a complaint about me. I sat there nervous in the chair, waiting for the other shoe to drop. I was hoping for the best but thinking in the back of my mind that this couldn't be good. Why was I sweating? Fuck. Even the leather chair I was sitting in felt uncomfortable. Something was making my skin itch, though I had no idea what it was. I sat there looking across the desk and a cyclone of thoughts and crazy shit started swirling in my mind. I was scared and was waiting to hear those words, "Leave your badge and gun on the desk." Can you say paranoid? See those first 18 months as a cop, they don't even need a reason to fire you. He looked at me and asked me if I needed anything; coffee, a cigarette? Back then you could smoke anywhere. We spoke for a few minutes and then he made me an offer that sounded pretty good - you know, like too good. Everybody else has turned it down so now I'm coming to you. The playbook was doing security and some driving for a local family. What rookie cop gets that privilege? I thought that's what all the old timers get. The benefits were that myself and two other cops were going to live rent free in a three-bedroom house, "The Cottage," on an estate in the south end of town. The family who we were going to be working for had some reasons to be concerned. The neighboring, whose last name was Parnes, was a real estate guy doing major deals and in the process must have pissed somebody off pretty good. There were threats made against them verbally and when that didn't work, two guys showed up in the woods behind their home with automatics. This guy was pretty lucky. Both guys from that incident surrendered, but how many more were on the way? Since I had moved out of my parent's home in 1985, it was hard to save money paying that monthly rent so this could solve a few problems. The lieutenant advised he would be living there also, in a small studio apartment above the garages, and would contribute with some of the driving. Sounds great, right?

The estate itself was on a semi-private road that only had four homes on it. When you drove onto the property, up a slight incline, the main estate was on the right in stone and dark chocolate hues. The property covered about six acres. It consisted of seven bedrooms and seven baths and a few libraries and studies thrown in for good measure. Behind the estate was a pool, tennis court, open slate patio and outdoor kitchen. The garage was off to the left, where the owners black Lincoln Town Car was kept. Further down the drive, off to the right, was a paddle tennis court and at the very end of the driveway was my home for the next year and a half - or what we liked to call, "the slave's quarters". The three of us moved in with high expectations and after a short meeting with Jim, the lieutenant who had set up the whole gig, we made some basic schedules as to whom would perform what jobs and when. Someone had to pick up the homeowner, Arthur Lipper, at 6 a.m. Monday thru Friday to transport him down to New York City. His office was at 52nd Street and 3rd Avenue. His pickup time in the evening would vary depending on meetings, dinner engagements, and more meetings. We always thought there was a side piece in the mix, but we could never prove that and really couldn't have cared less. Arthur was always prompt in the mornings and looked as if he had been up for hours. He opened the door to the car himself and would never make you feel like you were the help. I would then wait at the end of the street for the New York Times to be delivered. If it wasn't there by 6:05 a.m., I could tell his whole schedule was about to be thrown off. We would then drive to the city and I would head back to work to make it for roll call. In the winter at the estate, it was snowplowing and shoveling the driveway. In the fall, raking and blowing the leaves. Summer consisted of mowing the lawns and keeping up with the pool and courts. Springtime was painting and getting flowers planted around the home. The phone was always ringing. They also had a boxer who required attention as well; walk, feed, bathe, clean out his run, fresh bedding. There was always something to do. And just when everything was finished, Arthur's wife would call over and need a ride to the train station or need to have her dry cleaning picked up. We were all working seven days a week plus our regular jobs. I knew it was too good to be true.

Shortly after taking on this new role as security/chauffer/pool boy, I made it a point to seek out the security team that was working the estate next to ours. There were two New York City police officers sharing the detail at this residence. We spoke in length about the recent events and that the homeowner, who was often away, needed protection for his family. These guys had weapons everywhere; in the sofa, in the fridge, not to mention those on his person. Security cameras and motion detectors were also set up around the perimeter of the home. I thought to myself, *Well I'll be next door dragging the clay tennis court if you need us.* Back in 1988-89 when I was driving Arthur around, he had a cell phone in his car the size of a shoebox. Everybody else in the world was still using pay phones or soup cans. He was an entrepreneur and investment banker who was always doing business. He told me he had subsidized one of the first Subway sandwich chains in New York City. How's that deal looking? His bio included lectures at Harvard, Yale, Stamford and Georgetown. In 1969 his corporation filed the first prospectus for a stock index fund; this is a disclosure document that would give the investor information regarding the company and a description of the firm's business. I never really pried into his background, he seemed very private and was not the boisterous type. When he wasn't on the phone or reading the Times or Wall Street Journal, I would sometimes catch him staring out the window and rubbing the whiskers of his beard. He was always thinking. One morning as I was driving him, there was a call that he immediately answered. With his briefcase beside him, he began speaking to some guy on the phone from California. Its 3 a.m. on the west coast and this guy is pitching an idea to him. "So what do you have so far, just a prototype?" The conversation went back and forth for a good five minutes and I got a really good feel for what was taking place. This guy was looking for an investor to build a full scale jet engine. He had already produced a smaller one with his energy efficient system that would allow the aircraft to use 1/3 less fuel and produced the same output. I just drove the car, made the necessary stops, and looked for good parking spaces.

Arthur was a quiet man that probably never would have thought of having a security team living on his estate. His wife, on the other hand, had those teacher fingernails and I'm sure she dragged them down the chalkboard a few times making her feelings known. "Arthur, there were two men in the woods with guns!" She was all business too and rarely smiled. I'm not sure what size stick was up her ass, but it must have hurt like hell. I would often think to myself, "How rich do you have to be to crack a smile?" She had me cleaning up the rear patio one morning, wiping down furniture, and throwing in some new plants. "We have some company coming over this afternoon." I didn't really care, but for some reason she felt it was necessary to continue the conversation. Bob Guccione and some of the ladies from Penthouse will be coming by for a while. See......these were the benefits to this job I was looking for. Just as I had hit the grand slam to win the World Series, she hits me with a laundry list of things to do that afternoon. By the time I had made it back, the girls were out of pool and the pitcher of margaritas was empty. There is no joy in Mudville. I think she did that just to piss me off...and she succeeded.

Life was like this for a while. There were several cops who lived with me on the estate; and most of them would do it for a few months then wave the white flag. Kevin was one of the first to leave and I couldn't even blame him. There was never a minute to yourself. If I could stick it out for a year and a half I would have enough money for a down payment on a condo or home. Free rent and some leftovers that were in the presence of Penthouse models is hard to beat. Then the phone would ring and it was another trip to pick somebody up from the airport. My ass spent more time in that limo than you could imagine. There were some good times there when the owners were away on vacation; the problem was they hardly ever went away. Imagine this: "We're having a party on an estate, want to come over?" The area was so secluded that there were never any complaints from the neighbors. You could blast the music and splash in the pool all you wanted. We had one party where I took an Alco-Sensor from work. It's the device used in the field to determine if somebody is intoxicated. There were a few friends who got to crash on the couch that night.

Things really started going downhill fast in the fall of 1989. Some of the guys I was living with weren't pulling their weight and it got back to the lieutenant. He was looking to clean house. I awoke one morning and threw my shoulder holster on. The 9 MM Beretta was well balanced with the two extra 15-round clips on my right side. I was half asleep but started the car and pulled in front of the sidewalk. Arthur should be out in five minutes. It was a grey damp morning with that kind of mist that just hangs in the air. Where is this guy? It's five after. When somebody is never late your mind starts to race. At quarter past I called the house but didn't get an answer. Now I was wide awake and walking around the property. As I approached the front door I wasn't sure what to expect. It could have been a medical condition or maybe he had enough of his wife's bitching and was cleaning up the crime scene. As I went to ring the doorbell, the lock turned in the tumbler and he exited the home. "Sorry I'm late." I put the gun back in the holster and snapped it closed. Kevin and I used to joke about it after we left - what a great feeling it was TO NEVER HAVE TO LIVE THERE AGAIN. It was an experience that allowed us to bank some cash, which eventually led to buying our future homes. Last I heard Arthur was living in Del Mar, California and probably doesn't remember me or the only time he overslept in two years.

CHAPTER 6

DEATH

After being sworn in as a police officer in November of 1987 and attending almost six months of schooling, it was a class trip to the Westchester County Medical Center where I observed my first autopsy. When you see a friend or family in a funeral home it's very clean and, to some degree, almost calming. It's not always like that when you are dispatched to someone's home. It can get a little messy sometimes. At the funeral home they have been cleaned up, their hands are glued together, and their makeup and hair have been done by a beautician mortician. That's an actual job; somebody who goes from funeral home to funeral home doing cosmetics for those who have passed. I had a friend that did this sort of work. She would sometimes respond to as many as eight calls a day; putting on lipstick, parting the hair just right, and applying the pancake rouge. She could make up to $125 a pop. The medical examiner on this particular day was a doctor who had a very dry sense of humor and saw things as they were. The class huddled into the lab and someone was smart enough to bring a jar of Vicks so we could all take a finger full to shove up our noses. The body that was laid out on the table was a male white, maybe 40 years of age. His arms had several puncture marks from the needle sticks. "Okay, we all know why he died, but now we have to prove it." That was the doctor in his best Korean accent. He cut his skull open with a vibrating saw to expose and remove the brain. The chest was opened with rib splitters to weigh the heart and inspect the cavity. After taking out the liver, he took a scalpel and sliced it up like he was cutting a block of cheese. He then held it up for us and fanned across it with his thumb, showing several cross sections of the organ. "It's like reading a book." The smell in the room never got any better. A few guys had to walk out. I remember him concluding the examination by putting the skull bone back on the head, but the brain was still on a scale near the table. After an autopsy, the brain gets placed in the cavity of the body due to the swelling. Class was over.

It's my first year on the police department (also known as "The Job") when I responded to my first death in the field. She was a young woman who had overdosed on the first floor of a nine-story apartment building. The detectives who had responded with me were both cracking jokes but very understanding at the same time. Both had been cops for a while and even knew her 15 years prior, when she had good legs and worked for a local taxi company as a dispatcher. She sat slumped over on a dingy couch in the living room of the apartment. There was a glob of mucus that ran out of her nose a few inches that was suspended in midair. It was 10 o'clock in the morning. One of the detectives went through her purse and threw the various pill bottles, condoms, and a needle in the trash. He said, "Her parents don't need to see that! " I learned a lot that day from two old school cops, Robert and Bobby, who treated her family with respect. I was the rookie still getting my feet wet and learning about what you can and can't do as a cop.

I was working a day tour that was coming to an end. It was a very mundane shift with nothing exciting or out of the ordinary. I received a call from headquarters dispatch of a male party in his 20's not breathing or conscious. After arriving at the home and grabbing the oxygen tank from the trunk of the police car, I hurried to the front door of the residence. I was greeted by family members who advised that the party was on the couch and pointed to what looked like a small family room. Nobody was in a panic or yelling, it was very calm. As I knelt on the floor, I looked around the home towards the dining room and even into the kitchen. It all seemed a little strange. There were maybe 10-12 people there and nobody asking me, "How's he doing?" or "Is he going to be alright?" A few parties were even throwing back what looked like a late lunch. The young man was cold to the touch and oxygen would not have helped. A crochet afghan blanket was wrapped around him. I asked the usual questions to those in the home but didn't receive the usual answers. There was a language barrier with many in the residence and everything I said was met with blank stares and looks of "Huh?" After trying to sort out the situation and speaking with members of the family, I was finally able to speak with a young lady in the home who said to me, "It's alright, he had AIDS and is no longer in pain." A young guy from the medical examiner's office showed up about four hours later as I stood by in the home with the family and the deceased. He was working all by himself that night and needed help wrapping up the body in the usual white sheet and black plastic bag. He gave me 10 bucks for the effort.

Cops will help another cop out usually. I've been stopped by other cops in various jurisdictions; South Carolina, Florida, North Carolina, Virginia, Maryland, and of course New York and never got a ticket. Maybe it was my charming personality or the times I pulled over before they could get their lights on. It's better to come clean, apologize, and show your ID. I usually didn't work for people on the weekends unless they were really good friends, but on this one occasion I made an exception. It was a weekend where I had nothing planned; no trips to Lowes or parties to attend. It was another quiet day until about 2:30 p.m. when a neighbor in an apartment complex called about a strange smell in the hallway. Upon arrival, the smell was overwhelming and newspapers littered the doorstep about four deep. Unable to gain access, I was able to contact the superintendent of the building that let me into the apartment. Five steps into the unit on the left laid a very large black subject on the bathroom floor with drug paraphernalia on the sink and floor around him. I'm sorry, did I say a black subject? My fault, all white people look black after lying on a floor and not breathing for four days. He was bloated and appeared to be in his mid-40's with brown hair. As I looked around the apartment that was spotless, but was decorated like a bachelor, I noticed a large assortment of black canvas binders 3-4 inches thick. They were everywhere - 75, maybe a hundred or so

- in very neat and orderly bookshelves. My curiosity got the better of me and I had nothing to do except wait for the medical examiner and collect some overtime. I grabbed one of the binders and opened to no particular page. Stamp collection? No. Coins? No. Ty Cobb? Yes. Here's a guy with pages and pages of baseball cards from the early 1900's through World War II dead on his bathroom floor and I'm in his apartment wishing I had a cigar to mask the smell. Each card was in its own protective sleeve with nine cards to a page. I called his sister that day, the only family member's number I could find. She didn't sound very upset or care about the items in question. The day was long - very long - and I always thought twice before working for somebody again on the weekend.

I had just finished a late meal break on a 4-12 p.m. shift; it was 9 p.m. or so. I was strolling through our communications room at headquarters when a call was received regarding a loud bang. The address was a high-rise upscale apartment a block over from our building. The concierge on the main floor hadn't heard it, but he offered to take me up to the apartment in question. I rang the buzzer several times and knocked, no answer. The neighbor who had called it in came out into the hallway and described it as very loud. I entered the apartment with the concierge's key. The kitchen was off to the right and behind that a small living room. I identified myself as a police officer and got no response. The only bedroom was in the far left rear portion of the dwelling. I walked past the bathroom and peered into the bedroom where a man laid in his pajamas on the bed. The loud bang came from a shotgun that lied next to him. Only a portion of his head remained near his neck; the rest was now part of the ceiling and headboard. I can still recall the tiny pieces of bone and flesh that would fall from the ceiling above as they dried, making a noise as they hit the end tables on either side of the bed. The shotgun had a Band-Aid at the very end of the barrel wrapped around it like you would apply to a finger. I found the wrapper, plastic tabs and red string neatly placed in the garbage can in the bathroom. Here was a guy about to commit suicide and he had the forethought to not only apply the Band-Aid to bite on, but to discard the trash as well. I was able to notify both of his children who responded quickly. The son pleaded with me and wanted to go into the bedroom to see his father; I shook my head and said, "No you don't."

When a child dies it's not the same as an adult. I was driving the last hour of my shift and trying to stay awake. It was just after 7 a.m. when I got the call to respond to a home on Parkview Court. The mother was in the bedroom trying to revive the small infant. In the room with her were three or four other children, all under the age of eight. We did CPR together while waiting on the ambulance to respond. And we waited. And we waited some more. She was frantic and I had a pretty good idea her child had already passed. I reacted by driving the child to the hospital while mom did CPR in the rear seat of the police car. Later that morning, after the toddler had been pronounced dead, I found myself in the detective division being accused by the ambulance driver of not waiting at the home for their arrival. Strange morning. Sudden infant death syndrome (SIDS) was the autopsy finding. Ambulance drivers still sleeping and trying to cover their asses was my finding. That's one of those calls you replay in your mind a thousand times. You go to bed thinking about it, dream about it, and wake up to your first cup of coffee still hearing the panic in the mother's voice.

It was a call for service "right out of the box" as we would say. The squad for the tour would finish roll call and receive assignments. You wouldn't even be able to finish inspecting your police car for dents from the previous shift and they were dispatching you on a call over the radio. Sometimes the calls were of minor nature and held over from the previous shift; not this one. Unresponsive subject in the Soundview area of town. The wife showed me to a staircase that led to the master bedroom one flight up. There was no pulse or sign of life. I had an automated external defibrillator that I attached to the gentleman without success. He was in his early 70's. Nothing looked out of the ordinary; an upper middle class home, Tudor in style, with a pristine interior. When I spoke with the wife downstairs and informed her of the passing of her husband, she looked puzzled and told me that couldn't be. "He was in perfect health, we just went out for dinner last night, and he played tennis the other day." The results from the ME's office showed a simple heart attack and nothing else. That's where the story took a twist. The wife did not believe in these findings and hired her own independent examiner to perform an autopsy. I found out weeks later from a funeral director who did the arrangements that the second autopsy had come back with a dissimilar result. Toxicology reports in this instance showed signs of poisoning. Then I thought to myself, *What if some pissed-off server or cook couldn't stand the guy and poisoned his fettuccini Alfredo?* To my knowledge, nothing ever became of the case.

Over the course of 20 years as a cop, I dealt with several cases of people dying. There were plenty of car, motorcycle, bicycle and pedestrian fatalities. I recall a young man getting hit by a school bus while he rode his bike one afternoon; the location was Tarrytown Road and Main Street. When I first got to the scene, he was pinned under the bus along with his bicycle. The best part about the day so far was that there were no children on the bus. After pulling him out from the undercarriage, the skin on the majority of his face had been peeled back over the top of his head to reveal raw flesh. Just like Travolta and Cage in Faceoff. There was also this strange odor - almost toxic. As both members of the ambulance crew started working on him in the rear of the ambulance, I jumped in the front seat and headed towards the trauma unit at Westchester Medical Center. A team of about 10 different doctors and nurses worked on that party while I stood by the door waiting to hear on his condition. He was still alive five hours later when I left the facility.

After responding to a psychiatric hospital in town, I learned of a female party that had just killed herself. The procedure at the front desk of the nut house was to turn your weapon over to them. I always kept mine. A friend of mine once said, "Nobody ever complains about having bullets left over after a gunfight." My partner and I walked into her room to find her hanging from over a door. The blood had already started to drain out of her facial area, there was no need to call for anybody. Nick, my partner that day, looked at me and said, "Well, if you're going to kill yourself, this is the place to do it." There was a jumper once who figured eight stories off the Sears parking structure should be enough; it was. I figured it would be a bigger mess, but it was pretty well contained. Every year somebody wanted to get hit by a train. It was just a matter of time until you got the call to respond to an incident of this nature. There's a guy walking down the tracks and you would have to halt all train service. I remember a party who thought walking in the street between traffic and parked vehicles was a good idea. He was struck by an auto and the force pushed his body into a landscaping truck. It was the type of vehicle that held the exposed handles of rakes, brooms and shovels on the exterior of the frame. His head snapped just about every tool handle and left fragments of his skull and blood in its path. The driver of the car that had struck him remained at the scene. He told me that this guy just ran out into traffic from behind the parked cars. They build sidewalks for a reason.

CHAPTER 7

BOATING

My next-door neighbor Curt has the loudest laugh in the world. I could be sitting in my house and hear him laughing in his kitchen. He drives a tractor-trailer for a major department store for a living and is often out the door at 3 a.m. and not back till 6 p.m. He's close to 65 years old and still has a full head of salt and pepper hair that doesn't need a comb over. When he's not working, his passions are keeping his home looking great and fishing. About four years ago he bought a fixer upper, a 22' Aquasport with a 200 horsepower Mercury engine, and started working on it weekends and whenever he could get some free time. Having owned a fishing charter service in the past, he has all the rods and reels and just about every toy you would need to go catch a fish. I, on the other hand, don't fish unless it's at the food store under plastic. Curt talked me into going fishing one weekend, something I haven't done since moving to Florida in 2007. I purchased an $18 fishing license from Wal-Mart and packed a couple of sandwiches and some beverages in a cooler for the day. We headed out early, before dawn, and grabbed some bait and coffee for the 30-minute ride to Sarasota with the boat in tow. Curt's plan was to go about 17 miles out into the Gulf of Mexico for grouper. This is going to be fun….right?

We launched the boat without any problems as the sun started to rise over my left shoulder. The ride out to Curt's "spot" took about an hour. I got more familiar with the boat and was watching the compass and fish finder. The fish finder is basically a transmitter that is converted to sonar and reflects on objects beneath your boat. This information is then sent back to a monitor where you can see objects below your boat, their approximate size and depth. We slowed to a crawl and Curt set up anchor; time to do some fishing. We threw out four lines off the back of the boat with sinkers and bait attached. Grouper is a delicious fish and I was hoping to catch just one for dinner. As the boat rocked back and forth, I looked over at Curt who said, "Did you see that?" I had no idea what he was talking about. "That's a 4' wave." We had only been there about 15 minutes. My fishing partner looked over at me again a short time later and said, "Did you see that?" I have zero clues when it comes to boats and was feeling like an amateur on the water. "That last wave was 7," he tells me, "we have to get out of here." We pulled up the lines and I thought to myself, *We just came all the way out here for 30 minutes of fishing?* I had no idea what was in store. Curt advised that this storm (that was not in the forecast for today) was now about to smack us right in the face. He set the GPS, powered up the engine and we were off, now heading east back to the coast. *This would be a good time to break out the life preservers*, I thought to myself. I looked over at my captain and thought, *If he's not wearing one, how bad could it be? The* waves were now crashing against the hull of the craft as the wind blew in our face with a steady gust of about 25 miles per hour. We were getting soaked and the clothes I had on were not waterproof. For the next three hours we battled the current, high waves and wind. My whole body was shaking from being so cold. I felt dehydrated and remember the salt water constantly hitting me in the face where I had to spit overboard. At least I tried to spit overboard. My back and kidneys were taking a pounding from the boat slamming against the water; we were getting beat up. This was supposed to be a nice October day with light winds and temperatures in the mid-70's and I couldn't have been any colder. Curt piloted the boat and, after three of the longest hours of my life, we found our way back to dry land. We figured it out that we were doing about five miles per hour. Thinking back on that day, there were several things that went wrong but I give him credit for knowing that some days are just not good days to go fishing. Was I scared? Hell yeah.

It's more than a year and a half later and Curt and I are still neighbors and friends. It's another beautiful day, 4th of July weekend, but this time his wife Martha, my wife Sue and two other friends are going out on the same boat to do a little cruising and partying. So, what could possibly go wrong? Sunscreen, towels, food and this time I'm packing vodka just in case. It was going to be a great day on the water. As we left the pier, the jokes were being tossed around and everybody was in a fantastic mood. It was a sunny morning with calm waters and I thought to myself, *Am I back on this boat again?* We had gotten about 500 yards from the pier when the motor quit. REALLY!? Curt started checking the fuel lines and removed a panel around the rear of the vessel. It was no use, we started drifting north in the Sarasota Bay. We were unable to get the motor started and fix the unfixable. Curt was on his hands and knees trying to figure out why the engine had just quit. He broke out a small tool box and started tinkering with just about everything – all to no avail. The tide was still dragging the boat north and into the shore, which is better than the other way. After about an hour of trying to be a mechanic, Curt grabbed the anchor and threw it overboard. We were approaching a stone jetty with a canal and I had bad visions of being on the news that night. There were million-dollar homes approaching fast on the shore line and all I can think of is that this boat is either going to hit that rock wall or smash into something hard. Better brace yourselves, girls. Curt continued to drag the anchor and pull it up, then throw it out again to slow down the boat's speed. He guided the craft between the rocks and into a canal that was about 60' wide. We were in the middle of the canal now and had just passed a boat dock on our left-hand side. Curt's still heaving out the anchor as we drifted further into the channel. The ladies are all yelling, trying to get anybody's attention. As we approached the second dock to our left, two young men came to our aid and were grabbing ropes and lines and throwing them towards us. We caught the second line as they started to pull us into their dock. You want to talk about relief? An older gentleman was next on the scene; he was the homeowner who appeared to be in his late 70's or early 80's. His first words to us were, "I see you have an Obama boat...it doesn't work." We tied the vessel up to their dock and thanked them immensely. We were all relieved to be on dry land. As the guys worked on the boat, the ladies got a tour of the home and grounds. The homeowner showed them around and when they came back they each had a small origami bird that had been made by his wife. As my wife explained it to me, she had taken her life just three months prior. These paper figurines were made by her and now the husband was passing them on to three people he had never met before today. Pretty interesting the way everything worked out. Curt told me later that the problem with the vessel was bad gas. He wound up taking a beating that day - from the cost of the fuel, parts he bought trying to fix it, and the few jabs I'm sure his wife got in on the way home. I'll never go on that boat again!

CHAPTER 8

BETTING

There are two types of people in this world; those who bet, and those who never bet. I'm a believer that everything is a gamble, whether it's getting on an airplane, hiking in the woods, or eating that mystery meal you just bought off a food truck. For every person that doesn't bet that means that I have to bet twice as much to make up for what they're not losing. Who doesn't play Powerball or Lotto when it gets up to 400 million? Here's five bucks, I'm in. Sports betting is the best though. I would have to rank football, golf and horse racing as my personal favorites. I knew a guy by the name of Sal who would rather lose $2000 in Atlantic City than $20 on the golf course. There are good bets, long shot bets, and fun bets. There are no sure bets. If you're playing roulette in Vegas and you play your favorite number, you better find an ATM because you're going to need more money. If you are at the track and the horse you're wagering on is wearing your favorite color...ATM. Cleveland Browns are favored to win...ATM. Most people I know have no problem with the passive bet. Throwing down a couple of dollars on the Super Bowl, NCAA basketball finals or a few shekels in the slot machine; it's all fun and adds to the excitement. If you're that person at a party who won't lay out $5 or $10 bucks in a pool, stay home and watch daytime TV.

It all started for me sometime in the fifth grade. Mr. Majors was my teacher and I sat as far in the back of the classroom as I could. I started making bets with classmates, and it didn't matter what it was on. It was already halfway through the football season and basketball and hockey were just as good to gamble on. We bet dimes, quarters, and sometimes a whole dollar. I was ten years old in 1972 and I was taking the action for our class and anybody else that wanted to get in. Everybody had their favorite team - or at least knew who their dad rooted for - and would come to me to place a bet. If they had no money, I would bet their Chips Ahoy cookies against my Devil Dogs or Ring Dings. I wasn't winning a lot, but then again I wasn't losing. The turning point that year was a bet I made with a classmate named Lance. We shook hands on a Friday about a football game that was to be played on Sunday. Monday came and I wanted my money. Lance had a different opinion. He told me that he was not going to pay me and that there was nothing I could do about it. He was a lot taller than I was and had a few pounds on me as well. After a brief discussion in front of the school, the pushing started and then he kneed me in the balls. I went down like the Hindenburg. I guess he figured he had won the fight. Las Vegas would have never been built if a little ass kicking was all it took to get out of owing some cash. In hindsight, I should have used a little common sense but I was 10 years old and that was out of the question. Word on the playground got around fast and before gym class the next day I could read the minds of all the gamblers in my class. I would never get paid again if/when I won a bet. The school bell rang to end the day and I was approached by another student by the bus ramp. "You want your money from Lance, I'll get it for you." Finally, what all bookies need; muscle. He was going to take half the amount that was owed and nobody would ever stiff me on a bet again. The next day, Mr. Majors was breaking up that fight at the flagpole and moments later I was sitting in the principal's office trying to figure out my next move. I think I broke my mother's heart when she had to respond to the school and be advised of the situation. She dragged me to the car that afternoon and the look on her face said it all. I was the bad seed.

It was late January of 1992, and I was missing the Super Bowl. I was working a 4-12 evening shift that was fairly quiet and allowed me some time to catch part of the action. A few plays here and there, then off to another call. The Washington Redskins were up by two scores over the Buffalo Bills late in the game when a call for aid came in over the police radio. There was a hotel in town that had a large banquet hall that was having a huge Super Bowl party. Large projection TVs were set up and there were probably 250 guests in the room. The ambulance crew was right behind me as we entered the lobby looking for the individual having chest pains. As we entered the ballroom (which had been turned into a sports bar), we were directed to a subject close to the front row. He turned away from the action to witness myself and the paramedics as he grabbed his chest and said, "I think I'm having a heart attack!" The medical staff attempted to work on him, but he had other priorities. "Two minutes to go in the game, I got the winning numbers!" He was in the betting pool at the hotel and was about to win some serious cash, serious *tax-free* cash. He clutched his chest as we watched the sweat build up on his forehead and cheeks. We didn't blame him. He continued to view the game and I just thought, *That's dedication; he'd rather win than live.* We wheeled him out on a stretcher after the game in his navy blue suit and white shirt. He won and I got to see the end of the game.

Danny and I went to the Police Academy together. He was in the middle of a nasty divorce with his wife (often referred to as "that fucking bitch"). I think he might have been married to my first wife because she had the same first, middle and last name. We had both gotten into the traffic division after six years on the force and were riding Harleys for a paycheck. We usually met around 10 p.m. with a few other cops, at a disclosed location, to drink some java and talk about the events of the evening. On one particular night, after discussing car stops and the hottest girl we saw that day, Danny made mention that his wife was raking him over the coals and he was looking for work or any side jobs that were available to make some extra cash. We were in the basement parking garage of the White Plains Public Library. The usual crew was present; radar and bike cops with a few outsiders from the patrol division that we trusted. There were maybe six of us standing around drinking some

Dunkin Donuts coffee and watching the clock, waiting for the shift to end. If Slate would blow the whistle, Fred and Barney could go home. Bordering the library was a federal courthouse, a county courthouse and our own police headquarters in a city of 55,000 people. I'm not sure who came up with the idea, but I know I said, "I'll take that bet, there's no way you fire your gun." "Oh yeah, how much?" "100 bucks", I said. Without a second of indecision, Danny walked over to a flower planter some ten yards away with a dead geranium in it. He drew his service weapon, a 9MM Smith & Wesson, and fired a round into the dirt at its base. It happened that fast. Never bet against somebody who needs money. The sound was enormously loud and reverberated off the concrete walls and columns in the garage. We all stood there laughing hysterically. Danny had a great career and left the department shortly after I did. I paid him the next day and nobody ever spoke a word of it, until now.

I was partners with Eric in a Super Bowl bet we made every year from 1996 – 2007. The football pool was run by a friend of ours in the fire department. There was always a standby list of guys trying to get involved in the pool. We would split the box each year, putting up $250 apiece. It was your typical 100 squares box pool that cost $500 per box and paid the winner $25,000 for having the final score of the game in the right order. For example, if the final score was 21-17 the person with 1 and 7 for the correct corresponding teams would be the winner. There were a lot of other payouts, including 1st, 2nd, and 3rd quarter scores, plus reverses and boxes touching the final score. It sounds a little confusing but is really very simple. We had won some small action in years past and were still playing with house money. In 2003 we had terrible numbers; 1 for the Oakland Raiders, and 1 for the Tampa Bay Buccaneers. With 1:18 left to go in the game, the Bucs intercepted a pass and with the extra point the score was 41-21 Tampa. I began thinking of what I was going to do with half of 25 large. The game, for all intents and purposes, was out of reach and over. I doubled checked my numbers to make sure I wasn't screaming for nothing. The Raiders were just playing for pride now and with less than 10 seconds to go in the game Rich (I hate you) Gannon, quarterback of the Raiders, threw his fifth interception. It happened that fast, but it still felt like it was in slow motion. There was a knife in my back and I was looking for the ninja that threw it. The ball was returned 50 yards for a touchdown and $12,500 was just taken from my wallet. My jaw dropped and mouth opened. Did that idiot just throw a pick with 10 seconds left in the game? Did I mention that I hated Rich Gannon?

I was in the Bahamas last year with friends and we were strolling around the grounds of the Atlantis Hotel. I played some slots for about an hour, winning a few dollars on Wheel of Fortune. I've had the opportunity to play in Vegas, Atlantic City, Mohegan Sun in Connecticut, the Hard Rock in Tampa, on the island of Antigua, and on several cruise ships. Three weeks ago, a group of us went to Tampa Bay Downs racetrack for an afternoon in the picnic area. My wife and I won enough to make the day very enjoyable. It's nice when you win, but you have to be prepared to lose. This is the money you worked hard for and you can bet it on anything; just remember sooner or later you're going to win. If you bet with a bookie on Saturday and lose over the weekend, you pay him on Monday; if you win, he pays you in five days. That's just the way it works. For every winner there are nine losers at a casino. Keep it in perspective, have fun, and remember where the ATM is.

There are two memorial football bets that will always be close to my heart. Actually closer to my bank account. On January 8, 2000, the Tennessee Titans were playing the Buffalo Bills in a playoff game. I was working a day tour that Saturday and had placed the bet that morning in the locker room. I took the Titans but had to give five points in the bet. With the score 16-15 and 16 seconds left on the clock, it wasn't looking good. The Bills had just scored and were kicking off to Tennessee. The ball was brought up field and a lateral pass was thrown to the left and caught by Kevin Dyson. He then ran 75 yards for the winning score and the Music City Miracle was born. Final score 22-16. The play was reviewed for several minutes which seemed like forever. You never know what's going to happen when the refs get involved. I stood in the squad room with some friends who had also placed a little coin on the game. Nervous time. That was a good win.

In November of 2001, I had taken the Buffalo Bills getting five points against the Miami Dolphins. Buffalo was up 21-10 at the end of the third quarter and I started looking at the 4 p.m. games to gamble on since I *knew* I was going to win this one. I reclined on the couch, sipping a little Svedka vodka, and thought to myself how smart I was. Long story short, Miami put up 24 points in the last quarter and I got my ass handed to me. Have you ever had your ass handed to you? If you are yelling at the TV and your neighbors are thinking about calling the police, there's a good chance your ass is being delivered by UPS. Final score 34-27, not even the points helped. Where's that ATM again!?

A friend of mine wanted to go to the horse races one day so we decided to ride our motorcycles north to Saratoga, N.Y. It was about a three-hour cruise and the weather couldn't have been better. I had been doing pretty good, winning two of the first four races, while my partner was tearing up his tickets. It was Labor Day Weekend of 1998 and I was looking to place one last bet before we headed home. I had picked out a couple of ponies that I thought had good pedigree, trainers and jockeys that were better than most. I decided on an exacta box bet and went over to the teller's window. An exacta box is where you pick two horses out of the field and they have to finish first and second, but in either order. As the horses broke from the gate, both my horses got a good start and were heading into the first turn when jockey Mike Smith was bumped by another horse in the race. Smith was first pushed into the hedges bordering the track and then was unseated. He was tossed up in the air and then landed hard on the turf. The horse he was riding landed on top of him. That's 1200 pounds of animal landing on your vertebrae. That was one of my horses. Smith broke his back and was carted off in an ambulance. Just my luck - not only did my horse lose, but my jockey winds up in the hospital.

Sitting around my grandmother's table for dinner was a part of growing up and being on vacation. It was an old farmhouse where 13 kids grew up in the eastern portion of Pennsylvania. Birth control in the 1920's and 30's? NO. I was probably 12 or 13 at the time and was feeling pretty confident about my next gamble. As we sat down for the meal one summer evening, I remember the huge pot of fresh corn on the cob being placed on the table. I was starving and looked over at my aunt with my boyish grin. This was going to be easy. "I'll bet you I can eat more corn than you." My Aunt May didn't even flinch when I offered up the deal. There were no secondary rules (e.g. how many kernels were left on the ear or how much time the contest would last for). The only thing I heard was, "You're on." My plan of attack was simple; stay away from my grandmother's homemade bread and the potatoes that were mashed with butter and heavy cream. It was a gentleman's bet with nothing on the line except for bragging rights. When I finished my sixth ear, I was feeling pretty good. When I glanced over at my aunt's plate, she had just knocked off number 10. I quickly gave up, throwing in the white flag and staring down at my stomach knowing the competition was over. I think she polished off another two ears just to rub it in my face; she was laughing at it. Never bet against somebody who sometimes went hungry as a kid.

CHAPTER 9

CONCERTS

I had been in Mississippi only a short period of time in late 1980. I was attending the Air Force electronic technical school there after basic training in Texas. There I met a group of good guys that I formed friendships with. I would find myself hanging out with the same four or five guys every weekend. While in school, we helped each other out with this new language of electronics we were learning and how to cheat on the next exam. The white sand beach in Biloxi was two blocks off the base and there were plenty of tattoo shops, waffle houses and bars in the immediate area. We saw a concert in town one night that featured .38 Special and a backup band called Molly Hatchet. They were both solid southern rock bands of the era. As we drove up to the event, it looked like a pick-up truck convention. I had never seen so many gun racks and good-looking girls in cowboy boots. Cheap Trick also performed there in January of 1981. We branched out after a while and started going to concerts in Mobile, Alabama, about an hour away. Bruce Springsteen and ZZ Top were well worth the trip across state lines. Bruce played so long that night that we had to leave before the show was over to make the voyage back to the base so we wouldn't be late for school at 6 a.m. the next morning. Who plays that long? Yet out of all the concerts I've ever been to in my life - from New York to Montreal, California, Florida and even in England - nothing compares to that night in Mobile on January 29, 1981.

If you have never been to The South, you need to go. If you're watching My Cousin Vinny and don't believe the Sac-O-Suds exists, you're wrong. We had put in a long week at school trying to figure out how electricity flows through a piece of wire and stuff like step-up and step-down transformers. What's the difference between a.m. and FM? Static. The group Styx was playing in Alabama that night and we had a full tank of gas. We cruised east on Interstate 10, driving 80+ miles per hour in my friend's white Ford Thunderbird. I was almost 19, which meant that being stupid on occasion came with the territory. The interstate takes you right into the downtown section of Mobile and you exit a block from the civic center. Mobile, Alabama looked like the Detroit of The South. After partying in the lot for the better part of an hour, we slammed a final beer and headed inside. The show was good with a packed house, and singers Dennis DeYoung and Tommy Shaw had the arena energized. After the show ended, one of my buddies stopped to buy a tee shirt on the way out. The four of us left pumped up with a great adrenaline rush but were dreading the trip back to the base. We were walking through the parking lot when a young kid about 15 came up from behind us and ripped the shirt out of my friend's hand. He took off running at full speed. I took one glance at my friend Carlton and the chase was on. Carlton was a big kid from the Boston area and had that Larry Bird look about him. Since we shared a common name, it created an instant bond. We crossed a street into a residential neighborhood and kept sight of the thief. I think we turned right, ran two blocks, and then turned left. We were getting winded. After about the fourth block we slowed and figured it was hopeless. We decided to make one last turn, doing a slow jog, and there he was about 30 feet in front of us. He darted across the street towards a brick home with a driveway that sloped downward towards a garage. We figured this was our last hope of catching him. Off to my right side I remember a car pulling up, but I was pre-occupied with what was in front of me. If the kid made it to the end of the driveway and could scale the retaining wall, it was over. As Carlton and I got about a third of the way down the driveway, I heard that unmistakable sound of a gun being fired. Oh shit! We froze in our tracks. The homeowner walked by us, giving us a glance as he continued with authority to the end of his driveway. Holy crap is that a big guy. He was dressed to impress. He had a tight afro and a tan leather jacket that came to about knee length. He towered over both of us and the revolver he was carrying added another three inches to his frame. So here we are, two white guys chasing a black male in Mobile, Alabama. If you watch the local news, you know nothing good ever happens next. He bent over and picked up the tee shirt the kid had dropped while climbing over the railroad ties. He walked back up the driveway, looked us both in the eyes and said, "I believe this is yours." We stood there in awe thanking him, but he wasn't in the mood to talk and barely acknowledged us. He proceeded up the driveway and met up with a very attractive female whom he walked to the front door. If nobody has a Valium, I'll take a Xanax right about now. We walked off the property and now realized we had no idea how to get back to the car or where our other two friends were. It took longer than expected, but we were all reunited and you can imagine the conversation on the ride home. All that for a $12 tee shirt.

Getting the chance to go to Hawaii was great. Some people save up for years just to say they have been there. Take a picture of me with Diamond Head in the background and drinking some watered-down cocktail on a crowded beach; yeah that sounds like fun. Pull out a folding map and be more like a tourist. My adventure started when nobody else from the shop wanted to go. Everybody had either been there before, didn't like the long flight, or knew they would be away from their family for an unknown amount of time. We were leaving January 1, 1984. I was packed and ready for the 10-hour flight from Okinawa that afternoon. My friend Anne and her husband, Fred, had moved to Hawaii about a year ago and it was going to be good getting back in touch. Fred was a native Hawaiian and Anne was happy to be out of the cold of Upstate New York. When Fred had to work one evening at the base, Anne invited me to a concert featuring Blue Oyster Cult and Aldo Nova. I thought to myself, *This is awesome. I'm in Hawaii, kind of working, on vacation, getting paid, going to a concert with this guy's wife. What could possibly go wrong?* "Ya wanna get some beer before we park?" I said. Anne pulled into a convenience store a few blocks from the arena and we got out of the car. It was quiet inside, a clerk behind the counter off to our left and one other guy in his 40's staring at the beer cooler. We walked up on his right side and opened the door to grab a 12-pack. That's when I knew something was wrong. He started mumbling under his breath and looked at us like we were hiding in the rice patties, ready to take out his whole platoon. The flashback got worse. As were walking away from him, he launches a beer over our heads. Thank god it wasn't a bottle. I looked back and the next one struck some shelving. He either had really bad aim or bad eyesight because we were only about 20-25 feet away from him. Anne and I got to the front counter where the clerk was already on the phone to the police. I was just looking to pay and get out of Dodge. He then ran towards the back of the store and threw another grenade which landed over the counter. The attendant checked us out and we made a beeline to the front door where another can clipped the glass and spider-webbed the lower portion of the door. As we got back into Anne's car, the police were pulling up and I let them know what was going on inside. Anne told me that in her whole life she has only had two experiences with law enforcement and both times I was there. I looked over at Anne and we just shook our heads, the night was off to an interesting start.

CHAPTER 10

JERRY

Last November, my friend died. His birthday was yesterday; March 27th. I'm not sure how or when I met Jerry, but it was a friendship that lasted some 15+ years. Soon after becoming a police officer, I was dispatched to his home that had just been the subject of a home invasion. Jerry and his family were not present, but his live-in housekeeper, Carmen, was. She was tied up, beaten up and the home was robbed. Both subjects were apprehended a short time later; I hope they are still being traded in prison for a pack of Newports. Jerry and I started playing golf together and soon it was weekend trips, golf outings, and New Year's Eve at their second home in Upstate New York. Jerry always had a story to tell and a quiet way about him. He grew up in the Bronx with stoop ball, Tony on the pony, and skully; the neighborhood games long before XBOX. If you were playing stickball in the street there was a manhole cover that served as home, first base was the fire hydrant, second was a chalk square outline, and third was the door handle of a turquoise Chevy Bel Air. My wife had known him and his wife long before me. Their home stood on the south end of town on a small knoll and had a driveway you wouldn't want to shovel in the winter time. He often told me, "I've got a pool in the backyard that nobody uses; why do I even bother to take the cover off?" His dry sense of humor and wit were contagious. There was a transitional period from my father's passing in 1998 and Jerry coming into my life. He was 20 years older than me and gave a lot of good advice, yet could act like a teenager if the moment was right.

When I got married to my second wife, Jerry was there. I had a timeshare in Hilton Head, South Carolina and the backyard was on a golf course in Shipyard Plantation. We were set to be married at 6 p.m. on the 8th green on September 22nd, 2002. We had about 50 friends and family members who had flown and driven there for the nuptials. The day prior was golfing, tying up the last minute loose ends, and dinner for all in the three bedroom house that stood in an area called Kingston Cove. Another golfing partner, who we played with weekly, was Terry. He was also there with his wife and daughter Dena. Dena was best friends with my soon-to-be stepdaughter, Amanda. They were both around 21 at the time. The food was great, the drinks were cold, and the evening was just getting started. At one point Dena and her boyfriend sat in the living room with Terry, me and Jerry. The conversation soon came around to relationships and Jerry looked at Terry and said, "So let me get this straight," he then pointed to Dena's boyfriend, "He's fucking your daughter?" Silence. The proverbial pin-dropping scenario. That's just the way Jerry was, direct and to the point, and I loved him for that.

Jerry said to me one time, "Have you ever noticed the birds flying overhead in that "V" formation?" Of course, everybody has. "Do you know how they decide on who's going to lead? Fastest bird."

It was late in the year and the golfing season was over in the Northeast. Our typical Sunday foursome had decided to all go out for dinner and beverages in New York City at a place called Sammy's. It's a Romanian steak house located between SoHo and the East Village, but feels more like an old Jewish deli on steroids. We feasted on chopped liver, potato pancakes and a strip steak that hung over your plate with a few cloves of garlic on it. Where's my Prilosec? The block of ice in the middle of the table encased a bottle of Polish vodka and the shots started immediately. Jerry made eye contact with two gentlemen that walked into the restaurant and he gestured a wave at them. A few minutes later he sent drinks over to their table, not having the faintest idea who they were. That was Jerry, very giving. We sat there laughing and telling stories and busting balls like guys do. After we had finished our meal, dessert consisted of egg creams with some U-Bet chocolate syrup and a couple of chocolate rugelach. As we continued to laugh and drink that night, the two men that Jerry had waved to earlier were leaving and stopped by the table to thank him for the cocktails. We spoke for a minute and one of the gentlemen handed Jerry his business card. The card had his name on it and his job description; Israeli Consulate to the United Nations. "If you ever need anything, call me" were his words to Jerry.

We made it back to Sammy's a couple of years later; the place hadn't changed. That evening, with the organist playing off in the corner and half the dinner crowd dancing, I watched as Jerry took his pants off and danced on his chair in his boxers. I believe there comes a time in your life when it just doesn't matter anymore. Jerry had probably already received news from the doctors at this point, and there was nothing left to do but be a kid again.

After I left the area we would talk on the phone a couple of times a month and Jerry had told me that five o'clock in the afternoon was becoming three o'clock in the afternoon. We would send pictures to each other of what we were drinking that day or if he was sampling a new bourbon. He didn't want to hear complaints or have to answer for a bottle being less than full when his wife got home. He conveyed to me how he would have one or maybe two, then fill the bottle up with water to make it look like it was full. I'm sure she knew all along.

Jerry and his wife had a second house, about two hours north of their home, where they would spend weekends and holidays together. It was decorated like you were living on a farm in Central Iowa. It sat on 55 acres with two large ponds in front and the driveway which bisected them. As you approach the house, a mailbox on a post was erected about 15' off the ground. There was a painted wooden bird on top and a sign which read *Air Mail*. The home had all the amenities you could ever want; pool table, hot tub and a fridge that was always loaded. It was New Year's weekend and we were doing lobster and steaks that evening prior to the countdown. Jerry was doing the grilling (with my help) and the water was set to boil in the kitchen. My other two golfing partners and their wives were there also. The ladies were holding court in the living room when Jerry got into a comical mood. It didn't hurt that we had been drinking most of the afternoon. He began a fashion show, first coming out of his bedroom in a full tux that he could have walked the red-carpet in. That was followed by another Halloween-type outfit. This was followed by his Farmer Bob get-up; it was an old pair of Lee denim overalls with one strap left unbuckled. He had a piece of wheat hanging from the corner of his mouth as he did his best Huck Finn impersonation. The beat-up old straw hat finished off the look. In a chair, off to my right, sat Terry's wife. I don't think she has ever laughed and tonight was no different. Jerry walked behind her, doing his runway modeling show. What happened next came so fast it was almost in slow motion; Jerry drops his manhood on her shoulder - right there in the living room for all to see. I was crying I was laughing so hard. Farmer Bob with the big grin and his straw hat. Dinner was fantastic, but the pre-game entertainment was better.

We went downstairs into his oversized basement that was a cross between a pool hall and a salute to every old-timer Yankee that ever played the game. Pictures of Yogi Berra, Mantle, Gehrig and DiMaggio covered the walls. I thought I had just walked into a new wing at Cooperstown. The old black and white pictures take on a different feel that seem to make it look more like a game than a business. I stared at the pool table and challenged him to a game. He was more than willing to remove the eight foot cover and let me rack the balls. He missed once and the game was over before I needed to chalk a second time. I was looking for the best two out of three, but that was not Jerry's way. He started walking up the stairs, "Cover the table."

I used to sit at the bottom of Jerry's driveway and do radar enforcement when I was a cop. I had access to his home and he had the best security in the neighborhood. You always knew where you stood with Jerry, he either liked you or didn't talk to you. My last meal with him was at a restaurant on Arthur Avenue in the Bronx called Mario's. We ate and drank and told stories about the last 15 years. After lunch I knew things weren't the same when he didn't want to take a walk down the block to get some cheese and bread. Jerry was a practical joker. He spiked my coffee with Jameson whiskey one morning, just prior to a round of golf - I think he did it just to see my reaction and get a laugh. He admired my wife Sue, which was a blessing because he despised everybody else's wife. You know you have a good friend when you can finish each other sentences or sit in the same room and not say a word. At 4:12 p.m. on October 30, 2013 he texted me for the last time, "Chemo stopped working, not talkative. Thanks for the call." I miss him every day.

CHAPTER 11

CELEBRITIES

I had been working overtime all day and my feet were killing me. It was my day off, but I made the 30 minute drive from my home to White Plains, NY to begin working at 7 a.m. Standing on asphalt all day is not recommended by the back and spine doctors of America. I looked at my watch and it was close to 4:30 p.m. A construction company had come to town years prior and started building high-rise (and high priced) apartments and condominiums. Cops were needed for traffic control, to assist with lane closures and to keep the cars moving. Concrete trucks and endless flatbeds brought in materials to the site. If it wasn't for overtime, I'd still be living in a shoebox. The first two buildings were 35 stories each and had gone up with the usual delays and problems. In 2005 a new project began on two more towers that were to house more condos and The Ritz Carlton Hotel. The main developer was Cappelli Enterprises who teamed up with Trump to build the 44 story towers. Every cop who worked that detail knew Louis Cappelli. He was the one writing the checks. He would often show up at the job site, toss me the keys to his Mercedes Benz CL600 and tell me to park it. The work for the day had started to wind down, which was good as rush hour traffic was approaching. The sales office for the project was located on Main Street at Mamaroneck Avenue. As I glanced over from the other side of the street, I noticed the largest person I have ever seen exiting the structure. It was like looking at the Alps or Ural Mountains. Shaq. He crossed the street, walking in my direction, as I took in the whole situation. As he approached, he held out his hand and we shook. "Just want to say thank you for all you've done." I've never been approached by anybody with that kind of fame who took time out of their life to appreciate what I was doing. We talked briefly and he mentioned he was in the area looking for an apartment for his parents. It's not often that a celebrity seeks you out. Damn did he have huge hands.

Bob Newhart came to our town in 1999 to promote the Arts Council and the newest building it was calling home. After his speech and the evening dinner, it was my job to drive him back to the hotel where he was staying that night. That's right - don't call a taxi, just have a cop drive you home. As he exited out the back entrance into the parking garage, he looked tired and a little pissed off. I pointed out his limo, an unmarked police car, and we headed off to The Crowne Plaza Hotel. It was close to 11 p.m. and from the look on his face I assumed he didn't want to talk. I was wrong. He began his story with a red-eye flight in from California that landed early that morning in New York. After getting to the hotel around 10 a.m., he was told his room wasn't available yet. He was annoyed at the hotel and his personal assistant who had set the whole trip up. All he wanted to do was wash up and take a nap. He spent that morning in the lobby of the hotel nodding off. He exited the vehicle and thanked me. It was one of those half-hearted thank-yous that doesn't come off very sincere. There's an old college drinking game where you watch the Bob Newhart Show that was on TV in the mid-70's (and still on reruns somewhere late at night). The concept of the game: you watch with your friends and everyone takes a drink each time somebody on the show says, "Hi, Bob." I was going to ask him about it that night but, using my better judgment, decided against it.

I was working a tour early in the 1990's and had just started the shift. I was headed south on Broadway when I observed a vehicle with an expired inspection. The driver had little paperwork to go with the auto, but did produce an expired license that turned out to be suspended. His name was Carl Williams. He was a professional heavyweight boxer with over 40 fights. He fought against Larry

Holmes, Mike Tyson, Trevor Berbick and Tommy Morrison, just to name a few. At 6' 4" and 220 pounds, Carl "The Truth" was known to have a temper. We spoke in detail about what was going to happen next; the car was going to be impounded and he'd have to come to headquarters to see the judge. I learned from an older cop years prior that telling somebody they're going to jail or prison just makes matters worse. By the time they realize that they got arrested, you're almost done with the paperwork. Carl assured me I wasn't going to need the rest of the police force to get him into the police car. "I'm going to cuff you in the front like a gentleman, okay?" I transported him without incident. We spoke about his boxing career, the last fight he had with his girlfriend, and when he could get his car back. At one point, he asked about any warrants he may have had that were outstanding. He looked a little shocked when I told him he was good there. He passed away in 2013 at the age of 53.

I was called to the home of Charles Oakley once as a police officer. He was living in the south end of the city in an area called Brook Hills. He was playing for the New York Knicks at the time and lived in a modest townhouse. It was a snowy winter night with some heavy winds and already about six inches of accumulation on the streets. It took me awhile to maneuver my way to his home, up a steep hill that the plows hadn't gotten to yet. Upon arrival, there were two kids near his sidewalk with shovels. Mr. Oakley was standing at the front door in a pair of sweats and a hoodie. He told me that the condo association takes care of his walkway and driveway, and that he just wanted these kids to leave his property. It was a simple call, "Guys, you're not getting paid for this, I'd think about trying another street." Mr. Oakley thanked me and asked if I needed anything from him. Everybody in town knew Charles and were probably always trying to hit him up for tickets, autographs, and gear. I told him we were good, "I've got all your information."

As I pulled into the driveway, the home sat on the right and there was a large metal wagon wheel that decorated the property. I could see three men off in the distance trying to cut down an old rotten tree. The chainsaw was doing its part and bark chips were flying everywhere. I exited the van that I was driving that day, your basic white panel type that had about $100,000 worth of furs in it. I was working a side job for a furrier and, being that it was mid-April in the Northeast, it was time to pick up all the coats and store them for the summer. I was in Greenwich, Connecticut, an upscale town in the southwestern corner of the state. As I glanced over the paperwork, the homeowner walked towards me while brushing sawdust off his black and red flannel shirt. He asked if I was there for the coats and motioned for to me to wait where I was - he would meet me at the front door. I looked at the paperwork again - that's Tom Seaver, 300 game winner and Hall of Famer. He opened the front door and invited me into his home. We talked a little baseball as he went through the pockets of his wife's coats. He pulled out a few recipes and some money. "Oh, that's where she's keeping it." He signed the receipt book and I was on my way. Being a New York Mets fan, it was a definite thrill and brought back distinct memories of me and my father watching baseball games at Shea Stadium.

There were always celebrities getting on and off airplanes when I worked at Westchester County Airport. The airport was convenient and you never had to worry about traffic. Hulk Hogan was taking a flight to Detroit once and he stopped to talk with us. He was very approachable and commented that his disguise didn't work. There used to be a senior golf event in the area and Chi Chi Rodriguez flew in late one evening on a private plane. As I approached the aircraft to remove his luggage he exited the plane and said, "What are you trying to do, steal my clubs?" He was joking, of course, and told us he wasn't too big to carry his own luggage. Superman (Christopher Reeve) used to fly in from time to time - not the nicest to deal with. He had an attitude, a chip on his shoulder, and thought his shit didn't stink.

The radar detector read 62 mph. There were three or four of us doing speed enforcement that day on Westchester Avenue where the posted speed limit is 40 mph. I stepped out into the oncoming lane of traffic and motioned the violator to pull onto the shoulder. It was early afternoon and the operator (also the starting center fielder for the New York Yankees) pulled to the side of the road. Bernie Williams supplied me with all the necessary paperwork for the auto and said he was just going to pick his wife up for lunch and apologized for the infraction. A couple of the other guys I was with that day came over to say hi and introduce themselves. Bernie was well known around town, walking down the main drag and shopping for guitars and parts at a local store. I asked about the upcoming season (2005) and whether the Yankees were going to pick up his contract. He was very non-committal about it and said, "We'll see." Do celebrities get a break every now and then? They sure do.

For about three months the movie Unfaithful was filmed in our town. Cops were needed daily from 7 a.m. to 11 p.m. We were directing traffic, handling pedestrians and onlookers, but mostly just hanging out by the food service truck. The caterer for that movie had everything. Egg white omelets with spinach and feta for breakfast? No problem. This wasn't your typical roach coach that services construction sites. You want almonds? They had four different kinds. Dried fruit snacks from mango to kiwi. The movie had a $50 million budget and I think half of it went to food and drinks. I never had to pack a lunch. I met Diane Lane early in the shoot. She had just come from filming at another location and was walking to her trailer. She still had fake blood on her leg from the previous scene. We spoke briefly and she appeared to be in a rush to get her hair and makeup done prior to the next take. One evening the studio rented out a restaurant at the end of the block that had been closed. A buffet meal was served by the caterer and I was invited to join them. Richard Gere was standing in line to my right as we filled our plates and exchanged hellos. I remember him as being quiet - almost shy - and he asked if I needed anything? "Pass me the hot sauce." He sat down for dinner at the table across from me and barely spoke with those in his party for the 20 minutes I was there. When the production wrapped up, it was sad to see them go. We had made great overtime money and did a minimal amount of work. I watched the movie when it was released the following May; I've seen worse.

There is not much to do in Nantucket. My girlfriend and I rode bikes around the island one day and did the walk downtown that afternoon. We had found a little bed and breakfast a few blocks from where the ferry stopped and spent two days there in the fall of 1990.

The cobblestone streets were littered with the fall leaves and the dark grey clouds lingered around all weekend. That evening we headed up to the second floor of a small restaurant downtown where the food and service couldn't have been better. At the table across from me was David Letterman, who was doing his Late Night show on NBC at the time. My girlfriend was hotter than his date that night. He leaned in a lot, pretending to be interested in her conversation, but I wasn't convinced. They finished long before us and I never spoke a word to him. As our server came back to our table I could tell she was visibly upset. She scraped the crumbs off our table with the edge of a knife and I thought she was going to go right through the fabric of the tablecloth. She took another drink order and we passed on dessert. "You know who that was sitting over there?" I gave a quick nod. "Yeah, well he just stiffed me on a tip."

CHAPTER 12

ONE-LINERS

When I was growing up we would vacation in the summer at my grandparent's home in a small town called Swiftwater, Pennsylvania. My mother's parents had a farmhouse there and about 40 acres. There was an old two-story barn on the north side of the property that housed equipment, including a tractor, tools that the Amish wouldn't even consider using, and the family car. When I was about 12 or 13, my grandfather had become ill and was using a walker. I remember him always wearing overalls with an old blue and white painters cap. He sat in the living room a lot and would read and watch the birds that he fed at the feeder. One morning, he pointed out to me several yellow birds that were flying around in the area of the bird feeder. They were keeping most of the other song birds away from the seed he had placed out. My grandfather picked up the Remington .22 pump rifle that was near his chair and handed it to me. I had never held a gun in my hands before. He wanted me to kill all the yellow birds I could. "Here's a box of ammunition, go to it." That was the training. I guess he hadn't heard of the child endangerment laws yet. It was almost surreal being asked in such a way. He could have been asking me to go make a sandwich. I asked if it was loaded and he replied, "It doesn't work unless it's loaded."

In January of 2013 my wife and I, along with our daughter and friend, attended a P!nk concert at the Tampa Bay Times Forum. We made our way to the third tier with beverages in hand. I was drinking Heineken that night and my daughter was kind enough to buy the first round. Our seats were good, directly opposite the stage, and I could almost see the paint peeling off the wall. As we waited for the concert to begin, the lights were turned off except for a few strobes that were flashing towards the stage. It had become fairly quiet in the arena. There were two girls that were directly behind me in their mid-20's who had been there since we took our seats. Camera phones flashed as the 15,000 or so fans waited for the opening song and P!nk to be introduced. It was then that the girl behind me yelled in her loudest voice, "I'd eat the shit out of her pussy."

My friend Kegger had a great line that he used more than once. "The only thing better than going to the bathroom on company time...is going on overtime!"

I first met Trey in 2008; he had become the head chef at the golf club where I was working. We had enough in common to become friends and played some golf every now and then. In 2012 we had entered a golf tournament in Myrtle Beach, South Carolina. It's a four day event that brings in some 3000 people each year to participate. After the first day of the tournament we were walking the six blocks toward the civic center from our hotel. The promoters for the event had dinner waiting for us, an open bar, and 200 vendors selling everything to do with golf. As we walked down the sidewalk we were approached by a homeless woman in her mid-40's claiming, "I'm not going to rob you, I'm just hungry." She continued her speech claiming to be a disabled veteran, POW, and Daughter of the American Revolution. Without hesitation Trey pulls his wallet out and hands the lady a dollar bill, "Here you go sweetheart, go buy yourself a cup of ramen noodles."

A guy I worked with, who was often called Montel but probably looks more like Steve Harvey, was dispatched to a call once. It was an animal in distress that could have possibly been deceased in the roadway. Upon arrival he radioed back to headquarters, "No, no - this squirrel ain't dead....it's just knocked silly." I almost drove off the road I was laughing so hard.

Montel backed me up on a call one day that was a dispute with some pushing and shoving between this guy and girl. It happened in a parking lot and involved a couple in their late teens/early 20's. He was accusing her of cheating and she was doing everything but answering the question. They were a good looking couple and I was trying my best to keep them apart as the "bitch", "fuck you", and "whore" words flew. As Montel came onto the scene, we got them separated and she began to tell her side of the story. "He thinks I'm cheating on him." "Well, are ya?" was Montel's reply.

In 2011 I was out in Las Vegas with some friends. Nobody should stay more than three days in Vegas, it's overkill. I was checking out of the MGM Grand Hotel at about 5:30 a.m. on our last morning to catch a flight back to Florida. I was approached by a very attractive girl in the hallway about 25 years old. She was somewhere between still being drunk and starting a hangover. I think we were on the seventh floor. She asked me, "How do you get out of this place?" The hallways there are long and it can easily take you 10 minutes to get from the lobby to your room. She was obviously a working girl finishing off a date. She proceeded to tell me she had never been in this hotel before and that it looked like a spaceship. First sign of a crazy chick - she's been on a spaceship. I escorted her to the elevators and we made small talk waiting for the doors to open. As the metal doors parted, a couple (also in their 20's) stepped out and walked past us arm in arm without saying a word. As we entered the elevator she said, "Damn, she's hot! I wonder how much she gets."

It was August 31, 2002 and there were about 12 of us headed out to the Meadowlands in New Jersey for the annual kickoff classic. This was the first college football game of the year. The game featured Notre Dame and the Maryland Terrapins. The contest was pretty much a blowout by halftime so a few of us exited the stadium and had decided to return to the cars to continue the partying. As we strolled back to the vehicles Greg, a buddy of mine, decided to take somebody's grill that was left in the middle of the parking lot. It was your basic 16" fire pit that used charcoal briquettes. He brought it back to our area and we started up the grilling again. We were all standing around joking and refilling our solo cups when three guys walked up to us and said, "That's our grill." Without hesitation, Greg (who had taken it) said, "Your grill? How do you know it's yours?" One of the three guys bent over, lifted the lid that was cooking some dogs and burgers, and pointed to the underside of the lid. "See those initials? Those are mine." With that, the meat was quickly transferred to the other grill and as they walked off all my buddy could say was, "Well, if those are your initials I guess it's yours."

My brother-in-law Larry and I were talking one day and had decided to get tickets to a New York Mets game. The venue was the old Shea Stadium in Queens, N.Y. Larry had started going out with this girl and the four of us drove down for a game that began just after 7 p.m. We got to our seats in the lower section on the first base side with a couple of beers in hand and about 30 minutes to kill before the first pitch. There were a few vendors walking up and down the aisles and Larry's girlfriend asked if she could get some peanuts. We were seated about eight chairs in from the aisle. As the vendor approached, Larry raised his arm and called out. The vendor then threw a bag towards us like he was throwing out the first pitch that day. It wasn't a toss or an underhand lob, it was a fastball that struck Larry's girlfriend right in the face. You could hear the plastic wrapper slap against the skin. We all had that *"What the fuck was that?"* look on our faces. Before we could even get words out of our mouths the vendor quickly realized what he had done and apologized. He then said, "Those are on me."

I was in headquarters one night and had just brought a subject in on a minor misdemeanor charge. He was a young kid driving around with a suspended license and an open warrant. He was handcuffed to the rail and sat on the floor waiting for me to finish up some paperwork and the booking process. One of my favorite lieutenants, a good looking Irish cop, was walking by and stopped to look at the party. "What's your name?" he inquired. The subject told him and looked up at him with a slight glare. "Wanna hear a story?" my lieutenant asked. The prisoner looked at him without a response. My lieutenant started the story of how when he was a rookie cop (about 20 years ago), he was walking a beat late one night in the projects - it was freezing cold, about 3 or 4 in the morning - when he came across this lady lying in the bushes. She was covered in snow and was barely alive. "We got her to the hospital but she was pronounced dead from an overdose. That night you were born, so if you ever hit Lotto look me up."

My grandfather spoke very little. With 13 kids to feed and a farm to run, I'm sure there were a few laws bent here and there. We were talking one time about the deer coming onto his property and eating apples from the orchard and getting into his garden. "November is when deer season usually begins, right Pop-Pop?" He shook his head and said, "No, deer season begins as soon as they set foot onto my property."

In 2009 I had gone to Myrtle Beach, South Carolina to participate in a four-day golf event. On the final day our flight of 50 golfers were playing on a course called Tigers Eye, situated just north of Myrtle Beach in Ocean Isle Beach. After parking the car, I was walking to the clubhouse and saw a guy in front of me walking with a hot girl who was barely wearing a sundress and the sunrise proved underwear was optional. In his right hand was a case of Bud Light, in his left hand a size 23 waist. Somebody from behind me yelled at him," Hey, you're not allowed to have guests at this event, you're going to get disqualified." "So disqualify me, I'm gonna have fun!"

Cops in town knew where the best food was, and if it wasn't the best it was at least the cheapest. There was a deli on Lake Street in our town run by three brothers and their aunt (who we figured had made over one million meatballs in her life). I ran into a guy there one day who had purchased a used car from a dealership and was now having some serious problems with it. He had taken it back several times for repair with no resolution. He was tired of getting the runaround and was looking for some advice from me and the typical crew that hung out at the deli around lunchtime. His choice was a simple one. He purchased a permit from the town to pass out free lemons in front of the car dealership. He would greet each car on its way into the lot with a free lemon and say, "Just want to give you a lemon so you can make an objective decision." He would then tell his story. The management team met him out on the sidewalk about an hour later and told him they would refund his money on the vehicle. When talking to people doesn't work, sometimes you have to get citrus fruits involved.

I began working in the pro shop at Palm Aire Country Club in late April of 2008. There were several computer systems there to learn, the phone was constantly ringing off the hook, and the 400+ members all needed their TLC. During that spring and early summer I was learning the ins and outs from the golf pro and his assistant. There was also another guy in the shop by the name of Robert, but everybody called him Bob. It was a fairly quiet morning after the golfers had taken to the course for an 8:30 a.m. shotgun start. Bob and I were alone in the shop when the new general manager walked in to talk with us. He had only been there a short time and was making a few changes and doing what managers of golf clubs do; trying to keep his job. He entered the shop in his usual up-tempo way with the same B.S. line he always used, "Tell me something good?" His latest plan was simple; starting the following week he was going to be closing the dining room, bar and lounge area, the kitchen and all unneeded offices one day a week. The only thing that would be open was the pro shop and golf course. Bob who had a lot more seniority then I asked, "Why are you going to do that?" John, the general manager, explained that closing every Thursday would save a lot of money. Bob looked at me then back at John, "Why don't you close every day? You'll save a lot of money." I chuckled to myself until John left the pro shop, then broke out in full laughter.

Bobby Bonilla, whose real name is Roberto Martin Antonio, played on nine different teams and for 16 years in professional baseball. When he was released by the New York Mets prior to the 2000 season, a stipulation in his contract kicked in; he would be paid approximately 1.19 million dollars per year till the year 2035. That's the agent you want working for you. Mr. Bonilla was playing golf the other day at the Esplanade Golf Course in Lakewood Ranch, FL, where I worked. After finishing 18 holes with his guest, another party in his group asked if he could take his picture. Bobby was more than accommodating and stood there in his black shirt, slacks and cap. As the pictures were being taken the gentleman made mention that the picture was going to come out kind of dark due to the apparel he was wearing. Bobby laughed and told him, "I've been black my whole life, of course it's gonna be dark."

Working side jobs as a cop is pre-destined since you will never get rich on a cop's salary. I had secured a job with a fur company in town picking up and delivering minks, sables, foxes, beavers, and whatever else we could stuff in the van. Did I mention chinchilla and rabbit? Pick up the coats in the spring, throw them in the company's air-conditioned vault, and then get them back to their owners in the fall. There were probably 10 or 15 cops on the payroll taking turns making pick-ups and drop-offs. Lila was the secretary of the fur company and handled all the ground balls and phone calls coming into the office. I walked in one afternoon with my partner who had paid a very nice compliment to her. She was 60 if she was a day, wore too much jewelry and had a love affair with cosmetics. She retorted in her best Long Island housewife slang that she was old enough to be his mother. The reply from my partner was, "You know what they say; old bones make good soup." Lila just blushed and went about her paperwork.

This guy came off the golf course the other day after playing 18 holes and was talking to a co-worker of mine. He was your typical looking douchebag, about 30, who needed a 7-iron to the back of his knees. He was one of those loud talkers who thinks being boisterous is a good look. "Hey, I heard you can get a blow job here from one of the cart girls after your round." My buddy looked at him and asked him what he shot. "88, why?" Without missing a beat he replied, "Missed it by one!"

CHAPTER 13

TRIPS

When I was stationed in Okinawa, Japan, serving in the United States Air Force, I had several opportunities to travel. Who doesn't like a vacation? There were two trips to the Philippines, a trip to the mainland of Japan to see Tokyo, a week's vacation to Korea, a 10 day adventure to Diego Garcia (I had never heard of it either), and three weeks in Darwin, Australia. There was also an overnight flight to Hawaii, but for some reason when you say "Hawaii" planes break and you're stuck there. That's a lot of packing and unpacking in the 18 months I was there, but they were all worth it.

When I was told I was headed to Australia, I had to break out a map -not having the faintest clue as to where Darwin was. The city lies on the northern coast and is home now to about 125,000 people. This was going to be a major military exercise called "Pitch Black." It involved the Australian, New Zealand, British, French, and the United States services. All branches of the military were scheduled to be there. We arrived at our lodging for the exercise and the eight of us who had come from the avionics shop in Okinawa were a little bit overwhelmed. This can't be right! As we stared out the window, the Army and Marines were still busy erecting tents and pounding supports into the ground in a field below us. The Navy was just off the coast with their fleet anchored. Here we were, a bunch of Air Force guys, viewing it all from the third floor of the Mindil Beach

Casino & Hotel. It was 90 degrees outside but we set the thermostat to a comfortable 72, then ordered room service just so we could tell everybody we ordered room service. We couldn't believe we had just stepped in it. For the next 21 days we lived like kings. We covered each other's shifts so we would have some time to explore and hopefully stay out of trouble. On the first day of the exercise, a French Mirage jet buzzed our work site at dawn and we all felt the heat from the engine and deafening noise that soon followed. The aircraft was about 100 feet above our heads. You don't forget that! We were all in our early 20's and getting paid by Uncle Sam to visit Australia and drink as much as we could. We learned to order beer by the color of the can. Blue = Fosters, white = Carlton Draught, green = Victoria Bitter, and gold was 4X. Damn, were we getting an education. Our AWACS aircraft only had a couple of issues while we were there and we were able to correct the problems without losing much beach time. There were signs posted at the entrance to the beach to warn everybody it was box jellyfish season so swimming was out of the question. Another sign advised where nudity was acceptable. *We're going there,* I thought, but it seems that the locals don't go to the beach if they can't swim. That's right - four guys on a nude beach without a soul around. Later in the week we rented a vehicle and drove into the outback, stopping to see crocodiles, wallabies (looks just like a kangaroo) and termite hills/mounds that were 15 feet in height. We posed for pictures in front of one hill and joked about it for the rest of the trip. The city had great bars and clubs and we would head out just about every night to do something. If you were working the next day, don't be late 'cause it would ruin it for the rest of us. We listened to a band one night play INXS music at a club called The Garage; I think that's where I lost some of my hearing. I met a girl there at a sports bar, and she started driving me around and keeping me away from the tourist traps. I met her family and we agreed to stay in touch, but you know how that goes. The party would soon be over and I had my last lamb sandwich for lunch at the mall. Australia was a good time, even the parts I can't remember.

My first trip after getting to Okinawa was to the lovely islands of the Philippines. It was poor and depressing. The streets were dirty with what appeared to be a lot of homeless people. Trash littered the back alleys and I thought, *Where's the garbage man?* The first time you visit a third world country it puts you on guard. Why? Because everybody knows you're from the United States and to them you're a millionaire. We had flown into Clark Air Force Base, the largest overseas base at the time, and were staying in Angeles City for a brief four-day assignment. We checked in to a semi-clean hotel where the pool was bordering on pond scum green. We were off till the next morning and I was lucky to have some friends with me who pointed me in the right direction (since they had been to the area before). Some of the homes in the area were gated and stood out from the other shacks. You could tell who the wealthy homeowners were; they would employ some 17 year old kid with a cigarette in his mouth and a machine gun to protect the residence. Where the fuck am I? The streets were crowded and noisy with the constant blowing of horns and sounds of motorcycles. The local taxis were called jeepneys, a cross between an armored truck and a small school bus. They were brightly decorated and painted to attract your attention. You could jump on, pay your 6 pesos, and jump off whenever. The local beer there is San Miguel. The problem with the product back in the early 1980's was that there was very little quality control in the processing and brewing of it. The alcohol content varied from one batch to the next. Three beers could be like drinking water and the fourth was 180 proof. It also worked the other way around. Girls were everywhere in the bars and on the streets and it appeared that prostitution was promoted by the local law enforcement. There were stages and platforms in the clubs and somebody was always dancing for an American dollar. Then there was the age issue; every girl was 18 and just had her birthday yesterday. Don't ever Google LBFM, its more information than you need to know.

"Hey, who wants to go to Diego Garcia for 10 days?" Hold on, let me check my map again - *where* are we going? The island lies in the middle of the Indian Ocean, due south off the southern tip of India, and is inhabited by American and British military. It's a horseshoe shaped island with a lot of banana trees and not much else to do. Nobody else wanted to go there from our shop so I raised my hand. After a refueling stop in the Philippines we headed west nine hours to our destination. The flight was seriously long as we sat in cargo net seats, not first class, for the takeoff. The seats were aligned down the fuselage so when you took off you were facing the wing and not the cockpit. Poker games broke out soon after takeoff, as we sat on the hard floor and adjusted our butt cheeks often. All the aircraft's center seats were removed to accommodate cargo that we would need for the 10 day journey. You made friends fast and trusted the guy to your left, the guy to your right always got your card. A meal was served in a box that may have contained some protein, but I knew better. The island was awesome and we had more free time to go fishing, hit the beach or go for a run. We had crossed the equator to get there and were now officially in the Southern Hemisphere. There was one large building on the island that served as the chow hall, sleeping quarters, and base operations. There was no air conditioning to speak of so it was more comfortable on the beach with the trade winds blowing than in your bed at night. Another reason why nobody wanted to go there. The whole time I was there I only saw the aircraft I was assigned to a few times. We played a lot of darts, poker and watched the sunsets from the hammocks we erected between the palm trees. Sometimes you have to believe these trips are done just so guys can get away from their wives. Let's spend 20 million on an exercise; see ya honey, be back in two weeks.

My friend Tim wanted to go on vacation and neither of us had been to Korea. It was an easy two hour flight from Okinawa to Seoul, or so we thought. We caught an early plane off the base and had hotel reservations for the week. Tim worked right down the hall from me in the radar/Doppler shop. We had a great relationship and we both played on the Air Force Rugby team on the base. When the captain came on the intercom system an hour into the flight we knew it was bad news. The plane had mechanical problems and we were diverting to another airport. We landed safely in the city of

Gwangju (pronounced like Kwang-ju). The day passed, and we were all confined to the airport since our passport destination was Seoul and we hadn't cleared customs yet. Finally around four in the afternoon it was determined that the aircraft wasn't going anywhere and that we were getting put on a bus to our final destination. There were probably about 20-25 of us who climbed into an old navy blue school bus for the three hour ride north. The roads were poor and a lot of them had just one lane in each direction. The operator was good enough to stop so we could get some food for dinner and Tim and I thought a case of beer should do it. We were on vacation. We had the last row of the bus all to ourselves as the party got going and were soon joined by two ladies who kept us entertained. After about 45 minutes it was time for a bathroom break, "Hey driver, next gas station can you pull over?" His response was, "No - we drive all the way, no more stops." I'm sorry, did he just say no? Tim and I looked at each other and the girls seated in front of us got that pale expression on their faces. There's no way we're going to make Seoul without draining our bladders. See, you can't buy beer - you can only rent it. The daylight had long since passed and there we are in the back of this bus trying not to urinate on our hands as we peed back into the empty bottles. Now we're laughing so hard it makes the job at hand even more difficult. We tossed the bottles out the window and littered the roadway all the way to Seoul. The bus pulled into the airport and Tim and I made a break for it out the rear exit of the vehicle, running like mad for the bathroom. The airport police chased us into the bathroom yelling and screaming at us. They were a little touchy on that whole customs thing. It was an interesting ride, we made some friends that night and didn't get shot going to the can.

Tim and I had a great time in Korea. We climbed a mountain one day in the middle of town called Mt. Namsan that had hundreds of visitors. The walk up is a definite quad builder. As we approached the top I solicited somebody to take our picture. The view in the background was the skyline of Seoul. Tim and I scaled a metal fence and then climbed up on a rock outcropping. "Hey, what's on the other side of that rock?" I asked. "About a 500-foot drop," Tim answered. The picture came out great. Don't ever let a spiked fence slow you down. After a few days in a boring hotel I moved into a girl's tiny apartment to experience how most Koreans really live. It was a 15' x 15' box that had a small kitchen, one chair and a bed that was almost off the floor. The bathroom was a hole in the ground just outside the front door and 10 steps down to your right. The laundry was hung on the roof where large clay pots fermented kimchi, a Korean side dish made of cabbage and vegetables. The whole adventure was an eye-opener and there I was with a beautiful woman, living in a shack. She had none of the simple comforts of life. Freezer? No. Washer/dryer? Definitely no. TV ….really? I bought her some lipstick and makeup at the base and she acted like I just bought her an Audi R8. I walked just to the outskirts of town one day where cattle walked in the street and a woman was doing her wash in a dirty river bed. She had a small child on her back as she squatted on the uneven rock. There were rice fields and farms and large steer pulling plows. Not a John Deere combine in sight. I left the country with a different appreciation for what I had. It's still a tough call as to which country is the poorest, the Philippines or Korea. Flip a coin.

My trip to Tokyo was very short, only about three days, but I made the most of it. There is an amazing part of Tokyo called the Ginza where on weekends there is no vehicle traffic allowed in the area. There are large department stores and restaurants there. People wander down Main Street without having to look both ways. No cars honking horns, no trucks spewing pollution. We had no idea what was going on until we found out later. The subway was the best way to get around; it's clean and runs on schedule. As I rode the train one day I had a tee shirt on from an old job I had that read "The Athlete's Foot, White Plains, New York." A Japanese man on the train said to me, "You from White Plains? I've been there." A half a world away and he's been to the town where I grew up - pretty wild. We were able to hit a couple of karaoke bars and sing with the locals. Karaoke is taken from two Japanese words meaning "without orchestra". The saké was usually served warm and brought to your table complete with a small Bunsen burner to keep it just the right temperature. We were accepted by the majority of the Japanese people; however, you have to understand that at this time it had been only 40 years since we were dropping nukes on them and they were destroying lives in Hawaii. Maybe it was me, but it felt like some of the older people there looked at us differently. Of course it could have just been my bad singing.

Before I started getting my things together for the trip to Hawaii, I was told by others that the plane was going to break down. Really? The pilots knew it, the crew knew it, and everybody who had taken the trip before knew it. The game was called "The plane is broken and now we're stuck here in Hawaii till we can get the parts to fix it". Every month it was scheduled to take a plane that had been in Okinawa for 90 days and return it to Oklahoma, the home base for the aircraft. The reason being that the plane would become compromised and systems would fail due to the high humidity in Okinawa. Sounds like a lot of BS if you ask me. So, keeping with the strategy, a flight crew from Oklahoma would fly to Hawaii with another AWACS plane and we would swap them out. We would then return to the land of the rising sun with the other aircraft. Like clockwork it happened again. The plane that we were going to take back needed a new fuel actuator pump. So instead of returning back to Okinawa that afternoon, we were stranded...in Hawaii. I called up a friend of mine who was a native of the 50th state and he and his wife put me up for three nights and showed me around the island. We headed up to the north shore on Oahu and watched 25' waves crash onto the beach. There were two surfers in the water that day that thought they could outsmart Mother Nature. I took a picture of everybody standing up on the beach that day as the helicopter pulled their bodies from the ocean. It was good to be with friends, staying away from the tourist traps and eating some of the best food that the locals cooked. They finally located that aircraft part (which was flown in from New Hampshire via carrier pigeon). Back to work.

CHAPTER 14

SKIING

After leaving the island of Okinawa, I was stationed at Minot Air Force Base in North Dakota. I had extended my service time by six months to get my resume in order and figure out what a 23-year-old was going to do for the rest of his life. I had flown back to New York to see my parents, bought a truck and headed west, it was October 1984. I had just made sergeant and was always confused when rookies saluted me. After getting to the base, I saw the brownish yellow grass of North Dakota for one week before it started snowing...and then it never stopped till I left. I found a small one-bedroom apartment 15 minutes away and three blocks from the college in downtown Minot. The house was broken up into four units. I lived downstairs across from a quiet couple with a small child. Above my unit there were four girls who were interested in the church and went to school to become ministers and keep their virginity. The last apartment was the largest unit which housed some 0members of the wrestling team from the college. Guess where I hung out? The parties were always loud on Saturday night after a match and even louder if they had won. There's a saying that goes, "There's a beautiful girl behind every tree in North Dakota." Problem is, the state tree is a telephone pole. Winter was just setting in and my boss took me shopping one day to get a block heater for my truck. Why do I need a block heater for my truck? Because it won't start when it's -26 degrees out. Some people would just leave their vehicles running all night, it was very bizarre. I worked on B-52 bombers there and vividly remember the pain in my hands and fingers as frostbite was always near. We worked outside all the time, there were no heated hangers or portable thermal units to stay warm. If you got lucky, the problem was inside the plane and not outside where the wind was howling. We had to do all the work by hand; there were no battery operated drills to assist you. There was a portion of the aircraft I dealt with often. It was a coupler that was connected to one of our radios and was mounted on the very top of the plane in the tail section. The unit was just a little bigger than a shoe box, but in order to get to it, one had to remove 96 screws on a panel three stories up. After the unit was removed and a new one installed, you guessed it, the 96 screws went back in. I couldn't wait to leave there; it was cold, grey, and miserable. Did I mention it was windy too?

I had 30 days of vacation saved up when I left the service in early February of 1985, and was going to go skiing till my bindings fell off. The first stop was Montana where my aunt and uncle lived. They had a home in Great Falls as well as in Glacier National Park. I took a break after a few days on the slopes and ventured north with my uncle to do some snowmobiling. When we arrived there some three hours later, several others were already there and had taken to the trails. My uncle called them the Hells Angels of the north. They all had massive snowmobiles and were outfitted with the best and warmest gear. After getting the sled off the trailer, my uncle gave me some quick pointers and said to have fun. I ventured into the woods surrounded by huge trees and two plus feet of fresh powder. I had been on the sled for about 30 minutes when I made a drastic error of leaving the trail and attempting to create my own path through the woods. I held onto the machine as it rolled on top of me and I started to slide down the side of a hill. Luckily, the sled went out in front of me as we both tumbled about 40'. So, there I was, full of snow, a lot colder than I was a minute before and unable to start the engine. I climbed my way back up the ridge to the trail and then that eerie sensation came over me... where's the main road? I wasn't sure whether to go with my gut feeling or head in the direction that I heard sleds. The sun was setting fast and I knew there was a time limit on this adventure. Everything starts to look the same after a while, another tree, more snow, and the footprints left behind by me. There were no posted signs or a gas station to get directions. It was a good hour walk till I made it out of the woods and to the main road just after sunset. My uncle was there talking with a few guys and drinking a cup of hot chocolate. He looked up at me and said, "It's kind of funny to see a kid from New York coming out of the woods without his snowmobile." I explained what had happened and one of his friends offered to help. This was after about five minutes of laughter and reliving the tale. I jumped on his sled and we rode back to the scene of the crime. He towed me out and we even got the snowmobile started. It was now pitch dark as we loaded up the sled. Looking back on that day, things could have gone really bad; if you ever have an uncle who tells you to stay on the trails...stay on the trails!

   I left Montana headed for a friend's home in Moses Lake, Washington. John was in the service with me and was working on a dairy farm that had about 250 cows. He taught me how to milk them at 5 a.m. and again at 3 p.m. We washed down stalls and equipment and he showed me the latest invention for knowing when a female cow is in heat. It looked like a road flare that gets inserted into the cow and when her temperature increased, the flare would glow a bright red. It really stood out at night. Send in the bull. After a couple of days of playing farmer, I was on the road to ski in Oregon at Mt. Bachelor and then to California to test the slopes at Kirkwood Mountain. I made my way through Nevada, but not before falling asleep at the wheel late one night near Ely, Nevada. I wound up somewhere in the desert and had to wait for headlights in the distance so I could get myself back on the road. I was driving a 1984 Toyota pickup at the time and there wasn't a scratch on it. I was thinking of taking a right turn and heading straight to Vegas after that. I wanted to ski in Colorado and was making my way across Interstate 70, looking for a place to sleep one night and then ski in the morning. There wasn't a hotel around that had any rooms, all I saw was 'NO VACANCY', so it was looking like a night in the truck. It was about dusk when I came across a guy hitchhiking on the road. I slowed to a stop and he entered the vehicle. I asked if he was from the area and if he knew of any motels that weren't packed to capacity. The conversation was relaxed and he said that I wasn't going to find anything around here. The place was sold out. He told me he was working at a ski resort called Arapahoe Basin and invited me to sleep at his apartment, which turned out to be a trailer a couple of miles up the road. There was only one stipulation. He was 18 years old and couldn't buy alcohol yet in Colorado. We partied all night and got along well. It was Jack Daniels and Coke for the both of us. In the morning, I drove him back to the mountain and he got me a discount rate on a lift ticket. I was his brother from Wisconsin who had come out to see how he was doing. He was able to get the afternoon off so we could do some skiing together. He showed me the mountain and his favorite trails and took me up to the summit just over 13,000 feet. We jumped off the cornice – an overhanging mass of snow around the outer edge of the bowl. That was pretty insane, and the landing was less than perfect. I'm not sure how far we jumped in the air, but it felt like forever. I left a garage sale upon landing, poles and skis everywhere. That night, we hung out again and said our goodbyes in the morning. He was hoping to make it to the end of the season in April to get his bonus check from the ski resort. I wished him the best knowing I would never see him again or remember his name.

I had learned to ski a few years earlier at White Face Mountain in Lake Placid, New York. (White Face was often called Ice Face due to the snow melting then refreezing.) It was miserable. Nothing compared to the snow and trails out west. The mountains are enormous and the lifestyle is a little more laid back. I headed north after leaving Colorado and made my way back to Montana skiing at Big Sky Resort and Bridger Bowl. Vacation was over for now and it was time to head east. The whole trip was close to 3000 miles and I enjoyed every minute of it. Did I say vacation was over? I still had money in my pocket and always wanted to go to Europe.

CHAPTER 15

MY BLOCK

Growing up in my hometown was pretty uneventful, or so I thought. My mother and father had purchased a single-family home that was on a corner lot and adjacent to a dead-end street. Nothing fancy, but a nice area of town to raise a new family. One house away and I was in a county park that was about 250 acres. There were hiking trails, a few ponds to ice skate on in the winter and endless hours of bike riding to new places. My parents were friendly with most of the neighbors and then there was the one family they despised. The Andersons were that family. It seemed that there was a verbal argument between them on a weekly basis. They would park their car on the street to make it difficult for my parents to exit the driveway or make it a point to throw debris in front of our home. They would actually rake leaves in the fall, walk them across the street and dump them near our hedge line.

I don't remember how old I was, maybe 10 or 11, when Mr. and Mrs. Baxter moved in. Because we lived in a corner lot, we had the front, back, and side yards to play in. The Baxters lived across the street from us and diagonally across from our driveway. It was early in the 1970's and the Baxters were the first African Americans to move into the area. I very vaguely recall my parents talking about it and what it meant to the neighborhood. Me and my friends from the block were too young and too busy playing ball and putting playing cards in the spokes of our bikes to give it a second thought. It was a typical afternoon in the summer and we were playing baseball in the street when I first remember Mr. Baxter approaching us. He looked at us and we all thought we had done something wrong. Did somebody go in his yard? Were we making too much noise? His first words to me were, "So, is this the team?" We all looked at each other not knowing what to say. He quickly put our minds at ease and said, "Well, if this is the team you're going to need some shirts." He motioned with his hand, "Come on, follow me." We walked down his driveway to his garage where he pulled out half a dozen tee shirts from a cardboard box, all with the same logo. They were white shirts with the words, "Everything's coming up roses," on the front and 4 red roses in the middle. We were 11 years old and could have cared less that he was a regional marketing representative for the Seagram's Liquor Company. We put the shirts on proudly and were now a team. He passed out some baseball bats made of ash and we ran up his driveway with our heads held high. Mr. and Mrs. Baxter were good neighbors and our friendship continued until he passed. I was at his funeral and went to the church for his service which was in Harlem, New York. I stopped in to see Mrs. Baxter a few weeks after the funeral and she was getting rid of all his clothes and belongings. She told me, "It doesn't mean I love him any less. I can't wear his pants, and looking at them every day doesn't do me any good." She gave me a gun he owned and asked if I would get rid of it for her. I did, no questions asked.

Next to the Baxter home on the right stood a brick two-story residence with a small front yard and a Japanese maple tree off to the left. The home was rented out for one year to a family from Brazil. The father was working in the area for IBM and they had two great children, Mauricio and Claudia. I always got along with them very well; they taught us Portuguese and, in return, I showed them every trail and cool place to hang out in our woods at the end of our street. They had only been there a few months, but we bonded very quickly. Two new friends that we could play ball and share our secrets with. It was early morning when the smell of smoke and fire ripped through their home. The fire department responded and saved the foundation. Watching a fire like that as a kid brings it all into perspective. What if this was my home? Where are they going to live? What about all their toys? The summer had come to an unexpected halt and our friends moved back to South America.

We heard the fire trucks and, later, the ambulances with sirens blasting. They were rushing up our hill toward the woods we knew like the back of our hands. It was the following summer and we ran into the woods to follow the uniforms in front of us. I was attempting to overhear what was happening, but with all the chatter on the radios, it was impossible. After about a five-minute walk, we veered off the trail where the smoke and smell was most pungent. Just off the trail were the smoldering remnants of an aircraft lodged between some brush and a few beech saplings. The plane was a small two or four-seater and there didn't appear to be any pilot. A large man looked at me and said, "Son, can you get away from the body?!" I looked down at the ground and it looked like a charred log that was still smoking. I don't remember what happened after that. In the weeks to come, we would take friends and neighbors to show them the crash site. I later found a wheel to the plane that wasn't near the wreckage and brought it home remembering exactly where I found it. My mom called the FAA and reported it, but nobody seemed to care.

Learning to ice skate came pretty naturally for me. I wasn't afraid of falling which is most people's number one concern. The problem with the majority of people is that you're so tense you can't even think about skating. You're trying to keep your balance without crashing to the ice and breaking bones. Everybody falls, Olympic skaters, professional hockey players, it doesn't matter. The guys in our neighborhood would always get together a pick-up hockey game going down in the woods. Everybody was welcomed and the ages ranged from 10-15. Quite often you would have to bring shovels to clear the snow, which then served as the perimeter of the hockey rink. There was a large lake that we loved to skate on which had a small island in the middle. This particular winter, it had gotten cold enough where it froze over and we were in heaven. We had been playing for over an hour and I can't remember if we were winning or losing. It was mid-afternoon, and the consensus was to grab a snack and something to drink over on the island and shoot the shit. As I was getting to the island, the ice collapsed and I was up to my shoulders in really cold water. Some of the guys were still behind me while a few had made it safely to the island. With the stick still in my hands, I struggled to find thicker ice and kicked, trying to reach the tiny bit of land. It seemed like it was miles away, but in reality, it was only about 10 or so feet. The guys were yelling as I reached out a hand and somebody helped pull me out. Being wet and that cold was uncomfortable to say the least. My fear now was to get back on the ice and skate over to the trail that would take me home. 20 minutes later, I was peeling off clothes and looking for a hot shower. I never skated on that lake again.

It was the winter of 1992 and I had been a cop for five years. Directly across from the front of my parents' home was the home of Mr. Gomez. I had known him for some time and he came across as a good guy with the usual problems we all face in life. This night was a little different. He had found out his wife was having an affair and he decided to barricade himself in his home with an arsenal of weapons. Being the sector car driver for that particular area, I got the call along with another cop. The call originated as a dispute between a husband and wife and we were attempting to obtain information regarding both parties. She had already left the premises, leaving one pissed off husband with guns and crossbows to his thoughts. Knowing the subject pretty well, I felt I might be able to unlock the magic key and he would permit me into his home so I could make sure he was safe and didn't need any further attention. That was not the case. He escalated the situation and it was going to be a long night. Supervisors were called and anybody looking to get a promotion responded. There was a Command Center established as there is for any major event and ideas and suggestions were tabled. I was assigned to the left side of his home and, every now and then, I could see his shadow as he walked past a window with the butt end of a rifle exposed by his side. There were no other members of his family inside the house which reduced the tension we all faced that night. The standoff continued for about three hours and then, for some unknown reason, Gomez walked out his backdoor and was immediately tackled to the ground by an officer. We seized all his weapons and the cold night came to an abrupt end.

Six houses up the street from my parent's home lived the Lopez family. The children consisted of two boys and two girls. The oldest was Frank who I think was 17 or 18. I was just getting into double digits myself and didn't have much contact with him. His brother used to hang around with me once in a while, but I could tell we were headed down different paths. The parents were blue collar workers and friendly with my parents. The father had a landscaping business and his wife worked with the School Board. Frank went to a concert in New York City with his friends one night to see Alice Cooper. I believe it was the Schools Out Tour, but it could have been Billion Dollar Babies. After the show was over, Frank and his friends made their way back to the train station at Grand Central Terminal. Somehow they got separated. Frank made his way to the top of a railroad car to get a better view of the platform and hopefully get a glimpse of his friends. He spotted them in the distance and yelled as he waved his hands to get their attention. When he came in contact with the overhead electrical lines, his life was over. It was the first time I could recall somebody that young passing away. My mom tried to explain the story to me and I thought there might have been more to it that she was leaving out. I felt sorry for his mom and dad, they were good people.

CHAPTER 16

EUROPE

After returning from a month of skiing out west and still having a few Jacksons left in my pocket, I felt this was the best time to book a trip to Europe. It was March of 1985 and I had come back to White Plains, NY, to a place I never thought I would be. The house I grew up in. It's difficult to return to your parent's home after being away for almost five years. I almost felt like I didn't belong. I was still waiting on calls to come in from Boeing Aircraft, Grumman Aerospace and a few other electronics companies. Nothing, not even a job interview. I'm still waiting, what do you think my chances are? I was hired on at the local airport but delayed starting till I finished my European trek. After being on top of the world for the last few years and having a steady paycheck, I gave it all away to be a free agent and shed the uniform. I hated that olive-green garb we had to wear every day. I made a call to Darwin, Australia and spoke with the girl I had met over there. We had stayed in touch and she talked about her aunt who lived in the South of France and invited me to stay with them for a week. Really? I always thought houseguests and fish have a three-day shelf life. As I remember, the whole itinerary was set up pretty fast. I was flying over to London for a few days, and then I'd stay with her and her relative, then back to London to start a 12-day bus tour of Europe. All sounds pretty great, huh?

My passport was packed, I got my airline and tour tickets and just enough clothes so I wouldn't look like a homeless guy or a tourist. It was late May/early June when the adventure began. I landed in London and found my hotel room for the next couple of days. The pubs were a block away and transportation on the subway (the tube) was easy. I did the usual Big Ben and Tower Bridge thing and Trafalgar Square freak show. Not too much amazed me at this point – remember, I've been to the Philippines. I stayed in an area of London that was predominantly Indian, turbans and robes, not 'can I buy your island for $24?' It was interesting listening to them talk. The toughest looking bad guy just doesn't seem that tough when he's speaking the Queen's English. I made my way to the South of France by Bullet train, passing through Paris and an amazing landscape. I was really looking forward to seeing my friend and I thought what an unbelievable opportunity it was. I arrived at her aunt's home which was situated in Nice, France, two blocks from the beach. It was a grayish apartment complex with a large garden and fountain in front that may have had 30-40 units. The place looked like it was 200 years old and it kind of reminded me of an old castle converted to condos. It was a simple two-bedroom, two-bath with a very tiny kitchen and just enough room for a small bistro table and three chairs. Every morning I would go out and buy fresh bread and we would have the best coffee ever. I know, everybody says that. I've got the best doctor, we had the best seats, how come nobody ever says I've got the best mechanic? They made the couch available to me which was all I needed come nap time. I was still pinching myself. The average day would consist of walking down to the beach, getting a late lunch, drinking wine, maybe doing some shopping and drinking more wine. Her aunt left us alone for the most part but would be home at night. She was very friendly and cordial. Back in the mid 80's, the beach in Nice consisted of thousands of flat rocks with a smattering of sand in-between them. They called it a beach, but it looked more like the rock quarry from the Flintstones. Everybody had these straw mats that they would lay on and pretend that they were comfortable. The point I'm trying to make is that it was a nude beach so I really didn't care if I was lying on rocks or getting third-degree burns. Things went very well for the first few days. There were no fights, I flushed the toilet, and bought items for the home as we used them. As I was walking back to the apartment early one morning with a couple of baguette rolls and some pastry for breakfast, I got hit with the bombshell as I opened the front door. Both my friend and her aunt attacked me with guns blazing. "Where's the jewelry? What did you do with it? I brought you into my home and you steal from me? Where did you put it, did you sell it?" I got this nauseous feeling and knew this was not good. Here I am in another country being accused of a crime and I can't speak French. The movie Papillion flashed through my head and I was not going to a French penal colony if I could help it. I spent very little time trying to explain my side of the story because they already had their story down pat. "A visitor in our home stole jewelry, officer. We want him arrested." I wasn't hanging around to hear those words. They held the upper hand in all ways. If I left on my own accord, they win, I'm out of the home. If I stay, they call the police and have me detained, they win. My head was spinning as I gathered my belongings off the floor and quickly shoved them into my backpack. I rushed into the bathroom and grabbed a few toiletries and I was out the door. No goodbyes, no thanks for the hospitality. My parting words were, "I didn't take it and you know that!" I spent the next hour on the streets, toying with the idea of going to the American Embassy or just getting on a train and getting out of there. What if her jewelry really was stolen and she's on the phone to the cops right now? *Don't panic*, I told myself. So far, it's just like getting kicked out of your girlfriends' house. I was worried to the point that it was almost making me sick. I was trying to put the pieces of the puzzle together but couldn't find any corners. Consulate...train? Consulate...train? I headed west and hoped the police weren't stalking out the railway station. On the train ride back to England, I had hours to go over the situation and evaluate what had occurred. To this day, I don't have a clue, not even a guess. I did flush the toilet, right?

I felt safer now back in the land where they spoke English, even though they still had bad food. The bus tour was still a go and it was the start of a new journey. I boarded the motor coach early one morning and we set off to Belgium. The 12-day tour had Germany,

Austria, Switzerland, Italy, Monaco, and France on the list. Am I really going back to France? The tour guide was pretty good; we stopped often for pictures and had a hotel waiting for us every night. I made a few friends the first couple of days that were all about the same age. There was only one problem: on the bus were five or six women from Pakistan or India that believed one should not take a shower or wash their clothes. Deodorant? Now you're just being silly. How about a little perfume, bitch? Several of us complained to the driver as well as the tour guide and got no satisfaction. What would you do? The smell on the bus was so rancid I wanted to throw up. We stopped for lunch on the third day and five of us from the tour decided to opt off the bus ride. We were leaving the tour and going off on our own. It was Survivor 1985. We got railroad passes for $176 and decided we would meet up every night for the hotel and meal that we were provided by the tour. Five people that had never met before were now the best of friends. We made the most of the time we had and because we were traveling by rail, we made it to the next hotel stop long before a bus could. That gave us more time to party and, realistically, how many German castles can you see? Switzerland and Austria were by far the two most special places. Between the people we met and the scenery, it was all really exceptional. Both countries were spotlessly clean and even though it was often overcast and raining, the five of us could always find a pub and, before long, the laughs were a daily occurrence. We were so glad to be off the bus and now we could do whatever we wanted with no schedule or smell to deal with. We made it to Italy and saw the Leaning Tower of Pisa, the Coliseum, Venice and the City of Florence. When we got to Rome, I was contacted by my parents through the hotel we were staying in to inform me that my cat had become very ill and was not expected to live. I had rescued him when I was out in North Dakota and brought him back east. This put a severe damper on the trip; he was in good hands though at my parent's house. The Vatican was crowded and the Swiss Guards that protected the area reminded me of the jokers on playing cards. The whole trip seemed a little surreal at times. On the one hand, it felt like I had paid all this cash for a tour and wasn't getting my return on it. However, when we met up at the end of the day with others from the bus and discussed our day, it seemed like we were not only seeing more, but having a lot more fun. I felt sorry for the older people on the bus who had no choice but to endure the odor that never faded. I did go back to France and see Paris. I caught a show at the Moulin Rouge one night. It kind of felt like the original Cirque Du Soleil, but a lot more polished. The Eiffel Tower, Arc de Triomphe and Notre Dame also made my list of touristy stuff to see. The people there hated us for whatever reason, their attitude was snobbish and trying to get service if you spoke English was a chore. One of the guys I was with ran out of money and had to sell his watch on a street corner. I told him he could always get back on the bus, but he wanted no part of that. It's just a watch, right? Our last night in Paris was our farewell tour. We ate and drank and promised each other we would stay in touch. We never did. In the early morning hours, we made our way to the subway for the ride back to the hotel. The only problem was that we were on the wrong side of the tracks. Instead of walking around like normal people, we were jumping tracks at 1 a.m. and running between pillars to the other side of the platform. The subway cars there had rubber tires which made them super quiet, so they didn't have that usual train clatter that is usually associated with trains. By the time the five of us made it back to England, we were ready for a vacation. The trip was over, and I was going home to a new job and a sick cat that I would have to put down.

CHAPTER 17

NEVER CONVICTED

The first home I ever owned was a 10 x 50 shit brown trailer in Plattsburgh, New York. Purchase price: $2500. I was 19 years old and a homeowner. Does a trailer count as being a homeowner? Walk up three steps and there was a small front stoop that led inside. The kitchen and table were off to the right and the living room/mud room/TV room was directly in front of you. To the left of that was the hallway which led to a tiny second bedroom, then a bath, and finally, another bedroom that was considered the master at the far end. The previous owners were also military and being discharged from the area. I knew them vaguely and they seemed like good guys getting ready to relocate. You know the old expression, 'you can always get laid living in the trailer park'. The setup couldn't have been any better; a 10-minute bicycle ride to work and, more importantly, I was finally out of the barracks lifestyle. I had closed early in the day on the property and then headed off to work feeling a little better about myself and my future. I was going home that night to my new casa. As I entered the trailer park, up a slight incline, there was my new home on the right about halfway down the lot. Okay, who the hell is this sitting on my front stoop? Being a little cautious, I got off my bike and before I could speak, a sincere voice said, "Hi, are you the new owner?" "Yeah, I'm the new owner." "My name's Harold, I come with the trailer, want a beer?" At his feet was a brown paper bag that contained a 12-pack of Genesee Cream Ale, minus a couple. We went inside and got acquainted and I tried to figure out if this was a dream or if I was just getting punk'd. Harold told me that he had known the prior owners and lived with his family just down the road. He worked with his father who was in the sewer and septic business. That's right, your #2 buys us steaks so we can go #2. Harold was 5 '8" and had a pit-bull mentality. He looked like a cross between an older Steve Perry from Journey and Alec Baldwin. I had never met anybody that knew so much about everything. He smoked Marlboro reds and told stories about the area like he was the local historian. Does this guy work in the town library? Harold was never at a loss for words and would lend a helping hand to just about anybody.

Soon after I moved in, I took in a roommate to pay for some of the expenses and he, in turn, moved in his girlfriend who couldn't cook. Mike was a good guy and his girl, Brenda, was easy to get along with. There was always a party to go to, something to do in town and when all else failed, Canada was 25 miles away. Two other regulars in the group were Fred, who worked in our avionics shop, and his live-in girlfriend, Anne. If we weren't at their house, they were at ours. We were all in our late teens and early 20's and partying until the sun came up or we ran out of ice. In the winter, when we did run out of ice, we would go outside and use snow to chill the beverages. It was like Woodstock 12 years later. It was early afternoon and Anne, Harold, Mike and I were just hanging out listening to the Moody Blues and talking about everything under the sun. Anne made mention how she loaned this guy 20 dollars a while back and hadn't heard from him in weeks. It's 1982 and 20 dollars bought a lot more than three Frappuccinos at Starbucks. She called his home and he said that he had her money and if she wanted to come over and get it, he would be there. Who wants to go for a ride? The four of us jumped into Mike's car and headed off some 15 minutes away to get Anne's money. Harold was riding shotgun and Anne and I were in the back seat. We pulled into the gravel driveway and we all got out of the car and walked towards the front door of the home. "Ring the bell again, what do you mean there's no answer!" Somebody pounded on the door and we got the same results. Weren't we just on the phone with this asshole and he said he would be home? We were all pissed off and returned to the car. I'm not sure how long we sat there, all with the same feelings and figuring out the next chess move. As Anne and I were talking, the guys in the front suddenly opened the front doors of the car and exited the vehicle. Where are they going? Anne grabbed my leg, pushing it down and told me to stay in the car. We sat there for a couple of minutes going over what they were doing and whether or not I should go get them. They walked around the side of the house and disappeared from my view. A few minutes passed before Mike and Harold returned to the vehicle. Harold had a slight grin on his face and Mike was hitting reverse, fleeing the scene. "Where did you guys go?" They were both talking so fast and rambling that neither Anne nor I could completely understand what they had done. I could hear the stones from the driveway hitting the wheel wells and undercarriage of the vehicle. We would learn that they had broken into the home through the back door which got my rabbit ears up right away. That was compiled with urinating on some furniture and then Harold bragging that he had killed this guy's cat. Mike exited the driveway onto the main road at about the same time as another car was pulling in. I'm thinking to myself, this is definitely not good. I'm not sure whose home we drove back to after that, but I recall some phone calls being made and, due to the severity of what had happened, it was not going away.

Three days later, there was a State Trooper knocking at my front door. I couldn't believe it took them this long to find me. As I started to open the door, he pulled on the handle and proceeded to let himself in. I was asked a couple of your run of the mill questions, "Is anybody else here?" "Do you know where Harold is?" He motioned with his hand to follow him as we walked outside. He then told me to get in the car. Anne had already been picked up, he advised. The trip to the police station was fairly uneventful, he asked the same questions over and over and just twisted the words around a little. The subject matter was all regarding the incident. We arrived at the precinct and I was still not in handcuffs as we proceeded inside. I was seated in one room with a glass wall between myself and Harold who was brought to the station by another officer. Harold was seated in a chair and being spoken to by an officer in uniform. The next thing I saw was that officer slapping Harold across the side of his head and he fell off the chair onto the floor. "That's an attention getter", said Buford T. Justice. Harold picked himself up off the floor and, within 15 seconds, was picking himself up off the floor again. Anne and I wrote out statements as to what had happened. One of the troopers said the best thing I did that day was to stay in the car. There was a plea bargain that happened months later and both Mike and Harold were found guilty. Mike had the better lawyer and with no prior incidents got probation. Harold wasn't so lucky. All this for 20 bucks. Don't ever loan anybody money, just give it to them if you like them that much. Harold did some jail time and after that was on probation. The friendship was no longer existent after that incident. I was told that Harold died a few years ago in an automobile accident. Mike went his own way, but his girlfriend remained in the trailer and we hung out for the better part of a year. A friend from high school came to see me one weekend and he wound up hooking up with her. They are married now and have a life together. Anne and I still keep in touch 30 plus years later. She married Fred, had a son and divorced Fred. I sold the trailer to a young couple from the area before I left for Okinawa, Japan. They were strapped for cash and he offered a motorcycle to complete the transaction. So, I sold my house for a bike. Not quite sure who got the better part of that deal.

When I crossed the bridge and stepped onto Rikers Island, the razor wire was the first thing I noticed. Home to about 15,000 prisoners at any one time, the place looked like a shithole before we made it to the first entry point. We showed our ID and told them who we were there to pick up. The gates opened and we parked as close as we could to the reception area. When you're a cop and going into a jail or prison, you get the privilege of waiting for the inmate you're transporting to be brought down to the receiving area. This could take a while. If you don't like the smell of old gym socks and feces, this will probably not be your best day. The odor in the room also contained that bleach stench. There's a lot of yelling and screaming and cold stares. The guns you came in with have already been confiscated at the front desk and you stand there naked with only a pair of handcuffs as inmates get escorted and searched in front of you by the guards. They open their mouths and spread their ass cheeks to affirm that they're not hiding any contraband. And you wait. You look at the wall to your right and notice it's moving. Never lean against a wall unless you want to become intimate friends with the local cockroaches. The prisoners you pick up come in all shapes and sizes. They were angry, talkative thugs for the most part. "I didn't do it, I got set up, this is another case of mistaken identity."

On the first Friday of each month, our town shuts down a section called Main Street, about the size of a city block, and turns it into a party. There is a band performing at one end of the block and a Budweiser truck somewhere near the middle. When I first moved here it was a few hundred people that turned out with a couple of lawn chairs and some beverages. Now, it's tough to find a parking space and looks more like a fashion show and who has the biggest watch or latest iPhone. The music wound up around 9 p.m. and my wife was looking for a bite to eat before going home. The eight of us who had been hanging for the last couple of hours had decided on a new place and sat down at the Main Street Trattoria. We weren't looking for anything fancy and got just that when the three pizzas came to our table almost an hour later. I was ready to walk out of there but got outvoted by the majority. If you're not eating pizza within 30 minutes from when you ordered it, there is a problem. It tasted like a rubber chicken. The bill came and we split it up. I grabbed the leftovers into a box, thinking it would taste better tomorrow, and with that, we headed for the front door. As my wife walked for the exit, there was a table to her left with a group of girls who looked like they just turned 21 and were on their second glass of red wine and giggling like school girls. One of the ladies was having trouble pushing her chair back as she attempted to get up from the table. Sometimes you got to lay off the carbs and do a little cardio. Her friend seated next to her then grabbed the back of her chair in an effort to assist her...and that's when it happened. As my wife is walking by, the chair swings backward and my wife gets her legs tangled up in the legs of the chair. She fell to the concrete floor, landing on both knees. I could feel the pain. It got out of hand pretty quickly from there. The assistant manager came over and started accusing us of being drunk. He had this smirk on his face and I was so close to dropping him. It's been a while since I have felt like that. "Check the bill, asshole. Three pizzas and eight waters." I got in his face and thought I might need a second hand for this, that's when I tossed the pizza box across the restaurant. My pissed off meter pegged out fairly quickly. My wife wanted an ambulance to respond to check her out. Now the manager is telling us we all had to leave the premises. Not once did he ask if she needed anything or assist her. Total piece of shit. The cops showed up a few minutes later and the restaurant wanted to have us barred from the establishment. That's fine with me, I thought, I'm never going to eat there again. So, the police took our thumbprints and we had to sign some form stating we would not enter the building for a period of six months. Guess that's the normal cooling off period where you would then go back and execute somebody. Six months and one day, come on in for the veal marsala, leave the Glock in the car please.

CHAPTER 18

RUNNING

I was on the "Rock" less than two months when I met Tim for the first time. That's what all the locals called it. Okinawa, Japan, was 70 miles long and about five miles wide. I had seen Tim in the building where we worked but never got a formal introduction. I was getting in a little exercise on the track one evening and he was playing some weird game with about 20 guys that reminded me of Kill the Carrier. Having never been overseas, I was still getting my feet wet and learning about this historic island that I was on and would call home for the next 18 months. I was an on-again-off-again smoker and he caught me in the middle of six months trying to get in shape and lay off the nails for the coffin. He introduced me to rugby that day and told me that the practices were harder than the games. I think he was just a good recruiter looking for another body. He told me that there are only two kinds of people who play rugby, "You either have to be big or fast." I could tell when he looked at my 5' 10" frame and 160 pounds that he wasn't going to put me in the scrum with the big boys. I joined the Air Force team that afternoon and figured I could be a bench warmer if nothing else. Somebody threw me a red, white, and blue jersey and started to explain all the rules. Good bunch of guys from the minute I met them. Our first game was 10 days away and we practiced for a solid week. Being fast had its advantages, nobody likes to get thrown down to the turf by a 280-pound giant, ho, ho, ho. I played out on the wing usually or inside the half position; it's a confusing game at times. We played the Marines as well as the Army teams that were stationed on the island. There were also independent leagues and a yearly battle with some studs – mostly rich doctors and lawyers who flew down from the mainland of Japan. They would come to the island for the weekend and face off with all the branches of military then go back home and brag about the experience. I had learned just enough of the native language to understand what they were saying. I played two seasons there and, like all rugby players, I got nicked up more than once. Mud, blood, and beer.

The fight was still going on a half hour later, it was July 31, 1995. My ex-wife and I had not even been married three years and were fighting more than we were fooling around. I sat on the couch smoking another cigarette, thinking to myself that I can't live with this crazy bitch anymore. Do you want to file the paperwork, or do you want me to? It was the last time I had a Marlboro Light and started running seriously the next day. I had run a few races prior, but now set my sights on a marathon. 26.2 miles of knee, back and whatever other kind of pain your body can throw at you. My first marathon was set for the following January at Walt Disney World in Orlando. I felt my training had gone well. Then you wake up to rain the morning of the race and are carving up a Hefty garbage bag to make an instant poncho. The skies cleared before we hit mile one and it turned out to be a great day. We ran through Epcot, the Magic Kingdom and Blizzard Beach with all the Disney characters there to root you on. I was still sore four days later and just stepping up from the street onto the curb caused my legs to cry out in anguish. I signed up for two more marathons that year, one in Burlington, VT and the other in New York City that November. The start of that race begins in Staten Island where 28,000 people hydrate and then relieve themselves in the world's largest urinal. It resembles the chute on a cement truck pitched at a slight angle and runs for about the length of a football field. Women would squat down right in front of you to relieve themselves without a care in the world. Certain things are acceptable at certain times. If you did that anywhere else, somebody would take offense to it and call for the local sheriff. Running across the Verrazano Bridge, I could feel the movement in the structure bouncing up and down with every stride. We ran through Brooklyn where store owners came out of their shops to offer pastries to the runners. In between those races, I was running at least a race a month. Anything to keep your mind off a failing marriage. The following year, I entered the Virginia Beach Marathon and posted a sub-four-hour race. The running continued, sometimes hitting the pavement in the morning and then again in the evening. I was addicted and in the best shape of my life... physically. I went running with a friend one afternoon and we had done a couple of miles when we hurried through an intersection and must have pissed off a motorist in the process. He got out of his car yelling at us, when we flipped him off, he took a couple of steps to chase us. He thought better of it when we told him we were doing another six miles if he wanted to try and follow along. At the Marine Corps Marathon (in Washington, D.C.) a year later, it poured. I was cold and considering dropping out late in the competition. It was another lap around the Pentagon and then the dreaded hill to climb towards the finish line at the Iwo Jima Memorial. Thanks to a really hot Naval lieutenant who rubbed some crap on my legs at an aid station, I was able to finish the journey. My last marathon was oversold in San Diego in 1998 and, of course, they ran out of water at about mile 23. It was nice to see a local brewery support us by bringing out cold beer - just what I need; alcohol and three more miles of asphalt.

In my years working as a cop, there were always a few foot chases. If you're wearing a uniform with about an extra 20 pounds of gear on, the advantage goes to the other guy. I never thought that anybody could outrun me until it happened one morning. I was working with a partner on foot patrol that day and we observed two subjects in a drug transaction. One passed off some contraband to the other and the chase was on. The rain had ended about an hour before, so my raincoat was unbuttoned and flapping in the wind. The faster I ran, the more I slowed down. By the time I made it across the intersection, I had been cleared for takeoff. How the hell is this crackhead outrunning me? When he made it to the rear basement door of the projects, I had come in a distant second - also known as the first loser. Damn, I hate raincoats; you wear them and you still get soaked.

My first foot chase wearing a badge was over in 30 seconds. Some guy had just stolen some electronics from a local department store and was now running down Main Street in my direction. As the call came over the radio, I watched him turn the corner with this brown box in his hands running like a cheetah on the Kalahari. If this guy running with a VCR can run faster than me, I better quit right now and open a bar. It's hard to fathom, but people used to steal VCRs. Times change. There were always those quiet moments on the job and then the next thing you would hear on the police radio was somebody yelling, "I'm in foot pursuit," at the top of their voice. This was usually followed by a brief description, location and a lot of heavy breathing from trying to run down some suspect. "Male, white, blue shirt, Post Road." Idiots…Post Road was like a mile long. I had backed up a unit one night on a car stop and was just getting off my motorcycle when the passenger from the vehicle bolted and started running. One block into the action and I knew I had him. "Why are you chasing me?" he shouted back. "Why are you running?" Two blocks in and I knew he was going to give out soon, he hadn't seen a gym or done any aerobics since he was in jail the last time. He crossed over the main drag in town and collapsed at the doorway to Baskin-Robbins. You just got run down by a cop in motorcycle boots, a full leather jacket, and helmet - that's pretty embarrassing. He was so tired that he didn't even put up a struggle. Now I've got a craving for ice cream, Moose Tracks or maybe a little pistachio.

There were a few of us involved during an investigation one afternoon. We had some good information from a source that there was a subject with a weapon in the area by the laundromat across from the projects. What a coincidence. It was the typical look for the time period; 18 years old, gold chains around the neck, wearing dark clothes. What, nobody in LL Bean? It was always good to check the footwear. Sandals or flip flops… not running. Felony fliers laced up… good chance. Two kids darted from the scene. These guys thought they were the next Jessie Owens. They ran up Dennison Street past the barber shop with a black bag and turned right onto Orawaupum Street. Two good sized hills and they figured they could outrun the average donut-eating cop. I grabbed them at the top of the hill with a nice assist from my partner. I'm twice your age, have a hangover that's still talking inside my head and I ran you two clowns down...must be the adrenaline. We got a couple of guns off the street that day and I got to bust their balls during the interview and booking process about how slow they were.

I'm not sure how many miles I've run in my life or how many I will be able to do in the future. Every day you get older, it's the law. My first knee surgery was recently and the doctor gave me the 'I'll see you soon' look, and 'I'll be needing a new BMW by then'. Have you ever seen anybody running that doesn't look like they're in pain? A few years back, I ran two races in the same morning. The first being a 6.2 miler followed by a 3.1 miler. It was to benefit three slain police officers that were killed in the line of duty in Tampa. What was I thinking? I actually came in third place in the second race for my age group. My daughter signed me up for a nine-mile run earlier this year that went from a bar to a bar. Nothing like a good daiquiri at 8:30 in the morning with your scrambled eggs. Every runner I've known in my life is either getting over an injury or is about to get hurt and doesn't know it yet.

My passion for running began in high school when I was working a full-time job during my senior year. We sold sneakers and running apparel at a store called the Athlete's Foot. My manager was an English guy named Martin who, whenever something went wrong, would say, "Bloody hell." He could be in full-blown anger mode but with his British accent, it made you want to go and have some afternoon tea. I was scheduled to work one Saturday morning at the store with a close friend of mine. Lee was going to be married soon and even after an all-nighter, I knew I could count on him to be on time. But on this day, he finally rolled in about an hour after opening with his excuse for being late. He was over in New Jersey and missed his turn-off for the highway. As he got to the end of the street, he had to turn around and that's when the cops stopped him. It wasn't the fact that he had a small amount of narcotics on him and got arrested; no, the reason he was late was because he got lost and couldn't find the highway. "If I had never gotten lost, I never would have been arrested." Lee always had a good story. At his bachelor party, we spent the weekend at a Boy Scout camp in the middle-of-nowhere Connecticut. On our first afternoon there, we went to the local food store in town that had two aisles for checkout and just as many people working there. It seemed strange that they would have a lobster tank, but there it was. "We're going to need 12 lobsters please." When that many testosterone-driven guys invade your local food store, the cashier, who became overwhelmed, called for backup. She summoned her manager who came over cracking her knuckles and preparing for the worst. One bag of potatoes, 12 lobsters, 24 ears of corn and seven cases of beer. I thought her head was going to explode.

Running was new to most people in the late 1970's, but I had a key to the front door and the Nikes and Adidas were flying off the shelf. I also had a lot of instant friends that wanted me to hook them up. Back then, gas was 59 cents a gallon and the most expensive shoe in the store was $60. People were appalled. $60 for a running shoe? Who's going to pay that kind of money? There is never a bad place to run; the beach, mountains, trails through the woods, even in the snow. It's an addiction that's hard to explain. I guess I could see a shrink a few times a week but that would require me to talk to somebody who can only ask three questions. "How did that make you feel?" "What do you think you could have done differently?" "So, do you feel better or worse knowing what you know now?" I'd rather lace up the kicks and try to run five miles and enjoy a beer afterwards.

I have been running since I was 15 and had a paper route. A lot of miles training and a lot of races from Block Island (off the coast of Rhode Island) to the polo fields in Quechee, Vermont. Running on January 1st is a great way to start off the new year. I have three basic complaints when it comes to running and races. If you're going to start a race at a specific time, it would be nice to blow the whistle, sound the air horn or do whatever it takes to proceed. There's nothing worse for a runner than to warm up and then stand there like a cow waiting for slaughter. I would complain about the lack of urinals, but everybody knows shitters cost money, so hit the bushes or pee between the cars like the guy who is pissing on your tires two rows over. When you get to that water station, if you're tired, need to walk a little, or you're just not ready to handle the next 10 miles, GET THE FUCK OUT OF THE WAY! That's right, there are people behind you who don't need to stop when they are drinking. This is not the time for you to set up camp and start roasting marshmallows. Finally, if you aren't wearing a number on your ass or chest, it means that you are a spectator. I don't need you to step out off the curb and run with your friends for 30 seconds to show your support. That type of behavior has caused me, more than once, to give that person a little push in the back and the fuzzy eyeball.

Kevin and I were returning from a night in New York City once and he was weaving his way through the usual midtown traffic. As he stopped for a light, a group of about five guys were crossing in the crosswalk in front of us. One of them thought it would be funny to place his hands on the hood of our car and push down on it. With that, Kevin jumped out of the car and identified himself as a police officer. They then took off running. I exited the vehicle and gave chase with Kevin. We chased this one kid down for about two blocks and caught up to him behind a restaurant in an alley. He crouched next to a dumpster and soon realized that having a 9mm shoved in his face was not the way he wanted to start the night. He was pleading for his life through the apologies. We made our way back to the car and couldn't believe it was still there, engine running, doors wide open. Remember, if you're out in the woods with your friend and come across a bear, you don't have to outrun the bear, just your friend.

CHAPTER 19

MOTORCYCLES

My first motorcycle accident was on an old Yamaha 400 Special II. That's right, the one I had sold my trailer for. It was the kind of bike that could get you from place to place, but you never looked cool riding it. I was working at the airport at the time and had done a double shift that day, arriving at 6 a.m. and closing up the last aircraft and putting it to bed just after midnight. There was a little drizzle and fog as I left the airport and started the 20-25-minute ride home to where I was living in North Tarrytown, NY. Everything was going well and I could feel the sheets in my mind because I was going to be in my bed within five minutes. I turned off the highway exit to the right and I felt the bike start to slide out from beneath me. This is not good! To make matters worse, I overcorrected, trying to throw my weight to the left side. The oil and grease from the roadway coupled with the moisture and some bad riding meant I was going down. The accident happened on the ramp and I remember hitting my shoulder first. I had hit the throttle just prior to the crash, hoping the bike wouldn't land on me. I rolled or bounced a couple of times and ended up in a puddle of muck next to a pothole. My ribs hurt and my left shoulder was on fire. I was trying to get my bearings and doing the self-body scan to check what still worked and what no longer worked, when I saw the oncoming headlights. It was an 18-wheel tractor-trailer with a load of cars on it and there I was lying on the exit ramp. Luckily, he saw me and pulled off to the side of the road and helped me get to my feet. The cycle was pretty well shot. I got it started, but it was stuck in second gear. I later managed to get the bike home and dropped it in the front yard. My shoulder and neck were killing me at this point and I could tell something was broken. I knew I had to take a shower and try to clean out the abrasions. That was painful. I woke up the following morning and finally willed the strength to go to a doctor. I had to take a couple of weeks off work after that to heal my collar bone which had a hairline fracture, along with some bruised ribs.

I was in my fifth year as a cop and switched tours one day with a fellow officer. I was trying to get a head start on vacation and was walking out the door just after 4 p.m. when a sergeant asked, "Where are you going?" "Exchanged tours today, got 10 days off coming." "The chief wants to see you." *You can't be serious*, I thought, *what the hell have I done now?* I rode the elevator up to the second floor trying to figure out whose Fourth Amendment rights I may have stepped on this week. "Chief, you wanted to see me?" It was the old knock on the open door and talk at the same time routine. He looked at me, wondering why I wasn't in uniform and I explained the schedule change. I took a seat in front of him and he stated that there were some impending changes in the department that were going to be taking effect soon. There were going to be openings in both the detective division and the traffic division and he wanted to know where I saw myself. At this point in my career, there were several other officers with more seniority than I had, and I thought he was just feeling me out. "Chief, if it's my choice, TRAFFIC." I didn't need a gold shield to feel important. Back in 1993, the traffic department was given the majority of the overtime. Verizon is digging up the street… there was a cop there on overtime. Somebody is paving a road… cop overtime. If your company was in town blocking a lane of traffic for five minutes, you called the traffic division, hired a cop and paid them time and a half. The chief asked me why traffic and I responded, "They make the money." Probably not the best answer, but it was the most truthful one.

After eight days, my blood pressure had returned to normal. I was getting sleep and didn't feel exhausted. Good vacation. The phone rang midafternoon and I picked it up, it was one of my captains. The call was brief and to the point; when I came back to work, I was going to be assigned to the traffic division. There was no big deal made out of it or congratulations from my superiors, it was all matter of fact and what was good for them. I had never thought I'd be considered for this type of position this early into my career. Cloud nine, party of one... your table is ready.

The first day of being in the traffic unit was a blur. Somebody told me I had to get measured. "Measured for what?" I asked. "For your boots and britches." "Boots and britches?" "Yeah, you're on the wheel." I needed to be fitted for the leather jacket, helmet, boots, pants and special gun belt known as the Sam Brown. This was the first time anybody had told me that for the next 12 years I'd be riding a Harley Davidson 1340 cc motorcycle and getting paid for it. The motorcycle unit consisted of seven guys; the entire police department was just under 200 at the time and the department I worked for had a lot of specialized units. The patrol division was the mainstay and where everybody who was in it was trying to get out of it. The detective division also contained the street crime unit, vice unit, youth division, along with those assigned to the case squad. In traffic, there was the radar, bikes, horses and a group of about five who were assigned a sector along with school crossings and church details. Another group of cops got indoor duty either in the records division, as a jailer, in the communications room, or assigned to the booking desk. It is really quite interesting how the whole department operates. The system appears to be set up so little cliques are established within the department and each subdivision of personnel gets their own set of perks and doesn't associate with others. Divide and conquer just like the Romans. Once you got out of the patrol division, it was always considered a demotion if you returned.

The traffic division at headquarters was in the basement of the building just off the garage. It was an office big enough for two desks, some file drawers and a couple of chairs. The motorcycles were all kept in the garage 50' away in an area called 'the cage'. My lieutenant, who was a cross between Dean Martin and Billy Batts from Goodfellas, welcomed me into the unit and asked me to submit my motorcycle license. This is where it got a little tricky. "Sir, I don't have a license." "What do you mean you don't have a license? I see you riding to work all the time!" I had bought a Suzuki 750 cc Katana earlier that year from another cop and had been riding it to work on days when the weather was good. That was a fast bike; 142 mph was my top speed one morning on the interstate. Pretty stupid looking back on it. I did the head shrug and confided that it was just a permit I was riding on – not a good way to start your first day in the unit. The veins in his neck started to expand and he shook his head. "Go down to DMV and make an appointment." Three weeks later, I was making figure eights and impressing the hell out of the DMV instructor.

Within the first few years of being a motorcycle cop, I had been on my ass three times and number four was right around the corner. In both of the first two instances, a vehicle had attempted to make an illegal U-turn across a double yellow line and, unfortunately for me, my right shoulder took the brunt of the collision. I was sore but refused to go to the hospital. The bike received minor damage due in part to the speed being less than 30 miles an hour when both accidents happened. There are so many bad drivers in the world that I'm often surprised there aren't more accidents and fatalities. When I retired from the police department in 2007, there were over 5000 motorcycle deaths recorded in the United States that year. At one point in my career with about eight years on the bike, I was called into my captain's office. I was tired of riding and was looking for a transfer to a radar car. He was practically yelling at me because I had another accident. I tried to explain my side of the story and that none of the accidents were my fault. Did he send me for further training? NO. Did he transfer me to a police car? NO. "Just be more careful" were his words. I walked out of his office laughing under my breath. Remember the scene from the movie Serpico with Al Pacino, "I have three things to say, I want summonses, summonses, summonses." There was no quota when it came to writing tickets, you could write as many as you wanted.

The bike unit did traffic control throughout the city during the rush hours; 7:30 to 9:30 in the morning and 4-6 p.m. in the evenings. Our town was somewhat unusual because it had a population of 55,000, but because of all the businesses, it was close to 250,000 during the day. We had our favorite spots for breakfast and that second cup of coffee. There was also a local bagel shop, a few diners and even a liquor store we would hang out in. When I was working the evening shift, there was the late-night coffee clutch with the boys to get you through the last hour. We had various spots in town where we would go and parking structures were always a favorite. Sometimes we were on the eighth floor, sometimes two flights underground. Somebody always had the job of getting the coffee. I couldn't remember my anniversary, but when it was my turn to get the java, I knew how everybody took it. It was a muggy humid night in the middle of summer and things had just started to quiet down. We rode our bikes up to the roof of a garage in town, unbuckled our helmets, and tried to catch a breeze seven stories up. We had done this before and knew the territory. Across from us was another parking structure where a girl was half naked on the hood of a car two floors below us. We could see them, but they couldn't see us. The show lasted less than five minutes. After they had finished, she turned and we got a look at her face as she collected her clothes. One of my partners said, "Holy shit, I banged that girl last week." She worked at a deli in town and was a familiar face.

One of the duties the motorcycle division performed was to do funeral escorts. We had three funeral homes in White Plains and were called on often. A typical funeral escort might have three bikes assigned to it and a couple of marked vehicles; one to lead the procession and a trail car as another set of eyes. We would show up at either the church or funeral home and then escort the vehicles through town, possibly going by the deceased's home, and then onto the cemetery. We would block traffic at intersections to allow the procession to remain together. We would also travel to other departments to show our support and respect when a service member had passed. A cop from New York City had died in a shootout late one evening and we traveled to Queens, NY to attend the service. Weeks later, his brother, also a NYC cop, took his own life over the death of his brother and I was back in Queens – same church, same cemetery. During one funeral escort, the line of cars was off to my left and I was on route to the next intersection to stop traffic when a lady attempted to walk across the street at the intersection. I had a green light in my direction and there she is, all 240 lbs. of her attempting to cross in front of me in the lane of traffic I was in. With cars to my right and left and nowhere to go, she was a human bowling pin. I locked up the brakes and laid the bike down doing about 50 mph. I fell off the bike to my left and got saved by my leather jacket and helmet. My back was screaming and I had that brain freeze headache like I just ate a scoop of Ben & Jerry's ice cream too fast. The bike never touched her. I rode to the hospital in an ambulance and took a few days off to recuperate.

In the winter time, we rode as long as it was above freezing and there was no precipitation on the ground. It was cold and by the time you got home, all you wanted to do was take a hot shower. In the summer with temperatures in the 80's and 90's, it was miserable. I wore a bulletproof vest that retained the heat and that coupled with the heat from the engine of the bike and wearing a helmet made for a long day. All you wanted to do when you got home was take a cold shower. People would often tell me how lucky I was to be able to ride a bike for a living, and I would always remind them it's still a job that comes with demands and the needs of the department. I did an escort one day in a snowstorm that took us into New York City. As we rode in a line with our bikes side by side, I looked over at one of my partners and said, "I can't feel my fingers." "Neither can I" was his reply. The snow and wind were so miserable that day, I don't think I thawed out for a week.

My last accident occurred in a parking lot where a vehicle backed out of a parking space and struck the front of the bike. It sent me in reverse, throwing me off the back of the bike and landing me on my tailbone. I came down pretty hard on my helmet and saw a few stars. A few weeks later, after I was back at work, I went to the guy's home who had caused the accident and issued him a summons for unsafe backing. He was in shock and couldn't believe I was giving him a ticket. I told him I was in shock too; you crash into a police officer and don't even ask how he's doing or say you're sorry?

There was a restaurant in town called Gregory's that was very well known and whose owner had passed away. Service was held for this gentleman and the funeral escort took the hearse, family and friends to the cemetery. Our lieutenant advised that we were invited back to the restaurant by the family for lunch. It was a cold winter day and we were all wearing turtlenecks and leather jackets. There were five of us there that day who sat down to a meal and broke bread with the family. We were thanked by several for the service we provided and the sendoff he received. The red ink started getting poured and we got the nod from the boss that this was going to be overlooked. He told us, "You're not a real bike cop until you can ride it back to headquarters with a couple in ya." We sat there telling stories, stuffed from the endless food that arrived at our table and drinking some of the best red wine I've ever tasted. Our shift was over at 3:30 p.m., but we were still there an hour later finishing dessert and saying our goodbyes. We rode back to the garage and put the bikes away in the cage. As we rode the elevator upstairs to our lockers, somebody made the comment, "Hey, you think we should put in for overtime?"

Being part of the motorcycle division, there were always times when we would do things outside the scope of our job description. Why? Because we could and nobody would ever question them. A commanding officer once asked me to escort his girlfriend to police headquarters. I drove two towns away, met her, and gave her a presidential escort in her white Pontiac to the front door. I was even asked to deliver flowers once to this girl who was attending an event. I pulled up to her on the bike where she was seated with friends. We were in a city park that had a large group gathered for the festivities. I reached into my rear saddlebag and produced a nice crushed bouquet of flowers. There was a lot of clapping and cheering; I just wanted to get out of there. I went on a domestic dispute one night between a couple where an infant child was involved. She wanted to leave with the child and go to a friend's home but needed formula. There I was at 10:30 at night buying Enfamil in aisle 5 at the food store. I took my own cash out to pay for it and wished her a good night.

In the 20 years I spent on the job, our department lost two cops to off-duty motorcycle accidents. Two other officers were also badly injured but returned to work. Jan (pronounced YON) was a great guy with a big smile and blond hair. He had that Norwegian look about him and got hit on every day – he was that good looking. A week before his death, I was locking a guy up and Jan assisted me on the arrest. We were both fighting with this guy and he finally complied after his face was smashed into the hood of the police car. I cried pretty hard at his funeral. Mike was assigned to the detective division and had two brothers, also on our job. I had bought that Suzuki motorcycle from one of his brothers. It was not very long after his passing that I sold the bike; I don't believe in karma, but I wasn't looking to find out if it existed either. Both accidents occurred due to another driver failing to yield the right of way to the motorcycle operator.

At one time, our city had four gay bars with names like Talk of the Town, Lads, Stutz, and a lesbian club called Darby's. I was 10 minutes away from calling it a night when the call came in about a fight at Stutz. It was a cool night to be on the bike and I needed the leather jacket and gloves. I made a quick U-turn, hit the lights, and shifted into second gear. I was only a few blocks away and pulled the cycle onto the sidewalk in front of the establishment. I walked in past the bouncers at the front door who were just pointing and wanted no part as to what was going on. There was a good crowd inside and I glanced at the bartender who had his finger out, pointing to the rear of the bar and the bathrooms. When I opened the door, there was blood everywhere; the floor, the mirror and around the sink area. The two guys who were inside had just gone a couple of rounds and I couldn't tell who had won. As soon as I opened that door, the fighting stopped and they both stared at me in my leather boots, jacket, and helmet. One of the guys spoke up and said, "Well... look at you." I was waiting on a Village People reference, but it never came. Neither of them wanted to press charges on the other, and I later learned that the fight was over one guy kissing the other guy's boyfriend. The bar just wanted them out. What are ya gonna do? People fight.

We did a lot of parades in the bike unit starting the year with St. Patrick's Day. That was followed by the Memorial Day Parade and Columbus Day Parade. We would sometimes travel to other towns to be in their parades as well. Being in the unit, we were usually positioned behind the color guard and flag bearers and in front of the horses. It's always good to be in front of the ponies. There was a guy that worked in the mounted unit with the horses that would actually be called out every time the horses took a crap. The code for it was a 10-65 condition. That's right, somebody had to sit down and establish a code for picking up horse crap. I always thought a #2 was the standard condition. The truck would pull up and out would jump Nick, a civilian who worked cleaning and feeding the horses, with his shovel and pooper scooper. After each parade, we would hang around the cage downstairs or office waiting on the word to dismiss us for the day. Depending on who was running the show, we usually got the nod and left via the back door. "Traffic division will be out of service for the remainder of the day." Those words were always good to hear over the radio. After 12 years of riding, countless tickets written, thousands of funeral escorts, courtroom trials and who knows how many hours standing on my feet directing traffic, it was time to take off the boots for the last time. I pulled the bike into the cage and collected all my paperwork. I stared at the coffee stains at the bottom of the saddlebags. Roll the credits, the show was over. Just like how I entered, there was no big fanfare when I left.

CHAPTER 20

COURTROOMS

Writing tickets and arresting people was part of the job and going to court and dealing with lawyers and judges went hand and foot. There are several categories when it comes to lawyers. There is the recent grad, fresh out of college and law school that has a whole dictionary of 10 letter words with their papers in precise order. There's the lawyer who is assigned as counsel to somebody who can't afford a lawyer. This is what I like to call the pissed-off lawyer. They get paid based on state guidelines and attempt to work out a plea deal for their client who has a rap sheet six pages long. Finally, there's the lawyer that has made it and just does it because it's still exciting to them and, no matter what, they're not losing any sleep over the outcome of a case. Lawyers came in a lot of shapes and sizes, but it seemed that most hadn't been to the gym in a while and should have stepped away from the buffet line at Pizza Hut. I admired that old lawyer with the more salt than pepper beard that always had a great story to tell you. I met one lawyer once who I don't think ever went to trial. Everything was a plea bargain. He was a great dresser and could talk the balls off a pool table. Lawyers hated coming to our city courts after a while because of the two full-time female judges who would stroll in whenever they felt like it. What time does court start? Nobody knew. People in the courtroom were always looking at their watches. "I've got a trial or hearing that's supposed to begin at 9:30 a.m. and it's 11 a.m. and the judge isn't here yet. That's not only an abuse of power by a judge, but flat out disrespectful." When I was on the stand being questioned by a lawyer, I always took my time and answered in short one-word replies if possible. The more that is said, the more room there is for interpretation.

I was working a 4 p.m. -12 a.m. tour and had been called to an apartment complex on the report of a subject making noise in the hallway. It was about nine or ten o'clock and was unusual for this particular building that housed mostly senior citizens. I responded to the floor in question with another officer who backed me up. A male party in his 70's was observed in the hallway with a beer in one hand and a cane in the other (which he wasn't using). We assisted him back to the room he was staying in and advised him that neighbors had complained about the noise he was creating. There was another female party in the room and he agreed to stay in for the remainder of the night. "Go easy on the beer, man, have a good night." We left the area, and before I could finish writing the report, I got a call to return to the same location because the subject was causing a disturbance in the hallway again. *Great*, I thought to myself, *now I've got to lock up this old guy for being drunk in a public place and making unnecessary noise*. We returned to find the same party in the hallway and placed him under arrest. He had become belligerent towards us and was demanding his cane that we took away. He hadn't been using it since we got there and now he wants to play the victim. Never argue with a drunk or an idiot. He walked to the elevators and down to the car, cursing us out the whole way. Pretty simple situation, right? A few days passed and I got called in by my supervisor to explain what happened. We were both being sued along with the desk sergeant for our actions that evening. Over the next few months, we met with our attorneys and gave deposition after deposition. The lawsuit filed against the city was in the amount of one million dollars. The defendant's lawyer argued two main points in the case. The first was that a hallway in an apartment building is not considered a public place, therefore, we should not have affected the arrest. The second was that by taking away his cane, we had infringed on his "handicapped status" and we had violated federal law. After a ruling in city court by a judge, the defendant was found guilty of being in a public place and our arrest that night of him was deemed to be good. We now went to the federal court on the other aspect and were in the lobby waiting to be called in for the trial. It had been almost a year since the incident took place. The two opposing lawyers met, looking to work out some sort of deal, but I knew the attorney for the city wasn't ready to cut one. The defendant's lawyer said, "What do you got?" Our attorney answered back, "I've got three cops in their dress uniforms with medals and exemplary records, what do you got?" We never made it inside the courtroom. The trial was dismissed and all charges against us were dropped.

In our building, the two divisions of White Plains City Court were the Criminal part and the Traffic part. Basically, if you were alleged to have committed a crime, you were in the criminal portion, everything else was in the other courtroom. There were two full-time judges and two part-time judges that sat on the bench. One of the judges that was there in my early years was known as the 'Hanging Judge'. Imagine you work your whole life to become a lawyer and judge and get hit with the nickname of the 'Hanging Judge'? Prisoners having to go before him knew that there wouldn't be any leniency and that nothing they could do would help their situation. He was an old Naval officer who had not only been around the block but helped to build it. "Bring in the guilty man," he would say over his glasses that sat halfway down the bridge of his nose. He had a little smirk that let you know he loved his job. We would make runs to the jail and bring back prisoners to appear in court and the first thing they wanted to know was who the judge was. He was not only a good guy because he was on the cop's side most of the time, but he made it fun while you were there. He was very sarcastic and I always left the courtroom in a better mood.

My wife once worked for the city court which was housed on the main floor of White Plains Police Headquarters. The new public safety building that had opened in 1990 was state of the art with five floors. She had a dual role there as both secretary and court reporter. That's how we met. I was giving testimony in a trial and she was banging on the keys of her steno machine at 225 words a minute. She would later move on and work for a judge in the guardianship sector of the 9th Judicial District. While she was employed in city court, she worked for Judge Jo Ann. They never really got along very well, so when she was invited to her wedding, I thought it was kind of strange - and guess who got to tag along? This is going to be boring. It was an afternoon reception and I was looking for the bar as soon as we arrived. Three hours of my life I'll never get back.

Jo Ann attempted to run for a supreme court position and during her second go at it, we exchanged some nasty words just outside the courtroom in the back offices. Like a lot of politicians and people seeking elections, she posted her name on signs and placed them throughout the county where she was trying to get elected. At just about every major intersection and traffic light, it was not uncommon to see 10-15 signs of various candidates stuck in the ground. 'Vote for me on Election Day'. I had finished trials for the day with Jo Ann and was picking up some paperwork when she approached me and accused me of stealing her signs in front of several people. "Let's go right now to the chief's office if you want to file a complaint," was my reply. We stood there, toe to toe for about a minute, exchanging words; me, an officer in uniform and her in her black robe, until she backed down and walked away. I knew she had no evidence or proof, and to this day can't understand why she would come out of nowhere and make such an absurd accusation. She refused to follow up on the grievance and walked off to her chambers. My next stop was the chief's office where I explained what had just occurred and that her actions were slanderous towards me. He tried to smooth it over and went down to her workplace to meet with her. What was comical was that she had accused both me and my wife of the theft of her signs. I called my wife to tell her what had just happened and she left her office a block away and stormed into Jo Ann's chambers fuming. This was all happening at the same time the chief was trying to figure out why one of his police officers was being accused of sign-stealing by a judge. It got a little nasty in there and the chief was on the fringe of having my wife removed from the building. My wife was calling her Pinocchio and never backed down from the issues at hand. There was never an apology from her nor did I expect one. I appeared before her many times after that in the courtroom and she acted like the event never occurred. That is one wacky bitch.

Have you ever gotten one of those notices in the mail to appear for jury duty? I just throw them out now, but at one point I thought, *Hey this will be like a couple of days off from work, why not? They're probably not going to take me anyway being that I'm a cop and would perhaps be biased.* Wrong! Wrong! Wrong! They couldn't have cared less whether I was a cop or John Dillinger. I got assigned to a grand jury which hears a case and determines whether there is enough evidence to proceed to trial. On the first day, I sat in the back row hoping to keep my head down, sunglasses on and not be noticed. The prosecutor started with a case that involved a young man in his early 20's who was accused of burglary, assault and criminal mischief. He had entered the residence of his uncle and, being a little intoxicated, decided this would be a good day to throw some haymakers and do a little barroom brawling. The argument started in the living room and quickly moved into the bathroom area. During the scuffle, the glass top on the coffee table broke as well as the lid to the bathroom toilet. The officer who had arrested the subject was put on the stand to explain what had happened and was questioned by the prosecutor. The uncle was up next and appeared to be a little apprehensive in his testimony. Did he want to see his nephew go to jail? Probably not over a little fight and some broken items. Finally, the kid takes the stand and proceeds to tell his side of the story. He mentioned that he and his uncle have a 'no-knock' policy when it came to their homes. If the door was open, you could just let yourself in. Never heard that one before. You can't be arrested for burglary if your uncle tells you to just come on in. I voted not to proceed on the indictment and got enough of the jury to follow my lead to get the kid off of another felony charge. Those notices keep coming in the mail and I haven't been back since.

It's been close to 25 years since the trial of the century. On June 13, 1994, just after midnight, the bodies of Nicole Brown Simpson and Ronald Goldman were found stabbed to death just outside her home on Bundy Drive in the Brentwood section of Los Angeles. The OJ trial will always be remembered as the standard that set the mark. The courtroom drama played out every day on Court TV and replayed every night for those of us who worked all day. The trial lasted over eight months and just before the verdict was read, I looked at my friend, Greg, and said, "Not guilty, 20 bucks?" He said, "You're on." We stood there staring at the TV along with the rest of the world. It didn't shock me like it did some of my friends. When you take any trial either to a jury or have a Judge rule on it, you can never be 100% sure how it's going to come out. There's a great scene in the movie Training Day with Denzel Washington and Ethan Hawke. A guy is on trial for countless burglaries and, before sentencing, he gets a hold of some peanut butter and packs his ass crack with it. He proceeds to pull out a handful of extra chunky Jif in the courtroom and licks his fingers clean. The judge says this man is insane, so he can't go to jail. Off to the puzzle factory for six months and never sees the inside of a prison.

Over the course of my time as a police officer, I would plea out 90-95% of my traffic trials. If you got caught for doing 64 mph in a 40 mph zone, would you take a deal to pay $100 with no points on your license and no increase in your automobile insurance? You would if you were smart. I'm talking not even going to traffic school at night. Our courts were so backed up that it was almost a two-year wait to be seen. It was the dreaded Catch-22 scenario. The job wanted more tickets written every year, but that meant more trials. More trials meant more time off the street not writing summonses. We needed to find a solution. A section was found in the Vehicle and Traffic Law Book that allowed us to do this. That's the book that encompasses all the rules of the road for the State of New York. Are you ready for this? Section 1101 states, "It is unlawful, and unless otherwise declared in this title with respect to particular offenses it is a traffic infraction for any person to do any act forbidden or fail to perform any act required in this title." The first time we started throwing it around in court, the judges had to open up the book and explain it to themselves. It's a backup plan written by the lawyers in case they left anything out and you still wanted to charge them with an infraction; and because it falls under the Administration Section of the law… no points. We could knock out 40 trials in a day without ever taking the stand. Isn't that what we're all looking for in this world? I'll pay the fine just don't hit me with those points. If you drive a car, sooner or later you are going to commit a traffic infraction. From the second the cop activates the lights and sirens, it's how you handle it that will make a significant difference when your case comes to court.

CHAPTER 21

EARLY YEARS

For the first three years of my career as a police officer, headquarters was located in an old stone building that had seen better days. The police department was smaller then with fewer cops. It was your basic Barney Miller looking building which consisted of three floors. The basement housed the locker rooms and cell block area for the prisoners. There were showers downstairs that were stained with brownish crud and green looking crap. Up one flight of stairs was the main level that encompassed the communication room, booking desk, records division and various offices for detectives and higher-ranking personnel. The top floor was the courtroom that, by today's standard, had no security whatsoever. I had the privilege, or maybe it was the misfortune in some cases, of working with a lot of cops who were brought up by the old school method. Our squad was comprised of about 10-12 guys that rotated tours. Day shifts from 8 a.m. – 4 p.m., evenings from 4 p.m. - 12 a.m., and the dreaded midnight tour from 12 midnight to 8 a.m. Most of the guys I worked alongside with had worked with my dad and I'm sure there were the cops who didn't get along with him. He made it to the rank of lieutenant and retired prior to me being sworn in. As a rookie cop, a lot of the senior officers spoke to me about my father. His deep voice was made fun of as well as his ability to save a buck or two. Each one of them had skeletons in the closet and told me about some of the stuff they had done and the trouble they had gotten into. This was always followed up with, "I can't believe your father never wrote me up for that!" It was a different time back then.

Sal drove 11 car. He was usually in a good mood and had a passion for golf and gambling. With a thick black mustache, he looked like a Super Mario clone. It was midnight and we had just finished a 4-12 tour. Who wants to go to Atlantic City? Sal was leaving in five minutes and had a comped room at the Claridge Hotel and Casino. How do you get a free room at a hotel? Win a lot of money or lose a lot of money. Sal was the latter. It would take the average guy three hours to get there, but Sal could do it in two. He told me once he was getting pulled over by the New Jersey State Police for doing over 100 mph on the Garden State Parkway, but he kept driving and just held his badge out the window. Only Sal could do that and get away with it. Back then, the casinos closed at 4 a.m. and he needed two hours at the tables. He loved to play craps and smoked more Marlboros than the Marlboro Man. Guys who had gone to Atlantic City with him said they would never get in his car again. He drove that fast. He would show checks of his winnings as we awaited roll call. $4000 here, a week or so later a check for another $6000. I thought, *That's great, but how much are you losing in between?* Sal and I bonded very quickly, and we played golf together every chance we could. He knew the rules and had his steady game. He would rather lose $2000 in Atlantic City than $5 on the golf course. Sal also had a side business doing security. He would contract corporate offices or private residences, then employ cops that were off-duty to watch these buildings at night. It was great for us to make some side cash and Sal would always spread it around so everybody could get a taste. He was one of the most likable guys in the department. Picture this: a police car parked in line at a municipal golf course at 5 a.m. to get tee times. That was Sal.

Bobby drove 12 car. The first time I rode with him we got a call to respond to a bar fight involving a weapon. We were a block away and as we turned the corner, the front window pane of the establishment shattered onto the sidewalk. There was a crowd inside the bar as we observed one guy exiting the front door. He had a knife in his hand and was walking towards us. I was reaching for my gun and Bobby yelled at him, "Give me that fucking knife, asshole!" That's not what they taught us at the police academy. The guy made a quick 180-degree turn, took a few steps towards the street and threw the knife down a sewer opening. That was Bobby, nothing fazed him. He was working two jobs, pushing a taxi cab during his off-duty hours and burning the candle at both ends. When we worked midnight till 8 a.m., Bobby had his favorite place to catch a few winks. The gun belt would come off and the handcuffs were neatly displayed over the rearview mirror. "Get in the back seat, kid." He did everything but put on pajamas.

Dennis drove 13 car. If you looked in the dictionary, under 'salty' there would be a picture of him. We were working a snowy Christmas Day tour and none of us wanted to be there. There is an unwritten cop rule that unless absolutely necessary, nothing happens on this day. No tickets, no arrests, nada. There were only a handful of cops working and I was lucky enough to get a car and not be assigned to a foot post. Dennis drove past me early that morning in car 13 and waved. He was wearing a Santa Clause suit with the red and white droopy hat and fake beard. That was Dennis, bucking the system and doing what he wanted to do.

Rich drove 14 car. It always seemed like Rich was looking for something for nothing. He would drive around and see things left on the curb and search through them like a vagrant. Firewood on the side of the road didn't have a chance. He would be loading it into a truck before his tour was over. We worked a side job together once that took us into New York City. We were traveling past the west end and Rich spotted a prostitute doing the morning stroll and looking for a date. It was 40 degrees out and she's walking around in Daisy Dukes, baby hooker socks, and no jacket. Rich invited her into the van to warm up and she asked if we could drive her to a liquor store. Sure! We drove up town where she knew of the only liquor store that was opened at 8 a.m. She cracked the seal on the bottle of Remy and took a large swallow then said, "Ya want some?" Think I'll pass.

Rob drove 15 car. He was a little bit too spit and polished for me and the rule book was his best friend. If you don't get your hands dirty, it's tough to be a cop and other cops will pick up on it right away. In a perfect world, he probably would have been the ideal cop, but we know better. His shoes had that patent leather shine where the rest of us were using a brick and a chocolate bar. Rob always looked like he just stepped out of a band box, sharp creases and a military gig line. There was just enough brown on the tip of his nose that we all knew he wouldn't be in patrol for very long. He was a company man and liked working inside for the brass.

Don drove 17 car. Whenever you got assigned to ride shotgun with him, you knew two things were going to happen. You were going to eat like a king and, sooner or later, you would be stopping at the hospital. It wasn't like he even had a girlfriend there or was visiting someone. He had a very calm demeanor and took everything in stride. It was almost unnatural because as a cop your adrenaline will fluctuate from one call to the next. Don was different. He never raised his voice in my presence. He wound up being terminated by the police department; seems those little trips to the emergency room were profitable. The last time we met, he had a small deli and was making breakfast and lunches for the locals.

Nick drove 18 car. Nick hated people. He probably hated me. He probably hates you and doesn't know you. To this day, I think I've only seen him smile twice and once was at a bachelor party. We were just leaving the diner one night for that last cup of coffee when a call came in which required us to lock this guy up. As we were driving him back to headquarters, this guy wouldn't shut up. F this, F that, F the police; it went on for a couple of minutes. Nick took a large swallow of coffee from the container, turned his head over his right shoulder and proceeded to spray hot liquid all over the defendant. He didn't say another word. Back then, the police cars were separated with a grill or cage from the front seat to the back. If some guy in the back seat is giving you a rash of shit, it's time to stop short. Waffle time. See, back then, nobody got buckled in so their face would slam into the cage leaving a nice impression. You want some syrup with that? Nick was referred to as 'Mad Dog' and had a great eye for the job. 4:30 in the morning, see that guy over there? Remember his face, he's a burglar. The old police building (which had no cameras) was the perfect place to get your frustrations out. After you brought a prisoner in, booked and processed him, you then had to take him down a flight of stairs to the cellblock area. A lot of things can happen over the course of 13 steps. As a rookie, I saw him knee this guy in the stomach and thought, *Well, he just broke a couple of ribs.*

Donnie was the jailer. Picture a cross between that annoying kid you always wanted to beat up and Napoleon. He would walk around headquarters muttering, "You got a hairy ass." It was a frigid winter evening with the snow piling up and gusty winds. A couple of guys were locked up in the basement waiting to be arraigned in the morning by a judge. I had been on the job for less than a year and was told to report to the cellblock area to assist Donnie and learn about how the operations there went. As I made my way downstairs, the cold air hit me from the back door that somebody had left opened. I went over to close it, but it was shut tight. Donnie must have heard me and let me into the cell area. "It's freezing in here," I said. One of the prisoners had been causing some problems and Donnie's way of handling it was to open the window and let some fresh air in. He explained to me, "Rookie, this is how we deal with shitheads." The guy was pleading with him to close the window or give him a blanket. "Keep it up and I'll throw a pail of water on ya." That was my introduction into watching prisoners. Being the new kid on the block, I didn't want to rock the boat or go against policy so I grabbed my coat from my locker and went along with the game plan.

Danny drove a post car. It's hard to describe Danny because deep down inside he is a good guy. Problem is he had two different sides to him. He was that guy that was usually the brunt of a lot of jokes and most of it was because of his own doing. There was about a half hour left in the shift and it was getting close to midnight when a gun call came in with possible shots fired. That's when you drop everything and respond to the area. Maybe Danny was a little gun shy, but guys were there from two miles away before he could make it three blocks. Situation was that this happened more than once and a trust issue comes about. I don't want this guy backing me up! He had words one night with the sergeant over a similar incident and Danny got big and brave and called him out to fight in the rear of headquarters by the gas pump. They never threw a punch which made it look even worse for Danny. At 2 a.m. one morning, the entire squad - about 15 guys - were starving and the order was placed to go get White Castle burgers. Everybody chipped in and 150 burgers with onions and cheese were ordered. Danny didn't want any. What do you do with the cardboard containers from the burgers? They were shoved into the vents of Danny's locker.

Lieutenant Doc: This was my first lieutenant and from the outset we did not get along very well. I stopped a lady one night for going through two red lights at excessive speed. When she finally pulled over, her license was found to be suspended along with a couple of other minor infractions. She was a little jumpy at the scene and refused to cooperate with some of my simple requests. "Lady, you're going to headquarters, how you do it is up to you." She had a laundry list of all the cops she knew and thought by telling me all their names she was going to get a free pass. After arriving back at the station, I quickly learned that she and Doc had a friendship also. After writing her a couple of summonses, the lieutenant told me to drive her home since I had impounded her vehicle. Really? This bitch just gave me a hard time out on the streets and now I'm her Uber driver. Doc and I had that sparring relationship. He told me to go get coffee one night right after roll call; great, now I'm your chauffeur and server. I was on my way down Central Avenue, it was 12:06 a.m. when I stopped a vehicle that was parked at a green light for two cycles. Negative on that coffee, I've got one in custody for DWI. Six minutes into the shift and I have four hours of paperwork ahead of me. He gave me crap for that for over a month. He could be a real moody bastard. He had a limo company and was always looking for people to do runs for him to the airports or an occasional wedding or prom. I guess he was stuck one day and offered me a job driving a father and daughter from the area to Rochester, NY for her graduation. The trip is well over five hours each way. It was early June and the thermometer outside was in the upper 80's. The AC broke on the way home and we sweated like pigs with the windows rolled down. Doc asked me the next day if I got tipped and how much. "Sure did, $100." "Good," he replied, "then that's your pay since now I have to fix the car's AC." I never drove for him again. As the years progressed, he developed a bad heart and got put on the list for a transplant. It was soon after that he became the recipient of a new ticker from a 22-year-old kid who had passed away in a car accident. This is where the story gets good. He goes on to marry a girl that was in my academy class. I was at Nancy's first wedding when she married a guy with a Coca-Cola route, maybe it was Pepsi, doesn't matter. I looked around the room during the reception that evening and noticed that I was only one of three cops she had invited to the ceremony. She was on the job for about nine years and then retired. Here she was in her early 30's and Doc had to have been 55 plus. They both moved to the east coast of Florida where they hooked up for a while, but it didn't last. Nancy went on to work with the Palm Beach County Sheriff's Department. Here's the encore: my friend, Nancy, took her life in January of 2012; she was 46. Doc ended his own life about 10 years earlier; two people I worked with that both committed suicide.

George and Ronnie walked post 4. They were two of the four regular guys that had this post and they couldn't have been more opposite in nature. Ronnie on a good day was lazy and did the bare minimum. I had to work with him a few times and it was dreadful. His idea of policing was to go to the ambulance headquarters and find a couch to fall into. He carried a pair of sap gloves with him at all times. These were black leather gloves that had lead sewn into the material. If you made a fist, the striking portion of your hand was like hitting someone with a pipe wrench. Post 4 was the projects. Five buildings that were nine stories in height and had a total of 450 apartments. The elevators were rancid with urine most of the time and garbage was thrown throughout the building. It only takes a small percentage of people to make it miserable for the rest. George had a natural way about him and was very easy to like. The first time he took me under his wing, we were across the street from the projects in a small wooded area. George had his binoculars out and was observing the activity in the doorway of one of the buildings. "There it is." He had just observed a hand to hand transaction where one drug dealer was passing off the product to the buyer in exchange for money. We hurried down from our location and ran across the street to find our two subjects now in the foyer of the building. George grabbed one party while I took the other. My subject resisted arrest and we both went crashing to the hard tile floor, knocking over a shopping cart that had been left in the lobby. The next thing I saw was red liquid flying everywhere and I thought to myself, *Where is all this blood coming from?* My next thought was, *Can't somebody make a shopping cart out of soft plastic?* The struggle ended soon after it began, and cuffs were secured. The red stains on my uniform were from a juice box or drink that had been left in the cart. Damn, another trip to the cleaners.

CHAPTER 22

FIRE

Being a cop, there was a lot of interaction with the fire department. Most of it was positive with jokes and humor spread around. Then there were the bad days when you know that some firemen just don't like you and will go out of their way to piss you off and get under your skin. In the town I worked in, the fire department saw very little action. There would be that occasional stuck elevator or carbon monoxide alarm going off that they would have to respond to, but on the whole, it wasn't that they were responding to calls on a steady basis. It was mostly false alarms or an automobile accident and the usual mundane crap like checking bars for overcrowding on the weekends. When the shit did hit the fan, it was front-page news. As a fireman, there was very little overtime like the cops got so most had to rely on a second job. On a typical day when I would stop by one of the firehouses, guys would be in the kitchen reading the newspaper or making something to eat. They also spent a great amount of time in front of the boob tube watching Judge Judy or a movie. There was no separation like it was on the police department. Picture a dayroom filled with 10 firemen all shouting answers to Jeopardy. I was jealous, getting paid to watch TV and hang out. When I was thinking about becoming a cop, my father said, "Take the fire department test." They worked a great schedule also; three days on then three days off. Remember, there are only two professions in this world where you get paid to lie on your back, the other one is a prostitute. I wound up hanging out with a few firemen and had my share of dinners at the firehouse. Some of those guys were really good cooks and knew their way around a kitchen.

In my fifth year as a police officer, a call was dispatched for a fire in a residential area. The apartments were Section 8 housing that was subsidized by the government. They were two-story units with residences on both the ground and second floors. I knew of a few people who lived there and had been to several of the homes in the past. There were approximately 60 units in the complex that lined the street. I was a couple of blocks away and knew I'd be there long before the first fire engine left the garage. As I turned the car onto the street, I could smell the smoke and advised headquarters to have the FD expedite. I drove north of the complex leaving plenty of room for fire apparatus and hoses. I exited the vehicle and ran towards the northern units where most of the flames and smoke were emerging from. A small crowd had started to gather in front of the sidewalk. It was about 9:30 p.m. or so when I started pounding on doors and advising people to exit the area. I came across an elderly couple inside one unit, "Get out, fire!" I was yelling in my best and deepest cop voice. He and his wife were in what appeared to be a small studio or one-bedroom apartment and looked like they were just getting ready for bed as they were both in their underwear and looked confused. He looked at me and asked if he had time to get some belongings. If you're ever involved in a fire and a cop is pounding on your door and telling you to exit, you don't have time to get the family portraits or wrap up the good silver. I told him to bring his wife and his boxers. At this point, I felt I couldn't continue any further and had breathed in enough smoke to last me a lifetime. I exited the buildings as the FD was arriving and stepped off to the side where I had a well-deserved throwing up session. I had probably banged on 10-15 doors and yelled at a few people that may not have observed or knew the gravity of the situation. I threw up for the better part of an hour and couldn't stand the smell of my clothes. All I could think of was trying to get more air into my lungs. Everybody that night got out alive, even the crackheads and dealers. People are never prepared for a fire and when it happens there is panic, frustration, and the unknown. Save your ass first and worry about everything else later.

I bought a small condo when I was 28 years old in Brewster, NY. It was a simple layout and 1100 square feet. It was all I needed being single; two bedrooms and a bath. I shared a common wall with my next-door neighbors who were in their late 50's or early 60's when I moved in. Drew was a nice enough guy who was looking forward to retirement with his wife. They were quiet and pretty much kept to themselves most of the time. The condo was a fourplex unit with two units above and two units below. It was about 7 a.m. one morning when I awoke to the sound of the fire alarm going off in the building. Fuck, I threw on some underwear as I crawled out of bed and immediately smelled the smoke. As I got to the front door and opened it, there was Drew on the other side. He had a fire extinguisher in his hand that was kept in the front hall closet in the common area of the condo. He looked at me and said, "I can't get it to work." On most household fire extinguishers, there is a colored plastic seal and a cotter pin that needs to be removed prior to using it. I had already glanced inside his home where the galley style kitchen was. His stove was on fire and the flames had spread to the backsplash area and the cabinets above. After removing the cotter pin, I walked into his home and started applying the chemicals to the fire. The whole ordeal took less than a minute and the fire was out. Drew and his wife told me that it started when she was boiling water for tea and a couple of potholders caught fire on the stove. The fire department responded and vented the area with large fans to remove the smoke that was still in the home and hallway area. Both Drew and his wife thanked me for all I had done in saving their home. Saving your home? I was saving my home. Who has two thumbs and puts out fires in his underwear? This guy. About a week later, I came home after work one day and there in front of my doorstep was a bottle of white Beringer wine with a note attached thanking me again. Cost of condo saved from fire: $180,000... bottle of wine: $5.99. Is it the thought that counts? I don't even drink white wine.

In the 20 years that I was a cop, I am proud to say that we never lost a police officer in the line of duty in our city. Was it great training by the department? Maybe, or the fact that the guys you worked with were there to back you up when the situation called for it. Or was it just dumb luck? On February 24, 1993, the City of White Plains lost a firefighter in a South Lexington Ave. apartment fire. The fireman, Warren Ogburn, became trapped in an elevator on the eighth floor and was unable to radio for assistance. He died when his respirator quit working. The cause of death was asphyxiation. The fire had broken out in a kitchen when a gas stove burst into flames and quickly spread to the hallway of the complex. Back then, it was common practice for firefighters to take the elevators and proceed two floors below where the fire was. They would then exit the elevator and lug the necessary gear up the two flights by stairs. I remember working that evening and how chaotic it was. It was not just firemen and cops there but ambulances, news crews, displaced families from the apartments, the mayor, and hundreds of onlookers in the frigid cold. In the months to come, the Firefighter's Union would blame the city for poor equipment and not enough staffing to handle a blaze of that nature. The city retorted and explained that the older building where the fire occurred had insufficient fire sprinklers. Just to set the record straight, the fire department was using a ladder truck that night that did not operate properly at the scene. That truck was purchased from a neighboring fire department. It was built in 1948. I'll let you do the math. He was the only fireman who passed during the time that I was a cop.

Living 30 minutes away from work was great. When I left the job at the end of the day, it was almost like being on vacation. I was out in the sticks as they say and had no idea what was going on a half an hour away. So, when I awoke on July 27, 1994, it was just another day. I put the coffee on and threw a load of laundry in the washing machine. Darks, lights, and towels all got cleaned together. I was working a 4-12 tour that afternoon and left for work just before 3 p.m. Little did I know that earlier that morning a tractor-trailer carrying 9200 gallons of liquid propane had crashed on a highway in our town. The driver of the vehicle was traveling eastbound on

Interstate 287 just past midnight when he slammed into a bridge abutment, causing the vehicle to burst into flames. The propane tank became an instant missile dislodging it from the truck and landing about 300 feet away. Within seconds of the accident, several homes were on fire and everything within a 400-foot radius was engulfed by flames. The driver of the tractor-trailer, a 23-year-old man with a questionable driving record, was dead. 23 people were also injured. I walked into the locker room to change and listened to the information and news of the event. I dressed faster than usual and found a ride to the command center where the neighborhood was a dismal black and smelled of burnt toast. A friend of mine who lived there lost his home, but he and his family had gotten out alive. It was just after 4 o'clock in the afternoon and rush hour traffic was in full swing. Guess what I was doing for the next four hours? Electricity was still down in the area which meant no traffic lights or common sense for your average driver. The fire had destroyed three homes and caused major damage to eight others. Streetlights were now droopy metal ornaments. Lawns that were bright green were now charred with black soot. Trees were leafless and still had smoke emitting from them. Somebody handed me an award a year or so later that congratulated me for the work I had done that day. All I did was direct traffic for a few hours.

I was working a fire scene one day on Westview Ave. when an off-duty fireman approached me. He was attempting to drive his own vehicle closer to an apartment fire where several trucks, engines and ladders were already present. I had been blocking traffic for about a half an hour or so. "What do you want to do?" He advised he was looking to help out the other firemen that were already on call at that location. "Are you working today, did you get called in?" "No, I just want to help out." Nobody hates a fireman. They don't write you tickets for speeding, they don't lock up your loved ones, and you never see them in a Dunkin Donuts getting a couple of glazed and coffee at 11 p.m. - know why? Lights out at 10 p.m., bedtime.

CHAPTER 23

MY SHIELD #

   I had been working at a golf course in Florida after retiring from the police department when I met one of the members out on the driving range. It was a chilly February afternoon. We got to talking about golf, his career and where he was from. Given the chance, most people would rather tell you about their lives than listen to yours. He was a doctor from Boston, Massachusetts and was the Chief Internist with the New England Patriots football organization. He told me the following story which still haunted him to this day: It was the second game of the 2001 football season, September 21st, and the Pats were playing the New York Jets. After dropping back to pass, quarterback, Drew Bledsoe, scrambled to his right and raced up the sidelines where he was hit by the linebacker, Mo Lewis of the Jets. The severity of the injury was not immediately known but would later be diagnosed as a sheared blood vessel in his chest. Bledsoe was cleared to return to the game a short time later by this doctor who was on the sidelines that afternoon. After another series of plays, Bledsoe was not himself and was replaced by backup quarterback, Tom Brady. The game was soon over and lying on a medical table in the Patriot's locker room was Bledsoe. He was losing blood and everything that was being done for him was met with negative results. He was slowly dying. Bledsoe was taken to Mass General Hospital in Boston where he had lost almost half his blood supply and was bleeding internally. This doctor sat there in the waiting room wondering why he had allowed Bledsoe to return to the game. He was all alone in his thoughts and his only comfort at that time was the one football player that sat there beside him, some rookie named Tom Brady. Nobody else, not a coach, a teammate, not even an assistant medic trying to get a promotion. The two waited there for the better portion of the night until they learned of the good news that Bledsoe was stabilized and resting. Due to the nature of the injury, he remained in the hospital for six days until his release. The doctor finished the conversation by stating how much he respected Brady and his thoughtfulness that day.

In June of 1999, our family took a trip to Orlando, Florida and we stayed at the Grand Cypress Resort. It was a golfing vacation for me while the rest of the gang was hitting the pool during the day and Disney at night. The villa was the perfect three-bedroom and came with all the amenities; plus, I could walk out the back door to the first tee. During my stay there, I met the shoe room attendant who was a native of New Jersey and had gotten tired of driving taxis and finally made the move south. Besides being great at his job, he was also a fantastic storyteller. A member from the club had headed onto the course one evening and was playing alone on the East course. He stepped up to the par 3 island green on the 5th hole and seconds later he watched the ball disappear into the hole. That's when the problem arose. See, if you get a hole-in-one and nobody is around to witness it, did you really get a hole-in-one? There off in the distance at the club's golf academy stood a man hitting balls in the late afternoon sunshine. He saw the gentleman clapping and thought to himself, *That's the guy who is going to attest to the hole-in-one*. He drove to the green and retrieved his ball and then proceeded to the driving range area. "Hey, did you see that shot, can you sign my scorecard?" The guy hitting balls on the range was nondescript; shorts, a polo and baseball hat. "Great shot, man, congratulations." He signed the card and handed it back to him. "Hey, what's your real name? Why did you write Payne Stewart?" After winning the U.S. Golf Open Championship just a few days earlier, he was back home getting in a little practice and gearing up for the British Open. That

October, the airplane he was flying in would experience mechanical problems and crash in South Dakota, killing all six onboard.

My friend Mike was sitting in an airport minding his own business and making a few phone calls. His flight was taking off soon and the gate announcer was advising on flight information. The guy a couple of seats over was doing the same thing, typing away on the laptop and looking for a little conversation. "What kind of work are you in?" he asked. Mike is a very private person and he's not looking to become somebody's best friend at a moment's notice in an airport terminal. The two would kill a few minutes talking about how they made bread to support their families. Mike worked at a bakery in Florida that smelled delicious when you drove by it and was pumping out loaves 24 hours a day. The two exchanged notes, Mike working for the #2 bread company in sales in the United States and Jim working for a company called Big Lots. The conversation went back and forth and soon came down to the questions of how long you keep bread on the shelves in supermarkets. Mike responded that three to four days would be the absolute maximum since they want their product to be fresh for the customer. If the product is not sold, there are a few options as to what can be done with it. That's where the deal originated and the plan was set. I've got bread that is not up to our standards for sale and you have people wanting to buy our product at a reduced rate that's a couple of days old. Flash forward to 2010, a few years later, and Mike is invited by Jim to spend the weekend in Ponte Vedra Beach, Florida. It's May, and The Players Golf Championship is center stage. When he told me we were going, I had to sit down and have a drink. They had a condo for us and tickets for Sunday afternoon in the suites overlooking the island green 17th hole. This is going to be awesome.

We started out early on Saturday morning, a four-hour ride over to the east coast. There were six of us in the SUV. Mike and his wife, Amy, Pete and his bride, Peg, and me with my gorgeous, beautiful, sexy, vivacious wife, Sue; it's my book, so I can write what I want. The 'six-pack' off to another adventure. We chilled out at the pool most of the afternoon smoking cigars and drinking some of the finest vodka from Russia and France. The condo was perfect and the atmosphere energetic. We woke the next morning after a night of partying and I was looking for some coffee. Jim told me coffee was on the counter and that he liked his with a couple of shots of Baileys – a good eye-opener. I couldn't resist. A 10 minute ride to the golf course and we were walking onto the grounds at the Tournament Players Course at Sawgrass. We entered through the gate behind the 16th green and walked past the 17th hole. The girls who were all walking together were approached by a local newsman with a camera crew. He asked if they would like to be on TV, just doing a little piece on the golf and wanted to ask some questions. They looked at each other and started fixing their hair. Three women who are never at a loss for words and could start a conversation about anything stood there like stick figures. A few one-word answers, a couple of head bobs, it's such a beautiful day, and then Amy said she was rooting for Phil...Phil Mickelson. Mike, Pete and I stood in the background watching the interview and couldn't stop laughing. Talk about being camera shy! We walked down the ninth fairway and headed to the clubhouse for some early morning drinks out on the lawn. I walked into the massive clubhouse where there is a framed $1 bill in the hallway around pictures and the history of the course. The $1 was how much the PGA Tour paid for the 415 acres there, glorified swampland. The day was going along great until we made our way over to the 9th tee box around noon and were told by a marshal that Tiger Woods had just pulled out of the tournament on the 7th hole with neck pain. There were two unusual events that happened during that tournament. For the first time, an intoxicated spectator was locked up and tasered during his arrest. The other event was a car being driven onto the 8th green by two guys who must have made a substantial bet between themselves. As we walked back to the club suites, Mike and I noticed a guy walking down the cart path. "Look, Peg, that's Wilt Chamberlin, the basketball player!" She didn't believe us at first, but we convinced her to at least go and ask him. Peg shyly walked up to the gentleman who stood 7' in height and could have been mistaken for a sequoia tree. The conversation was brief and she walked back to where we were standing, shaking her head, "So, I asked him and he said, "why would I want to be Wilt Chamberlain? He's dead.""

I was playing golf one afternoon and was teamed up with a guy who had been an on-field reporter for the New England Patriots. The 2000 season was just beginning and July was time to get back to practicing. That football buzz was in the air again. He told me he had made his way down towards the end of the bench, walking, jotting down a couple of notes and snapping a few pictures along the way. A pretty routine day until he saw Robert Kraft, owner of the team, walking towards him. He was thinking of the right question to ask him, something different that wasn't your everyday yawn, ground ball question, I've heard that before garbage. He never got the chance. There sitting on the bench was some rookie quarterback with a large pizza in front of him and a slice in his hand. Mr. Kraft walked up to him and they made their introductions. "Mr. Kraft, I'm Tom Brady, I'm going to win a Super Bowl for you one day." My playing partner thought that was pretty hilarious since Brady sat fourth on the depth chart of quarterbacks that year. *Who is this cocky dude sitting there eating pizza like he owns the place?* he thought. They only spoke briefly and the Patriot's owner moved on and Brady went back to his lunch at the end of the bench.

I sat at a wedding once and was picking through the salad portion of the meal that didn't taste like anything. With about 125 people at the nuptials, the room was crowded but the bartenders were keeping up. The five-piece band was just finishing up their first set and was getting ready to take a smoke break. As they left the stage, some college kid strolled up to the piano and adjusted the mic. He had just been sitting a couple of tables to my right and looked as if he wasn't impressed with the iceberg lettuce either. He was a little overweight and his suit jacket he would have to grow into. As he pulled the bench up, he began singing. "A long, long, time ago, I can still remember how that music used to make me smile." He knew and sang every word to American Pie by Don McLean. Not only could he play the ivories but he had a fantastic voice also. He got a standing ovation and blushed as he went back to his chair. *That's not the first time he's done that*, I thought. Impressive.

My friend had just completed his tour of duty in the Middle East and was telling me about one of his last assignments. He was sent to an outpost in the middle of nowhere with a couple of guys and met up with some local militia enforcing the area. Picture looking 360 degrees and not seeing anything but sand. He walked into the makeshift barracks, unloaded his gear and got his bearings. Where is my bed, where is the shitter, and when do we eat? That's about all you needed to know. He greeted the new friends wrapped in their headdress and got a quick tour. Next to the camp was a scene out of every Clint Eastwood spaghetti western, except this time it was a donkey that was tied up just outside the back door. It was a three-legged donkey. When he asked one of the guys what the donkey was for, they just smiled and pretended like they didn't understand. Really?

CHAPTER 24

SUPERMAN

When you're a cop, you have to be Superman. You may not look or sound like Superman, but you have to pretend; it's like Halloween every day. Once you jump into that phone booth and put on the shield, bulletproof vest and gun, you are Superman because that is what the public demands of you. You can't lose. There's a bat in my house, call Superman. My pet lizard is cold, call Superman. There's a bear running around the city, call Superman. Real calls that were part of being a cop. It's a job unlike any other because it's impossible to guess or even gamble on what the next call will be. Imagine Vegas trying to lay odds on that. It could be a guy on the railroad tracks stealing copper wire, a homeless guy who just killed a woman in the mall or a domestic fight where the wife is too scared to tell you the truth. Think about that for a second… You're watching two guys exchange drugs in a doorway one minute, doing CPR the next hour on an unresponsive party, clearing a traffic accident after that, and then looking for a missing child in Macy's. Your shift is half over.

Crane Avenue was a residential street in town that was just off North Broadway. The majority of the time it was very quiet, so when you got a call there, it usually involved the same two idiots. Tonight wasn't any different. It was about 10 o'clock when I answered the radio and began my response. I remember being in a pretty foul mood and was just looking for a reason to take it out on somebody. When I arrived at the residence, Idiot #1 was out front with a baseball bat yelling and cursing. Idiot# 2, his brother, wasn't around. The subject had just come home and parked his mother's car in the driveway. When he attempted to get his dog out of the backseat, the animal bit him. So, he did what any normal person would do; go into the trunk of your car, get a baseball bat, and start smashing the vehicle. Soon after I arrived at the scene, I could tell it was going from bad to worse. My backup arrived a few minutes later and he was also familiar with this party. We tried to do the reason it out thing, but that wasn't working. So, being in that nasty frame of mind, I decided to turn the table. "You want to hit something with that bat, hit me!" I could have cared less about the car he was destroying, I was worried about the dog inside. I had pulled my gun upon arrival and kept it by my side at waist level. He continued to rant and rave and curse at us and the animal. I told him repeatedly to drop the bat and get on the ground. Finally, I'd had enough and told John, my backup, I was going in. This was long before the days of tasers, even though I don't think they would have worked in this situation. I started toward the subject at a slow pace and he began to back up towards the front of the automobile. With John to my left, I quickened the pace and I think he realized, gun against bat, 2 against 1, odds not in his favor. He dropped the weapon and we got him cuffed without any problems. A few months later, I was in a bar in town and saw him there. He had a lot to say, criticized the way I handled the situation and told me, "You wanted to kill me that night." "Nope, just wanted you to drop the bat." He wanted to shake my hand, but I knew better. Never shake hands with somebody you locked up.

Sometime in my fourth year as a police officer, I was chosen to train new rookies that were fresh out of the academy and coming onto the job. It was a three-month training period that included every aspect of the job; from driving a car, report writing, and how well they could handle calls. There was no extra pay for it, but you did get an extra vacation day and there were some liberties that you could take. My first rookie was a guy named Dean. After about the first week, I learned he was pretty well hooked up with some of the bosses upstairs and I got the feeling he would be on a fast track to the detective division. That's how it works sometimes, friends take care of friends. It was almost time to go home after a fairly quiet day tour when the call was dispatched. "Respond to the intersection of Barker and Cottage, there's a subject there directing traffic, he's naked." It's never a 22-year-old Swedish model, so I didn't ask for a description. This subject was the brother of Derrick Lassic, who played a couple of seasons behind Emmitt Smith of the Dallas Cowboys. When we got to the scene, the directing of traffic had stopped and now he was doing pushups, pretty well as I recall for a guy 6' 4" and about 250 pounds on the cheeseburger meter. I looked at Dean and he looked at me. "You want the arms or the legs?" Dean was a couple of inches shorter than me so he stayed low and I went high. When somebody is on angel dust, you can't talk to them or even think about reasoning with them. We wrestled around in the street for a while and I think he knocked out a couple of one-arm pushups with me on his back. We finally got the condition under control and dragged him over to the sidewalk. We brought him straight to the hospital where he got fitted for one of those gorgeous smocks you get to wear with the opening in the back. Dean wanted to know if we were going to lock him up after he gets discharged from the hospital. He was guilty of disorderly conduct and exposure of a person; two violations that would be argued in court if it went that way. "You want to go home or do two hours of paperwork that's going to get flushed by the district attorney?"

The Kings Inn Motel was one step above living underneath a highway overpass. Nothing good ever happened there. Fights, drugs, thefts, an abundance of people who were waiting on their next fix or John to walk through the door. I was driving 14 car that night and had to come from the other side of town to back up Kenny who had the lead on the call. It was close to midnight and I could feel this was going to go into overtime. By the time I got to the location, Kenny had made contact with the parties involved. The two individuals living off the government inside had a dispute and it became physical. We separated the male and female and started to ask all the necessary questions. Kenny was very, very – did I say very? – low-keyed and never had much to say. Some guy beating on his

150

girlfriend didn't have the slightest effect on Kenny. He continued to inquire about what had happened and write in his notebook. Me, on the other hand, not as cool, and looking at this guy's smug face only enraged me more. I threatened the guy to take a swing at me since he liked beating up on women. "Hit me." I got right in his face and was hoping he would at least give me a little push to get the ball rolling. Nothing. Back in the early 1990's, the domestic violence laws were just beginning to change and, for the most part, they helped the cops out. We got her to press charges that night, but I'm sure a week later they were back living together in that one-room roach trap eating Funyuns and beef jerky.

I was very apprehensive about entering the apartment. I hate bats. The middle-aged woman was more scared than I was. The mammal was flying in circles from the kitchen into the living room, then the dining room. I watched it do this about 3-4 times and thought to myself, *I'm not that good of a shot.* "Miss, do you have any large pots with lids?" We both ducked into the kitchen out of the flight path and she pointed to a lower cabinet near the stove. I grabbed the largest lid I could find (about 12 inches in diameter) and swung for the fences. Strike one. The bat continued to fly in circles and entered the kitchen again a few seconds later. I was hoping not to break anything in the kitchen like the vase that was nicely displayed on the bistro table. This time, we had contact and it fell to the floor like it should have done the first time I swung at it. I got a dustpan and threw it into a garbage bag. "Miss, do you have a dumpster in the back of this building?" I was going to be a nice guy and take the dead animal out for her. Then she wanted to know what I was going to do with it. "Lady I'm going to throw it in the garbage." "Doesn't it need to be tested for rabies?" "No." People can be funny. She stood there thanking me as I left the apartment but, at the same time, wanting a full-scale investigation. How did it get in? Shouldn't we take it to the CSI lab for a full post-mortem examination?

When you meet somebody for the first time, you have a good idea as to their mental state. After speaking with them for only a few seconds, you're able to tell crazy, maybe a little crazy, or just boring like the rest of the world. For the first few years as a cop, I was assigned a couple of days each week to communications; answering phones and thinking, *This really sucks, I want to be out on the streets*. When you're answering phone calls for eight hours, you get a lot of the crazies. A homicide phone call wouldn't get you into any trouble, but not sending a cop to a lady's home because of a heating situation would start an investigation equal to the Warren Commission. "You have no heat in your home?" "Is there fuel in the tank?" "Okay, well you need to call a service technician." I sent two cops to her home that evening because she needed a hug and a little TLC. This woman was also worried that her pet lizard was going to freeze because she forgot to put oil in the tank. The uniforms on the scene determined that her lizard was probably going to be okay. "If you would like, we'll lift the tank for you so you can put an electric heating blanket underneath it." Sometimes you just have to play along with the game. Make them feel happy and get the hell out of there as soon as you can.

Our department got its share of animal calls. Pit bulls were always on the top 10 list. Your basic cat stuck in a tree call - have you ever seen a dead cat in a tree? We had our share of rabid animals like skunks and raccoons and the occasional coyote sighting every now and then. When the call was received on this particular day that a black bear had come to town, it got everybody out of their chairs. If you live in Maine and there's a bear in your backyard, you might hear your mom say, "Kids, get off the swings for a minute and come into the house, mom is gonna scare off the bear with her Benelli 12-gauge." It's a little different when you're in a city of 60,000. The animal was first observed near the intersection of Mamaroneck Avenue and Bryant, a very busy cross street just on the edge of the business district. Sergeants, lieutenants, and captains scrambled for the doors. Members of the detective division also got in on the chase, and you could never find those guys anywhere. There were perimeters set up and traffic was diverted away from the area. A nice quiet afternoon turned into the hunt for David Berkowitz. One of the lieutenants thought he had an idea of the animal's whereabouts and got on the radio to advise that he was in the rear of the Italian restaurant with no sign of the bear. His next transmission was, "Oooooh, there he is!" The bear traveled back across the highway and into a wooded area that had an apartment complex on one side and a rehab hospital on the other. For the better part of an hour, I observed cops and newspaper reporters drive by me in search of this elusive bear. Minutes later, he wandered onto the 15th hole of The Ridgeway Golf Course which was just behind some apartments. The animal was met there by several members from our department and tranquilized. The paper had its front-page headlines. What probably surprised me the most was that there wasn't a car accident that day with the amount of reckless driving that was going on. The bear was later transported to an area in Upstate New York and released back into the wild.

One of the scariest nights of my career happened at 11:30 at night. 30 minutes later and I would have been leaving the locker room, changed, out of my cape, and headed home. Not that night. A subject had barricaded himself in his home and was threatening persons in his residence and those on the same floor of the apartment building. His home was in the projects right across from police headquarters. When a gun call is received, everything stops. That cup of coffee gets discarded out the window and that slice of pizza never makes it to your waistline. Mustafa, his street name, was a violent drug dealer and known by most of the cops. Myself and a few others arrived on the scene and made our way up to the ninth floor. From all the information we had, there were weapons in the apartment and at least two other individuals that Mustafa was not allowing to exit the residence. I took up a position just off the elevator and to the right of his front door. We could hear the yelling and screaming coming from inside the apartment and we settled in. We evacuated the floor and another cop went down to the eighth floor trying to clear those residences. We hadn't been there five minutes, trying to contact the subject and at least get him to talk to us, when he let the first round go. Deafening. That's the problem. When you go to the shooting range, everybody has headsets on or some type of ear protection. I had two guns with me that night; my service weapon, a Smith & Wesson 9 mm and a shotgun. I wish I had a third. The asshole pucker factor just went from a gun call to shots fired and now the whole department was racing to the area. He finally opened the door to the apartment after much pleading and advising him nobody was hurt. The two other women that were in the dwelling were also allowed to leave. One of them exited, saying, "He's fucking crazy, he's gonna kill somebody." Within minutes, the confrontation came to a complete halt when Mustafa got shot by our firearms instructor. Rule #1: "Drop the gun" means drop the gun. It was a good shoot and Mustafa got patched up at the hospital.

CHAPTER 25

CATS AND DOGS

My cat just walked into the room and was crying like a baby. He does that about three to four times a day when he wants attention and a couple of minutes of your time. So, I got down on the floor with him and he attempted to break my forehead with his. He left the room a short time later then went over to his brother and proceeded to jump on his back and bite his neck in that dominating male cat position. A quick smell of his ass and it's back to the food bowl. My daughter got my wife and I these two guys when she was in college; we named them Crockett and Tubbs. I was a big Miami Vice fan back in the day. They are two indoor grey cats that spend their days sleeping, throwing up hairballs, and eating like they just got released from Guantanamo. I'm under the assumption that you're either a cat person or a dog person. You can have both and love them the same, but you had one before you had the other. They have both passed since I began writing this after a good life.

When I was very young, my neighbor across the street asked me if I wanted to make some money one summer taking care of her dogs. School was out and I was probably about 10 years old. The job would consist of walking them, cleaning out their pens and feeding them. Sounded good to me. She was a breeder and the dogs were Great Danes. Sometimes in life nobody tells you the little things and you have to find out for yourself. I've never needed to use trigonometry.

It was that summer when I learned that it's not a good idea to go near a litter of new puppies when Momma is around. As I bent over to see one of the new pups, she proceeded to latch onto my right forearm, taking a nice chunk of skin with her. I had just been attacked by Godzilla and the blood was gushing from my arm. That summer, I became the fastest runner in track and field. Sprinting home and crying to my mother that I was now permanently scarred and that I was going to lose my arm. Cats scratch... dogs bite.

I was leaving Montana and was returning to New York after a month of skiing and seeing some family and friends. I was officially retired from the Air Force and planned on being home in three days. Four plus years in the service had gone fast and it was time to look for work in the real world. I had packed up my Toyota truck with a duffel bag that held some clothes, my skis and a cat that I had rescued a few months earlier. He was still a kitten and had those claws that were like razor blades. He was orange with a little bit of white on him and I named him Otis. It was early March in 1985 and, being the smartest traveler in the world, I had packed up his food and water bowl and placed it on the floor in front of the passenger's seat. Otis had a place to sleep on the bench seat of the vehicle and I kept my eyes on the road looking to do about 12 hours of driving the first day and make it to Fargo, North Dakota. I was on Highway 200 in eastern Montana when the crying began and he started looking around for a place to go to the bathroom. How did I forget a litter pan? Told ya I was the smartest traveler in the world. I pulled off onto the graveled shoulder of the road and down a small dirt path that may have been a road at one time. The sky was grey above me and there was not a soul around. Off to my right was a large corn or wheat field that had a few patches of snow scattered about. I picked up Otis and walked him over to the world's biggest urinal; the great outdoors. I put him down and thought I had pretty good control of him with both my hands on his sides. He bolted from my grasp and began his own journey in that field. Holy shit, cats can run fast! There I am in the middle of bumble-fuck Montana chasing a cat around in a field in 20-degree temperatures. Sounds like fun, no? He finally got tired out and sunk down real low and I was able to corral him. "Do you have to go to the bathroom or not?" The fear had left me and I was now in the yelling mode. I've done some pretty dumb things in my life, this was in the top 20.

In 1990, at the age of 28, I bought my first real home. I was single, so I had that going for me, and figured I had the next 30 years to pay the mortgage off. I was working a 4-12 shift one night and got called to a residence off Old Mamaroneck Road. I responded to an upper-middle-class home and met with a woman who needed some information documented. The situation was a divorce case and, of course, her lawyer had told her to call the police if the sun doesn't rise in the morning or anything is out of the ordinary. Call the cops, because you can't reach your attorney after 5 p.m. We talked for a while, I wrote down her information and she walked into the next room saying, "I have to check on my cats." She motioned me into a den/TV room where her cat had a litter of kittens about six to eight weeks old. There's a sucker born every minute, right? Four cats and a mother laid in a makeshift basket with a few towels and blankets arranged in no particular fashion. Otis had died before he was a year old and I really wasn't in the mood to be a stepfather. It was getting late, close to 11:30 p.m., and my shift was going to be over soon. She told me to think about it and that she would be up till 1 a.m. if I wanted to come back and take one of the kittens home. It was pretty simple - go to headquarters, turn in my reports, get changed, then get in my car and drive home. I got to her house about a quarter past midnight and Sambuca now had a new address. He was another orange and white tabby with a good personality. He was easy to take care of and as he got older, he started venturing outside. There was a large wooded area in the rear of my condo, so I felt safe allowing him to be out. One weekend, I took a perfectly good wooden door from my kitchen that led to my rear deck and cut a rectangular hole in the bottom of it so Sambuca could come and go as he pleased. It was the perfect setup, no litter box to worry about and no smell to deal with. I awoke one morning to the sounds of screaming and cat cries that were scary to say the least. Sambuca was in a knockdown fight with an animal he had brought in from the great outdoors. As I pulled the shower curtain to the side in my bathroom, I found my cat and some other animal in the bathtub with blood splattered everywhere. It looked like a scene from The Godfather. The noise ended within seconds and my cat, covered in blood, began licking his fur. I stared down at the dead animal in the tub and said, "What the hell is that?" My pulse slowed down, Buca retreated to the kitchen to finish cleaning himself and get some food, and I began cleaning the walls and tub to get rid of the evidence. The dead carcass was a weasel. Where the hell did he find that? The bathtub became Sambuca's favorite place to bring his prey; the list included mice, birds, and an occasional rabbit. The Clorox was always nearby.

Later in his life, Sambuca developed cancer in his eye. It was interesting how it occurred. One day your cat has two green eyes, and a few weeks later one of the eyes had turned a golden brown. I didn't really think anything of it. He was still eating, catching everything he could from outside and still getting his mandatory 16 hours of sleep a day. During a routine checkup, the doctor advised he has been blind for a while in the eye. The cancer was encapsulated in the eye socket so removing the eye was the next step. The lids were then sewn closed and I had a one-eyed cat. He was still the same mush as ever and he adjusted better than I did. About a year later, I found him one morning under the Christmas tree with his back towards me and not wanting to be disturbed. He would later be crying in pain and another trip to the vet was scheduled. His blood test came back positive for hepatitis C. How the hell does a cat get hep C? The vet tried to explain it was due to the animals he caught in the wild and that maybe one of them was infected. Maybe it's just me being skeptical, but I wondered if the operation the prior year was done with the cleanest of instruments. We will never know.

When the call came in about a dog loose in the area of Central Avenue, I was half nodding off in the patrol car. It was another freezing night and I had the heat cranking and the window cracked a couple of inches. Every cop who works the midnight shift has his or her own favorite place to catch a few naps; mine was the cemetery. There was a point in time that I knew the names of the deceased where I would always park. There was a huge elm tree just off to my right side that was often used to get rid of the last cup of coffee. When I got to the area, I did my best to search for the stray dog and finally located the animal about two blocks away. When I went to approach it, he quickly fled under a car that was parked on the street. The dog was black and white and I was hoping to get it off the streets or find its owner on a cold night. My mistake. As I knelt down to look under the vehicle, the Japanese Akita took a bite out of my hand from underneath the automobile. His teeth ripped through my glove and the pain was immediately felt. You know the old saying, "When was the last time you had a tetanus shot?" Well, if you can't remember, it's time to go get one. I drove myself to the hospital and vowed I would never try to rescue another dog for the rest of my life.

In early 1999, my wife and I purchased a home in Sunset Beach, North Carolina. It was a two-bedroom, two-bath townhouse in a gated community that was going to be our retirement home. There were three golf courses on the property and I could hit a 5-iron from my front yard and be on the driving range. The beach was a 10 minute bicycle ride away across an old swing bridge that crossed over the Intracoastal Waterway. The year the house was being built, Hurricane Floyd hit the area as a category 4 storm with 155 mph winds. 24 inches of rain in 24 hours and the place was still standing. We would usually drive down there a couple of times a year, which took about 11 hours from our home in New York. On one particular trip, I had borrowed my mother's car to haul down some furnishings for the house. We had spent about 10 days down there and were headed home. It was always a long journey north, back to work, hit the food store and the favorite grind of unpacking and laundry. Our first stop on the way back was a trip to McDonald's where my bride could hit the bathroom and get us a mid-morning snack. We were in Selma, NC and I pulled into the driveway of the golden arches. My wife moved the cats, Crockett and Tubbs, off her lap and made her way out of the car. It's amazing how stiff you can get sitting in the same place for three hours. I pulled the Ford off to the side and Crockett began crawling onto my left shoulder and down my left arm. His paw struck the window down switch and he jumped out the window. Panic had officially set in! There I was with only one word to describe the situation - okay, maybe two. I got the window back up and jumped out of the vehicle in pursuit of my cat that had run a short distance into the playground area at the restaurant. We've all been to McDonald's and know that each playground is protected with those steel iron posts. Keeps the pedophiles out, but allows your cat in. This can't be happening. I'm on my hands and knees trying to call for him when my wife walks out the door with a couple of bags in her hands; sausage and biscuits and another round of coffee. "Mark, what is going on?" You thought I had a panicked look on my face, you should have seen her! I'm thinking that the video cameras around the playground have already been activated and the middle-aged white guy on his knees with his hands sticking through bars has sent out an alarm across all of the east coast. The cat was running around amongst a few bushes and those plastic slides. I was worried that he was going to find another set of metal bars to exit from and he would be gone. He got frightened by a noise coming from his left and started a dash toward me. I grabbed him and never let go. By the scruff of his neck, I slid him through the rails and back to the car. Half the ordeal was over... now I get to listen to my wife yell at me for the next two hours as we drive home on Interstate 95.

After moving to Florida, you become accustomed to certain things. Each year, starting in October, the migration of the snowbird begins. People from up north rolling back into town with their out-of-state plates. The lines at the food stores are ridiculous, traffic sucks, and going out to eat becomes a chore. You get used to it, like you would seeing alligators and armadillos. The noise I heard this one morning was unlike anything I had ever heard before. I had let my cat, Crockett, out on the back lanai where our pool is and started working on that first cup. The area is enclosed with screening, so he has free reign to walk around the pool and chase the occasional gecko. Sunrise was still about 20 minutes away and the first sip of the Columbian was hitting the spot. When a child cries, you know what it is. If your vehicle has a loose belt and makes that noise, you know what it is. I slowly opened the slider onto the lanai and the sound became stronger. After taking about 10 steps to my right, there was my 12-pound house cat nose to nose with a 30-pound wild bobcat. His fur was extended as far as it could go. I thought to myself, *That's one tough cat.* The only thing separating them was a piece of screening. I watched for a couple of seconds not wanting to scare him. The pool's edge was directly behind him. He held his ground and the bobcat gradually retreated into the dense brush behind my home after seeing me. It was a pretty amazing sight to witness. My cat had defended his property and not fallen into the deep end. The morning was off to a good start.

It was the dead of winter in the Northeast. You know how a snowflake is pretty on Thanksgiving and an inch of white powder on the ground for the holidays in December is the perfect Hallmark card? When you've been shoveling snow all of January and February, the power has been out a few times, and there's been a couple of close calls driving in icy conditions, it's just not that cute anymore. Let's not even talk about the various potholes that eat your tires and cause your alignment to go into chiropractic shock. I had made it through another week of freezing temps and that rodent out in Pennsylvania declared another six weeks of hell. It was a quiet Sunday afternoon; football season was over and spring training was still a couple of weeks away. I had walked into my kitchen to check the clock to see if it was 5 o'clock yet. Yep, 5 o'clock comes twice a day. That cat door I had made a few years earlier was now being used by Felix and Oscar. Both cats had come after the passing of Sambuca. The door was on a flapper that swung both ways to allow the cats access in and out. I heard it bang briefly and I knew both cats were outside with a foot plus of snow on the ground. Then I saw my cat, Oscar, attempting to come through the door backwards. So, his butt is in the kitchen and he's attempting to pull something with him from the outside. He's working feverishly on getting his latest accomplishment into the house, and I wasn't about to interrupt his fun. Moments later, he was able to jockey the animal through the small opening and presented me a frozen rabbit that could have been from the ice age. It was covered in snow and now began melting as it hit the warmth of the kitchen. Nice present.

Dogs bark, I get it. But every day that my upstairs neighbor went off to work, this little French Bulldog would bark his fucking lungs out. He was a cute little black and white pup that needed attention. She was single and needed a companion, and the occasional guy who I would see leaving in the morning just wasn't cutting it. I get it, nobody cares if a cop is trying to get some sleep because he worked all night. The landscapers are going to mow the lawns, the postal jackass is going to slam the metal boxes for each tenant and dogs are going to yap. The barking continued. "Hey, Jamie, did you know as soon as you leave in the morning your dog barks for hours?" She always had a flippant answer and that 'it's all about me' look and attitude; she couldn't have cared less. It was more important for her to get her nails done. It went on for a couple of months and then I got the animal control officer involved. He told me he would take care of it, warning her with a citation, then a fine. Next thing I knew, we were in court giving testimony in front of a judge for a dog barking. It's amazing how some people can be so inconsiderate.

This is a little disgusting, so if you want to go on to the next chapter, please be my guest. Fair warning. My brother-in-law is in town with his girlfriend staying at our home. It's always good to get away from the snow for a week. They have been here before and they are very low maintenance. "You want eggs, toast, cereal?" He was happy eating a Snickers bar for breakfast. On this one occasion, the girlfriend also invited her twin sister and her boyfriend. My one cat obviously didn't appreciate all the newcomers in his home and let me know about it one morning just before I woke up. He hopped up onto the bed and, being the king of his castle, decided to piss on my face as I was trying to get 30 more minutes of REM sleep. It was like somebody shooting you with a garden hose. I'm half asleep and fighting with the comforter. I thought there was a leak in the ceiling, but then I saw his ass aimed right in my line of fire. Are you allowed to kill your cat after that? The bill for the dry cleaning came back at $82. Okay, maybe I can't kill him, what about waterboarding?

CHAPTER 26

CRUISES

After getting off probation from the police department in the spring of 1989, it was time for a much-needed vacation. I had been a good boy for 18 months and needed to unwind. In layman's terms, that's getting drunk and chasing women. A buddy and I had booked a cruise leaving out of Florida and going to Mexico, Grand Cayman, and Jamaica. Having never been on a cruise before, I had no idea what to expect. The Caribbean is a lot of banana islands where it's great to be there for a week or so, but let's face it, nothing beats the U.S.A. We got to our cabin just after 2 p.m. and found a note along with a bottle of champagne from our travel agent. Blah, blah, blah, thanks for booking with me, have a great time! We did a quick change into pool attire and headed four flights up to find the party. On each cruise, before sailing, there is a mandatory fire drill or evacuation drill where you have to report to a section of the ship. They don't call it an iceberg drill, or what happens if pirates start shooting at us drill. It's 30 minutes of your life you will never get back, so make sure you bring a cocktail with you. You stand there like a bunch of cattle thinking this is an awful start to a vacation.

We made it to dinner the first night and met three other couples who were already working on their appetizers. Yeah, we were a little late. Two guys on time for dinner on their first cruise ain't gonna happen. I surveyed the table and knew that there was at least one minister, a stay-at-home mom, and somebody who worked in a feed store from the Midwest. They were looking at their watches by the time dinner came and were already getting ready for bed. There was one couple there that was pretty cool, they both worked for the phone company and were having a good time. What's the best part about being on a cruise? The endless drinking and food? No. Gambling whenever you wanted? No. How about the fact that if you want a jazz, piano, or dance club, they are on the next deck? Comedy shows are usually pretty good, hit up the late seating. No, the best part about being on a cruise is that you will never see these people again and that you don't have to drive home blowing a 1.4 worrying about the DWI stop. How do cruise ships make money? They pay their staff crap and a cocktail is $12.

After drinking and dancing with two nurses from Boston all night, we were headed back to our cabin when we met some late partiers just down the hallway. They were playing the ever-popular toilet paper game on the ship. Slow down, tree huggers... it all gets recycled. The toilet paper is rolled out along the hallway side by side with one end placed in the toilet. This night, they were playing against the room across from theirs. The toilet inside the cabins is flushed and because of the onboard suction from the ship, it pulls the paper for several seconds. The toilet can suck down 30-40 feet of paper at a time. The last room with paper on the floor lost. Just a little drinking game at 3 a.m.

We touched down in Mexico after a day at sea and decided to go to some Mayan ruins in Playa del Carmen. The bus ride was fun to get there; traveling with the locals who held their roosters in their hands and smelled like it was time for a little Speed Stick. We traveled back to Cancun, or maybe it was Cozumel, in time for some dinner and a stop off at Carlos N' Charlie's. If you're under 70, you should definitely go there. Waiters shooting red wine out of a bota bag into your mouth from across the table. The next day was Grand Cayman Island and an absolutely perfect day at the beach. You never have to move because waiters walk up and down the beach serving everything from cocktails to sunblock and towels. You got money? They got it. The seas were pretty rough that day and the ship was unable to dock on the pier, so they have smaller boats called tenders to bring passengers to and from the boat. We made the last one back to the ship at 5:30 p.m. and we sailed a half hour later. That night, for some reason, we never made it to dinner and missed the lobster and steak night. The fact that we had been drinking and partying in 90-degree heat had absolutely nothing to do with it. Then there was the knock on the door at about 9:30 p.m. and our entire table that we had been eating with burst into the room with red, white, and blue confetti and streamers. Our friends of four days had brought us dinner and told us how much they missed us. Cold lobster is still pretty good.

The following morning in Jamaica, I got off the Carnival ship and was looking for someplace to play golf. I walked down to the end of the pier and was greeted by several taxi drivers. I asked, "Hey guys, anybody know of a good golf course in the area?" Two of the guys turned to an older gentleman and he replied, "Runaway Bay, mon." I looked over at the taxis parked by the side of the road and couldn't believe what these guys were driving. "Come on, mon, I take you." I opened the door to a 1968 Chevy Chevelle and we headed off. We hadn't gone 10 minutes down the road from the port at Ocho Rios when the driver pulled over to get something from a small convenience store. "You need anything, mon?" "No, I'm good." He walked back to the vehicle moments later carrying a six-pack of the local beer and offered me one as he twisted the cap on his. It was at this point that I thought to myself, *When in Jamaica, have a Red Stripe, mon.* It was just after eight in the morning and the golf course was a left turn onto Rickets Road then down a gravel two-lane path. He told me he would pick me up after I finished the round. "Sounds good, how much do I owe you?" "Don't worry, mon, you can pay me later." It was astonishing to me that this guy would just leave me at a golf course without being paid for his service. I checked in, got a caddy and was teeing off 15 minutes later. The course was nothing special, I can shoot an area code without much effort. Four hours later, we were walking up the 18th fairway and I was getting ready to hit my approach into the green. I looked over to my right and saw the sand and gravel spewing into the air from the flat-black two-door sedan. I was laughing so hard inside I could barely hit the ball. He met me as I came into the golf shop and I asked him if he was in a rush. "Nobody in Jamaica is in a rush, mon." We killed a couple of beers in the bar and then he drove me into town, giving me the lowdown on the drugs and the merchants; who to stay away from and what to say to the locals. Best $40 cab ride I've ever taken. Because we all know that is what Jamaica is famous for: weed and pushy store owners.

On another cruise, I sailed out of New York City going to Bermuda. If you ever get the chance, GO. It's clean and fun and I never felt like I was looking over my shoulder. We sat down for dinner the first night and were met by three other couples. It was the late seating for supper so it was well after eight when the first round was brought to the table. They were all drinking Coors Light and were at least a couple ahead of me. We tried to converse, but they all had such heavy Scottish accents that I did more head nodding than anything else. By the third night of listening to their stories and drinking in their laughter, I was a baptized Scott. We talked about where we lived, kids, cars, jobs we had and just enough foreplay to keep the conversation interesting. That's when I put two and two together. Years prior, I had done a security side job over one summer that was at a home in Mamaroneck, NY. The house was located on Flagler Drive, a very expensive area that has a gatehouse with a guard. Problem is that the guard was about 80 and probably needed a walker with tennis balls just to get to his car. The family I was doing security for had a good sized home with a small beach in their backyard and were concerned with kids partying on the grounds from Memorial Day till Labor Day. They were hardly ever there and left the property in the hands of a caretaker to keep the keg parties to a minimum. He didn't want to get involved, so he hired us. The shifts were 12 hours long and paid enough to make it worth your while. I had relieved the day tour guy at 7 p.m. one night and did a quick once-around of the property. It was your typical mansion with the caretaker's home just to the right of the castle. I met the caretaker briefly on a prior date and had all the necessary phone numbers and the 'what to do in case of' list. I sat in the car for most of the time and would get out to stretch every now and then. It was about 5 a.m. and I was counting the minutes till I was getting relieved, when a car with music blasting entered the circular driveway. I remember seeing the passenger's side door open and a girl exit the vehicle in something less than lady-like fashion. The car quickly sped off and she stumbled to the front door, adjusting her mini skirt that showed more than just leg. It almost appeared that she was pushed out of the car, but she gave a half-hearted wave back to the trio of boys and appeared to thank them for the ride. She was in her late teens or early 20's - oh yeah, she was trashed. She entered the residence after fumbling for keys and disappeared into the home. I finally made the connection. Here I am in Bermuda having dinner with that girl's father, the caretaker of the property.

The ship we sailed on could only stay in the port of Hamilton, Bermuda for a couple of days and then had to reposition to another town on the island. My wife stayed on board and I jumped on the moped we had rented and took off to play golf. How can you tell the tourist on the moped? He's the only one with a golf bag between his legs trying to drive on the left-hand side of the road during the morning commute. My wife and I met up later to hit the beach, strolled through town and checked out a pretty neat old fort on the northeastern part of the island. I was talking to a police officer in town that afternoon and mentioned that I was looking for an authentic Bermuda Police tee shirt. He pointed me in the direction of the police recreational club located a few miles away. We got on the moped and, after getting lost a couple of times, came across the club. The building was in the middle of nowhere away from town and I felt that if I was going to get ambushed, this was the place. The area looked like an old western ghost town and we thought to ourselves, *This can't be it*. As we walked inside, the bar had just enough appeal to make it interesting; a simple pool table, a couple of beer signs, and the usual police memorabilia with some patches stapled to the wall. There were no markings outside and if it wasn't for a person walking by that gave us the heads up, we would have turned around and headed back to the ship. It was cops only in the bar and they looked us over as we came through the front door. It was late afternoon when we got there and we grabbed two stools as close as we could to the taps. Seconds later, we were met with a warm smile from the bartender and a couple of coasters placed in front of us. We must have made a good impression, and before long were telling cop stories and buying tee shirts like we had been coming there our whole lives. The beer was flowing and the guys couldn't have been nicer. When I told them I was a cop in New York, there was instant bonding. "We were just up in New York for some training." "Really, whereabouts?" I asked. "White Plains." I looked across the corner of the bar and did a double-take at the guy I was talking to. "That's where I'm a cop." I thought for a second, *This is too weird*. Reminds me of the guy who is playing golf and can't hit the ball out of his shadow and turns to his caddy and says, "You're the worst caddy I've ever had in my life." Then the caddy says, "No, that would be too much of a coincidence." The cops we met that day from Bermuda were open and honest. They told us some stories about their island that the tourists don't get to hear. Yes, there is crime and drugs on the island. We laughed and drank for the better part of five hours and realized it was time to get out of there. We knew that we were not going to make it for dinner onboard the ship and really didn't care. I hit the ignition switch on the moped and it fired up. My wife, Sue, held on to my waist as we tried to navigate our way back to the vessel. The sun was starting to set as we drove back across the causeway towards the town of St. George. It was one of those perfect days. There were over 3000 people on the cruise that week and nobody had a better time than we did that day.

The following afternoon, we left the island of Bermuda and I decided to relax with a good cigar on the aft deck as my wife got ready for dinner. After pulling out of the port, I watched the wake from the engines pour waves into the Atlantic. I have never smoked a bad Padron cigar and this one did not disappoint. I took another sip from the glass and watched the waves, realizing they were no longer in a straight line. We had begun to turn and were now heading back to Bermuda. This can't be good! There was no immediate communication from the crew and I headed downstairs to our cabin to see how my wife was doing in hair and makeup. It was almost dark when we pulled back into the port. I was sitting there making small talk at dinner and trying to figure out the math. We had sailed out of Bermuda for about three hours, then three hours back, and spent about an hour or so at the dock. So, we're seven hours behind schedule. This is when the stabilizers on the ship don't get used. Stabilizers are like airplane wings that protrude from the sides of the ship. Instead of the ship rolling from side to side by the waves, stabilizers can eliminate about 85% of the rocking. The result is the ship can go faster, but the throw-up potential also increases. We were finally advised that a party was seriously ill on the ship and that medical aid was needed. We both survived the day and a half at sea without seeing the porcelain goddess and made it back to New York on time.

I've had the good fortune of seeing a few of the islands in the Caribbean, 17 to be exact, and St. Maarten is probably my favorite. Not only did I get engaged there, but at one time, I had some friends who knew the place like the back of their hand. We were invited to spend a week with them on the island as they drove us to the places tourists don't go. When it was time to leave, we didn't stand with 300 people in line waiting to check in at the airport. My buddy spoke with an agent, passed him off $20 and we went to the head of the class. That's a lot better than standing outside listening to the wives complain about the heat. Our friend had a bar there on the beach called The Firehouse and we hung out one day as the parades from Carnival passed on the streets of Philipsburg. It was an all-day party that lasted into the night. On another occasion, we ate dinner one night that was literally in a family's backyard. The owners had a huge pool and the tables were aligned around it. He was passing out free samples of his rum punch that he was very proud of. There was a passion fruit that was smooth and he poured me another shot after my compliment. The catch of the day was red snapper and we ate like being rescued from Gilligan's Island. I watched as four guys in their mid-20's who had finished their meal walked out past our table. One guy gave his buddy a little push and splash, right into the pool. That got everybody's attention. I thought it was going to get nasty for a minute, but four drunken guys kept it together pretty well.

Didn't know there was going to be a show with the meal. The island is half Dutch and half French, but don't let that fool you, US currency is taken almost everywhere. The French side of the island has several nude beaches. Great place to do some people watching and laughing. Some people do not have mirrors in their homes. I went on a cruise once that had us in a different island almost every day. Where are we? After a while, it all starts to look the same; there is a small market just off the pier, a white sandy beach, and somebody serving drinks. It's like Groundhog Day. Most ports have a nice welcome sign so you don't get confused as to what day it is.

On one cruise, it was time to do some serious research and figure out just how to smuggle enough alcohol onboard without it being confiscated. There are several videos posted on the internet with different ideas and methods. Most ships allow for one bottle of wine to be brought on board per person. So, when you finish that last bottle of merlot, carefully rinse it out and don't get the label wet. Add your favorite rum, vodka, whatever and use your basic food dye to perfect the color. Dark wine bottles work best, forget the pale greens and yellows. The corking stage is next; the old one should work fine, just invert it so it looks brand new and tap it in with a hammer. You can always put a dime on top of the cork so the glass doesn't get chipped. Buy a few wine wrappers to finish off the project. You'll have to use a hair dryer to activate them and they will seal around the head and neck of the bottle. Having good props always helps. Keeping a bag from a liquor store with a receipt can't hurt. Besides the fake wine, we also had bladder bags that we brought onboard in our luggage. They can be purchased in any camping store or online. We hung them up in the shower in the stateroom like IV bags in a hospital. Nobody likes getting off a cruise with a $1000 bar bill. When in doubt, get the beverage package.

My last voyage was on a brand new ship that had only been in the water for about a month. It was built in Germany and had every bell and whistle on it. What it didn't have was a crew that knew what they were doing. The bartenders looked like they hadn't slept in a week and the wait staff could have been on mushrooms for all I knew. The Norwegian Escape did have a ropes course that was terrifying on deck #20. I hate heights and this wasn't helping. At one point, you have the opportunity to walk the plank off the side of the ship. I don't trust that window-washer's harness or that silly D-ring that's holding me up. The 5 O'clock Bar opened every day at noon and we were there. Car bombs and back-up drinks after the shots. By the second day, they knew what we wanted. Next year, it's the Mediterranean and a five-country tour.

CHAPTER 27

DECISIONS

There was that musty smell in the air that happens after a
rainstorm in the summer. The good thing about rain when you're a
cop is that it drives most people inside. Unfortunately, people still
have to get from one place to another and driving in the rain just
makes matters worse. A lot of people think they're a NASCAR driver,
but they're not. The streets were still damp and the tour was a little
more than half over. I was driving 14 car that night and it was fairly
quiet. It was just after 9 p.m. when the call from communications
was dispatched. I was driving south on North Broadway when the
dispatcher advised of shots fired in a section of town about a mile
and a half away. Here's a good rule to live by: If you're in a car and
you hear sirens, don't think 'where are they coming from'? STOP
your vehicle as soon as you safely can and, if possible, pull to the side
of the road. Then wait till every emergency vehicle has passed. I was
in my third year of being a cop and was trying to remember all the
training I had received regarding shots fired calls. It was a blur. Your
adrenaline starts pumping and you begin to focus on the task at
hand. You're taught that the most important rule of getting to any
call is to get there safely. More information was being received from
headquarters regarding the shooting and it was relayed to us that a
subject was now down in the middle of the street. The location of
the incident was Chatterton Ave., near a small deli/bodega where
the local kids/assholes were known to hang out. I activated the car's

lights and hit the siren as I sped down Broadway getting ready to make a right onto Hamilton Ave. There was a small pickup truck to my right approaching the intersection and he slammed on his brakes in the wet roadway. The ass end of his vehicle slid into my lane of traffic... crash. The accident was minor. When I say it was a minor accident, that means the car is still drivable and nobody is going to the hospital or morgue. I exited the police car and said, "Give me your license, stay here." I continued to the call and advised headquarters of what had just happened. The call turned out to be bullshit, and I returned to the scene of the accident where my sergeant was already waiting for me. We had a short discussion and he told me that I should not have left the accident scene. He went on to preach the book of rules that the police department has in place, and how I had just disobeyed them. He wrote me up for the offense and stuffed some more worthless paper in my file. Just so we are clear, do you understand what just happened? My sergeant responded to the accident scene and not to the area where the report of shots fired originated. Just in case you think that all cops want to be badasses, some would be better suited working for Microsoft at a computer terminal. Was I angry? A little. It would have been nice if he could have used some common sense. You learn very quickly about supervisors in this world. Some are really good and others just don't have a clue. I was lucky enough to have a few really good supervisors, guys that cared, taught and weren't afraid to get a little dirt on their hands. Years later, that same supervisor had the balls to ask me for a favor when I wrote somebody he knew a ticket. There was a running joke about him in the department that if he ever exhaled, he would take somebody's eye out with a button on his shirt.

I met my first wife, Liz, at the mortgage company where I was securing a loan for my first home. It was February or March of 1990. She was the secretary at the front desk and did some typing and filing work in her Monday through Friday 9-5 job. Soon after we began dating, she met my friends and I met hers. There was one particular friend that she cared a lot about, and they both could finish each other's sentences. Her name was Michaelann. I had the impression that the relationship was on its last legs or at least needing a little oxygen seeing how Liz was single and Michaelann was married to Joe. That's just how it works out; married people hang with married people. It was just over a year later in the spring of 1991 when Liz had asked if we could all go to dinner one night. I had never met Michaelann's husband but had heard a lot about him. He owned a limo company down in the Bronx and I believe he was also setting up a car wash company. From the way Liz had described it, there was always a lot of cash coming in. The plans were quickly changed after we got to their home and Joe was unable to make it. "I got some business things I got to take care of." Michaelann didn't want to be the third wheel at the table that night and asked her husband if she could go with another friend who just happened to be in the apartment when we arrived. This guy's name was also Joe and he said he would drive us down to Queens, NY to the restaurant the girls had picked out. Joe #2 worked across the street from Joe #1 and had an auto body shop. I imagine the two helped each other out at times and told customers "if you ever need a good mechanic or limo company, that guy across the street will hook ya up." Besides having businesses across the street from each other, they had one other thing in common: they were both in love with the same woman. We sat down for dinner and ate some really expensive Italian food that night. In New York City, everything is expensive. The restaurant was an old converted warehouse with ceilings that were 30 feet high with huge panes of glass making up the façade. I couldn't put my finger on it, but there was just something off about the whole night. Like, who would ask their husband if they could go out for dinner with another guy? What kind of husband says, "Sure, honey, have fun?" Maybe it was just me trying to dial in the situation and putting the cop face on. On June 10, 1991, a couple of months later, Michaelann and her husband drove back to their home on 14 Sweetfield Circle in Yonkers, NY. It was late at night and she ran inside telling her husband she had to use the bathroom. While he parked the car, he was met by several rounds of ammunition that would end his life. Joe #2 would be found guilty of second-degree murder and sentenced to 25 years to life. Two days prior to being sentenced, he and Michaelann were married in a jailhouse ceremony. She must have had a good story to tell the cops.

I was stuck inside communications again on a 4-12 tour. When most people become cops, the last thing they want is to be assigned some indoor job like answering the phones, dealing with prisoners, working in the records division, sorting paper into files and punching keys on a computer. I had just gotten off the phone with a party when I was informed that my home on Sycamore Lane had been broken into. Shit! I pictured the place being ransacked and my stereo equipment and TV gone. I checked with the lieutenant on duty and he relieved me to respond to my residence. There was a footprint about three feet up on a rear door and the lock had been broken. Remember, it's not how good your lock is, it's how good your door is. There was only one thing missing from the home; my off duty-gun that I had purchased when I was in the Air Force in Minot, ND. It was a 9 MM Italian made Berretta, and now somebody else had it. Nothing else in the whole house was disturbed or taken. Pretty odd, huh? My roommate, who had discovered the break-in, and I started checking the neighborhood for anybody suspicious. I had the feeling it was a lost cause and never put a lot of faith into our detective division when it came to solving burglaries. You know the old saying, 'they couldn't find a whore in a whorehouse with a fistful of fifties carrying a three-pack of condoms.' It was close to midnight when I shook down three youths hanging out at a bus stop. I may have invaded their Fourth Amendment rights a little, but I was pissed and didn't feel like getting shot with my own gun if they did have it. I took a little heat for being less than professional in dealing with them. Later that night, cops from another jurisdiction responded with dogs that did a little sniffing to no avail. I had a few of my own thoughts as to who did it and later questioned one guy in particular about the incident. He lied like he did on several other occasions; he had an alibi and complete story as to where he was that night. He was a square badge security officer but would tell people he was a cop. The case was never solved.

I'm not sure exactly how the call was dispatched, but it was involving a husband and wife, your typical domestic dispute where a weapon was involved and injuries had occurred. I responded to the upper-middle-class home just off of Gedney Esplanade. It was about 4:30 p.m. and I was the first responder on the scene. I was met by the wife at the front door, and I recognized her right away as being one of the emergency room nurses at a hospital in town. She explained she had just been pushed down a flight of stairs that led from the second floor of the home to the foyer we were now standing in. I asked, "Your husband did this?" "Yes." "Where is he now?" She explained that she was knocked unconscious and didn't know what happened. As I looked around, there were three children in different areas of the living and dining room and the oldest one spoke up. He said that after the altercation his father had come down the stairs and thought he had killed his wife. "So, where is your dad now?" About this time, I heard the sirens from the ambulance getting closer and then there were two people at the front door. A neighbor walked into the home along with some bearded guy that had to tell me he was a lawyer before he could tell me his name. The son pointed to the door near the kitchen which led to the basement and told me his father was down there. His story was that his dad, after fearing he had just killed his wife, went into the kitchen, grabbed a paring knife out of the drawer and plunged it into his own heart. I walked over to the doorway and there he was, lying at the bottom of the stairs next to oil burner with a knife handle sticking out of his chest. Okay, let's take a vote: Who thinks the wife did it? The 17-year-old son? Or did he kill himself? I checked for a pulse and breathing and got neither one. The ambulance crew was now on top of me and loading him up onto a stretcher. The guy looked to be about 300+ lbs. During the incident, I had radioed out for additional units because of all the discrepancies that were present in the home and to secure the scene until we knew just exactly what we had. The wife was complaining of back and neck pain as her lawyer was consoling her. With the conditions being what they were, several supervisors along with the detective division arrived. The husband was transported to White Plains Hospital. I attempted to get some information from the kids, but they weren't saying much. The wife was saying less. I was told by a supervisor to transport the Mrs. to a different hospital in town for treatment. She was able to walk to the police car, but when she found out where she was going, she told me that I was kidnapping her. She demanded to go to the hospital where she worked and where her husband was going. Being a nurse, you can move very freely around a hospital where you're employed and have a lot of co-workers. She was probably standing 10 feet away from the bed when the doctor told her he had passed. So, who called the lawyer and neighbor that were there seconds after me? She did. The three children who just watched their mom get thrown down a flight of stairs are emotionless. Dead father... even more emotionless. Things that make you go 'Hmmm'. Everybody gave statements and when it was all said and done, the verdict was that no charges were going to be filed against any family members. From all accounts of what I read and heard, he wasn't a very nice guy and now he's dead and the family can move on.

There were four of us from the traffic division getting dressed that afternoon in the locker room. We had our own little area that kept the unity and humor segregated to our own section. Sometimes you couldn't wait to get out of that place and other times, when the jokes and banter among cops were in high gear, you never wanted it to end. To this day, I don't know why but everybody called him Bing. It was a nickname that just fit his 275-pound frame, and that's probably being generous. He had a baby face and most likely only needed to shave once a month. He was getting close to retirement. 20 years can go pretty fast. Since I had known him, he had a steady gig Monday to Friday 8 a.m. to 4 p.m. with holidays off, a sturdy car, and enough overtime to make him happy. Yeah, he had a pretty good hook. That afternoon, a bike cop, Alan, was in rare form and was not going to let it go. "You're not gonna retire, where are you going to go, what are you going to do?" Bing acknowledged Al and said he was on the way out. Al then made the bet that if Bing retired in a month, he would buy him a steak dinner. I was standing there pulling off my boots and said to myself, *I've got to get in on this.* Myself and another friend, Eric, jumped in on the action hoping for a free meal. See, the thing is, when you have been doing something for 20 years, it's not only comfortable, but it's security. Al took the bet and said he would buy all of us dinner if Bing pulled the retirement string. A few weeks later, we were making dinner plans at the Chart House in Dobbs Ferry, NY. The restaurant was located right on the Hudson River with some fantastic views and seated about 250. The four of us sat down just after 7 p.m. and started throwing them back. Bing had a few stories that nobody had ever heard before and we listened while we looked over the menu. When the server returned, I ordered a porterhouse steak medium rare and a baked potato loaded with everything. One of the nice things about this restaurant was the ability to get your steaks a little thicker if you wanted it. Just ask for the Callahan cut. The four of us sat and ate like it was the last supper for over two hours, telling tales and laughing. When the check arrived, Al, true to his word, tossed his American Express onto the white linen tablecloth. After dinner, we decided to go over to the bar area and have one for the road, also known as 'one for the ditch'. Back then, smoking in the lounge at a restaurant was not a problem so we decided to light up a few cigars as we waited on cocktails. With that, the manager came over to us and said that cigar smoking was not permitted. We looked around and saw people smoking pipes and cigarettes and had a couple of choice words for him. Al just dropped $300 and now we're getting kicked out. Looking back on the situation, it was no big deal – we needed a change of scenery anyway. We left the restaurant and drove down Main Street in the small hamlet of Dobbs Ferry and found a local dive called The Eagles Nest. We ordered up a round and got permission from the bartender to light up our ropes. The night soon came to end, so we said our goodbyes and Eric and I walked to our cars. We had both parked in the bus stop across from the bar but had checked the schedule and knew that the last bus had already come through. It was close to midnight as we compared the two parking tickets we had just received. I looked at Eric and said, "What do you want to do?" The police station was just a few doors down and we decided to go and plead our case. We approached the thick pane of glass and were met by the desk sergeant who not only looked pissed off but had an attitude as well. We told him we were both cops in White Plains. He didn't care. "Can you tell me who wrote the summonses?" He replied, "I did." We walked back down the street talking about what a dick this cop was and whether we were going to fight it. A week later, I put a check in the mail for $25. Case closed, right? It's two years later and my chief wants to talk to me about an upcoming trial I had. When the brass called you in for a favor, it was always done tongue in cheek. "Hey, I got a call from a sergeant down in Dobbs Ferry, you wrote his brother for a red light." "Sure, chief, whatever you need - what's the last name?" Have you ever gotten a present when it's not your birthday or the holidays? Good stuff! When he told me, my whole face must have lit up. I left his office with a smile from ear to ear and knew that today was going to be fun. My trials usually started at 10 a.m. and I would meet with all the violators who never passed the stopped school bus, were never doing 53 mph in a 30 zone, and never made that illegal U-turn across a double yellow line. I met the sergeant's brother outside of the courtroom and I offered him a plea deal; no points and a $100 fine. He looked at me as if he didn't understand. "Did my brother talk to you?" "Yeah, he spoke to my chief." He was going to get the same deal everybody else got. I let on very little and waited till the trial was over and he had pleaded guilty to the reduced charge. "Tell your brother I said hi... and thanks for helping me out with that bus stop ticket." He looked at me like I was a real prick and I'm sure he was on the phone to his brother before he got to his car. You never know when it's gonna come around, so when it does, take full advantage of it.

CHAPTER 28

GOLF

We arrived at Carvel Country Club just after 8 a.m. and had a few minutes to warm up and get another cup of coffee before the first hole. I had played with John a few times before and always knew I had a challenge in front of me. The course had some interesting history. Its location was about an hour and a half north of New York City and owned by the Estate of Thomas Carvel who sold thousands of Cookie Pusses and Fudgy the Whale Ice Cream Cakes. Me personally, I think it was the same mold with a different name. Carvel started selling soft ice cream back in the 1930's when his truck broke down on a Memorial Day Weekend and he was trying to unload his product before it was lost. Soft ice cream was now the latest hit at Carvel. The dining room at the club was filled with pictures of Mr. Carvel and golfers of the past and some of the rat pack from the Las Vegas era. The course is now closed as developers fight over the last blade of grass. John had a pretty good game at one time and told me some stories about how many events he had won in high school during his late teens and competitions into his early 20's. He was always quick with a line or some gem to keep the conversation flowing. The day was going as planned; a lot of laughs and what guys normally do when they're out pegging it. The 16th hole at Carvel was a long par 5 down a hill and the green ran from front to back which made the hole that much more difficult. I stepped up to the tee and cranked one down the right center. Then

John sky popped a driver off to the left and into the deep rough or what we like to call 'the native fescue'. He had that look about him like, how did I do that? I had a pretty good idea where it was and started walking the 50 yards or so into the tall grasses. After locating the ball, John picked a club out of his bag and thrashed at it, sending it straight up about 12 inches and then falling back into the rough. Every shot makes somebody happy. He took another swing at it and, this time, he moved it some 20 or so yards. The rest of the hole was pure frustration and that look of bewilderment. By the time John reached the green, he was shaking his head and trying to figure out how many strokes he had just taken. He lined up his putt and railed it into the back of the cup. *That was a lot of strokes*, I thought to myself, but I didn't want to ask. We walked off the green and John said, "That was an 11." "How did you make an eleven?" "I sank a 25-foot putt!" he replied.

One of my wife's best friends lives out in Arizona with her husband, Frank, in an area called Scottsdale that was just north and east of downtown Phoenix. We were going to be in the area and we got the invitation to stay in their home. At one time, Frank had thought about joining Troon North Golf Course that was about a 9-iron from his house. He had met with membership from the course and got a complimentary round of golf to see if he liked the layout and course conditions. He told me the story how after hitting his tee shot on #1 he drove down the cart path and was going towards his ball in the fairway when he was told that he had to stay on the cart path due to the over-seeding on the fairways. Frank wasn't about to walk to his ball and told the guy, "That's it for me, I'm not joining here." He found another club to join about 15 minutes away called Tatum Ranch Golf Course and invited me to join him early one morning. Frank was always running late and had the habit of tying his golf shoes on the tee box of the first hole. We had just finished hitting our tee shots on the fifth and I got back into the golf cart with Frank at the wheel. It was a warm January sun with crystal blue skies. That was the last good thing I remembered about that day. As we drove down the cart path Frank decided to get a little too close to a cactus bush on my side of the cart. "Frank...Frank..." I'm yelling as the bush is coming closer. I tried to lift my leg and get as close to him as possible, but it was not happening. Moments later, I've got several thorns and prickers from the kneecap down just below my shorts. The F-bombs were flying. I've got blood dripping down my leg and Frank is telling me how they usually have those pruned. How the hell do you drive a golf cart into a cactus minefield? The rest of the round sucked and trying to remove barbs with a tee is probably not recommended by the American Medical Association.

I had always wanted to play Whippoorwill Golf Club in Armonk, NY and got the blessing early one Monday morning. It was an old Donald Ross course that had been redesigned from the 1920's. I was about two miles from the course when the police sirens came up from behind me and the Suburban raced past me, it was 7:30 in the morning. As I made the next right and drove another half mile or so, there in front of me were two vehicles that had just been involved in a head-on collision. The officer had already started working on one subject and had started oxygen. The parties from the other vehicle were out of their car and appeared to have minor injuries. I pulled over to the side of the residential road and yelled over to the cop, "You need a hand, I'm a cop in White Plains?" "That would be great," he replied. "Did you call for a helicopter yet?" "No, just an ambulance." Due to the severity of the injuries, I called over his car radio to his communications that a STAT flight helicopter would be necessary to transport the subject to a trauma hospital. STAT stands for stabilization, treatment and transport. We both started doing CPR on the party and did our best while we waited on the ambulance and helicopter. The subject was bleeding from several areas on his body and appeared to be in his late teens. We both worked on him and it seemed like the officer was very familiar with the male party. Within a few minutes, medics were there and directions were given to the helicopter crew to land on the 14th hole which was adjacent to our position just north of the roadway. He was still alive when the helicopter took off and I was 15 minutes late for my golf date. As I drove into the golf course property, my friends were there waiting for me and asked, "How are you going to play golf with blood all over your shirt?" As you can probably imagine, there were a lot of things going through my mind that morning when I teed off, and none of them had anything to do with golf. A few hours later, we reached the landing zone where the helicopter had been. The fall leaves were nowhere to be found having been blown earlier by the blades from the chopper off into the rough. Driving home that afternoon and going past the crash seemed a little surreal. The following day I called to follow up on the condition of the subject, but their headquarters would not release any information to me over the phone. I finally got my chance to play the "WHIP," as Whippoorwill Golf Course is referred to and can't remember much about it……. except for # 14.

Mr. Terry loves golf more than me. In a typical season, he would have a couple of new drivers, at least one new set of sticks, two or three putters and a bag that looked as if he had just been sponsored by Cadillac. He was always looking for the answer that he thought he could find by dumping his wallet on the counter and breaking out the MasterCard. It doesn't work that way. He had a swing that was almost corkscrew in nature. Every time he swung, I cringed thinking about the stress he was causing his lower back. It demanded perfect timing and a little luck. There were a few times I thought for sure he was going to fall over. If he had been right-handed, I would have had some really nice clubs. We developed a friendship and played almost every weekend for several years together. Sometimes it was really good, sometimes it was like arguing with your girlfriend. I invited him to spend a week with me down in Hilton Head one September, six days of golf and maybe a little drinking to break up the monotony. We were playing Shipyard Plantation one afternoon and Mr. Terry was having a pretty good day. At one point, he looked at me and said, "I've got a chance to break 80." He had never done that before. We finished the 17th hole and all he needed was a bogey 5 on #18 to shoot in the 70's for the first time in his life. His drive on the final hole went dead right off the face of the club and it was a miracle that it didn't go out of bound or at least catch the water that guarded the right side. He was now some 200+ yards to the green and his ball was nestled down in the thick Bermuda. He managed to punch it out and navigate it over a small stream that flows across the fairway. He was now about 60 yards out and hit a little wedge that rolled up the slope and stopped about 25 feet from the hole. I was rooting for him, but still knew he needed two good putts to finish the day. When he got to his ball, he realized that he had a putt with a severe break on it that was uphill for the most part, then broke down and to the left at the end. He lined it up and I could tell as soon as he struck it that it wasn't going to get there. He had left himself about a three-footer. He looked at me and asked, "Is that good?" I thought to myself, *No that's not good; you want to shoot a 79, you have to earn it.* "No." Mr. Terry looked at me like I had just kicked his dog. Now he's nervous, more nervous than he was five minutes ago. He stood over the ball and to his credit nailed the putt. I was happy to sign his card and attest his score. 48 hours later, our friendship would take a turn for the worse. We were betting a few dollars and the match had come down to the last hole at Rose Hill Golf Course just off the island of Hilton Head. Mr. Terry's drive went the republican way and bounced off every tree in South Carolina. We all stood on the tee box and nobody really knew for sure where it was. After helping him look for a while, I walked out of the wooded area into the rough and heard from behind me, "I've got it." There was only one problem with that, I was now staring at his Callaway golf ball that was right in front of me. I was pissed. Not only is he going to lie, but now he's going to cheat to try and win a bet. Play golf with anybody for four hours and it will tell you everything you need to know about their character. We finished out the hole and, of course, there were words when it was all over. I threw him his golf ball, "Your ball was in the rough, you played an incorrect ball. Learn the rules." A guy once said to me, "If you don't cheat in golf, you're only cheating yourself because the chances are the guy you're playing against is cheating."

Gus was 96 when I met him. A teaching golf pro from Pennsylvania who had moved to Florida and was still giving advice and lessons on the driving range. He played three times a week and told me he had won the lottery twice. Not once like everybody else in the world is hoping for, but twice. "Gus, what do you like to do besides play golf?" "Well, I like to go to the mailbox on Tuesdays." "What's the big deal about going to the mailbox on Tuesdays?" "That's the day when my check for $6000 comes in the mail from Lotto." Steve had just become the new head pro at Palm Aire Country Club where Gus was a member in the mid-90's. They talked about playing together someday and finally the match was on; kind of like the old man vs. the kid. Because of his advanced years, he said he would need some strokes to make the game fair. Steve was in his 30's and Gus 80+ at the time. After it was all said and done Gus agreed to take only one stroke over the 18 holes; the only exception was he could use it however he wanted to. The game began and each one of them parred the first hole. That's when Gus said, "I'll take 1/18 of a stroke on that hole." Beware of anybody who has won the Lotto twice.

In my junior year in high school, I had decided to try out for the golf team. Golf was not that popular back then and there were definitely no hot cheerleaders coming to the games or pep rallies held for us. Practice was held on the grounds of a nearby hospital where we would shag our own balls and get some advice from our Coach, Mr. Winterstein. The season was short and only consisted of about 10 matches from April till mid-May. The golf team consisted of six players who were ranked 1-6 with two alternates. I was hoping to just make the team and feel like a little part of something. We had a team meeting one afternoon before the start of the season and I learned then that I was going to be the #5 man on the team. There was a smile on my face as I looked over the paperwork the coach had passed around. There were the dates of the matches, times, courses we would be playing and which school we would be playing against. It was a low budget operation with no uniforms and about the best our coach could do was to get us some fresh balls for the matches, secure tee times and some bus service. We had our last practice scheduled in late March and a cold annoying drizzle fell out of the sky. I was there with an old pair of rain pants on and a wool cap. My hands were cold and swinging the club became a chore. As I looked around, there were a few guys who decided not to show up. Great, the nucleus of the team players 2-4 were the teacher's pets and got a free pass to stay out of the rain. Not the case. The following day, the coach told me they were off the team and I was now his #2 player. My first reaction was being scared and knowing I was going to let him down because I knew I was not good enough to compete against other #2 players. He told me, "You'll be fine, study up on the rule book." Our home course, Ridgeway Country Club, was directly across from the high school and we could jump the fence and cut across the sixth fairway to get to the clubhouse. I finished the season with a .500 record and learned about the rules of golf that year thanks to a really good golf coach. My opponents, well some of them, learned a few new rules also.

The World Amateur Golf Tournament is held every year in Myrtle Beach, SC. The event is for all amateurs and lasted four days with a playoff round on day five for all flight winners. On average, the headcount is about 3000 golfers that travel there from all over the country and from several countries outside the U.S. The first time I was there in 2009, the weather was as good as you could expect, but the play was obnoxiously slow. There were a lot of people lining up one-foot putts and taking way too much time to swing a club. Six-hour rounds of golf are not fun. In tournament play, you are required to keep your opponent's score. As we walked off one hole, the guy I was keeping score for said, "Put me down for a five." I kept walking to the cart and said, "You sure about that?" "Yeah, I got a five." "Ya want to count them up again just to be sure?" He began replaying the hole in his head, first one was down the left, then I punched out over to the right, the next one was over the green, I chipped on and made two putts. "Oh wait, that was a six." "I'll put you down for a 6." "Wow, you could have had me disqualified." "First one is on me, the next one is on you." A day later, guess who I'm playing with? His brother who had also made the trip in from the State of Washington. Once again, I'm walking off the green and I get the same story from him. "Ya wanna count them again?" I said. I looked at him and told him what had happened with his brother yesterday; you guys either had the worst math teacher or you skipped class every day.

Farmstead Golf course is not your average 18 hole track. The course was about a 10 minute drive from my vacation home and was always in excellent shape. The course lies in the town of Calabash and the property is situated in both North and South Carolina. What makes it unique is that their liquor license is in the State of North

Carolina. This makes it tough for the cart girl who can only serve beverages on certain holes. On my first trip there she explained in her best southern charm how she can't cross state lines, not even for a Gatorade. The finishing hole tips out at 767 yards and is a dogleg left par 6. You tee off in South Carolina and finish your day back in North Carolina. I've taken a few sevens there.

CHAPTER 29

THAT WAS EASY

I grabbed a barricade from the side of the road that wasn't being used by the construction company. Two plastic saw horses with a six-foot plank connecting the apparatus. Working overtime was usually boring and made for some long ass days. The money was right, and you did it because you had a family, or wanted a new car or were tired of eating peanut butter sandwiches. You stand on your feet for eight hours and assist with traffic while the crew digs a hole or installs fiber optics. It was just after lunch time and I needed to put something in my stomach. There was a deli across the street and I was a heartbeat away from taking a break when the call came over the radio. I listened half-heartedly. A car had just been stolen and the dispatcher was advising of the license plate number, year, make and color. I was standing on West Post Road with very little to do except watch the cars go by. As I dragged the barricade across the one-lane roadway, I knew this was a long shot but figured what the hell. I stopped the first car and advised the driver of some construction issues. A line of cars was now headed towards me and I looked at the color of the cars as they slowed for the vehicles in front of them. I was looking for a white Jeep Wrangler. "Repeat that plate number again?" After stopping traffic, I walked down the line of autos and there in front of me, seven cars away, was the stolen vehicle. It was being operated by a male driver with three of his buddies along for the ride. To this day, they will tell you two things,

"We didn't steal the car," and "We got caught by a cop on foot causing a traffic jam." As I approached the subjects, they had no idea what was happening. They could see the construction equipment just ahead of them and to the left and I told them that it was only going to be a minute or so. I wasn't crazy about the odds, four of them against one of me, so I stalled waiting on backup to respond. The dispatcher from headquarters radioed back the plate number which was a match and I advised I had that vehicle stopped. Several other units responded to my location and we were able to get all parties out of the vehicle without incident and into some nice bracelets made by Smith and Wesson. The guys working the construction company crew all stopped to watch the 10 minutes of excitement and had no idea what was happening till after it was all over. When you are making a felony arrest like this, every cop that responded has a weapon out and is making sure they get home safely. I drove into headquarters for the three hours of paperwork thinking, *Damn, I still haven't gotten anything to eat.*

The whole time I knew Walter, he was assigned to the detective division. He never said a lot, but when he did I would make it a point to listen. That's the kind of guy who goes about his business and doesn't have to pound on his chest to tell you what a great cop he is or how many brick walls he can jump in a single bound. Across from our police headquarters was a large mall called The Galleria that opened in 1980. It takes up two city blocks, has four floors of retail space and eight levels of parking. I don't think a day went by when some sort of incident didn't happen there; theft from stores, stolen cars from the lot, a homeless hangout, the usual place for kids to loiter and be annoying kids. Cops could sign up for overtime there writing parking tickets and being a second set of eyes. On one summer night, myself and Walter got the opportunity to cross paths. I was driving a car and he was on foot hanging some paper on windshields for expired meters. He had finished his rounds and I offered him a ride down to the office. The parking garage was almost empty and there were just a few cars left in the lot. We were on the seventh floor of the structure when he said to me, "Slow down here for a minute, I want to talk to this guy." A young man in his mid-20's

189

was walking alone, and I drove up alongside of him. Walter extended his hand out the window and the young man shook his hand. "I thought you said you were going to call me?" Walt waited for a response and got a head shake and a promise that sounded about as sincere as 50% of all marriage vows. I sat there behind the wheel watching Walt work his magic. I assumed he was an informant that had gotten a deal and was now paying back Walt for staying out of jail. He was still holding on to the man's hand and Walter threw another question at him that I couldn't hear very well. The answer he got back must have been worse. Walter looked over at me and said, "Drive." Walter had a grip that was like a vise as the car inched forward. The young man was now walking beside the car. It soon turned into a brisk walk as the two continued their conversation. After a quick tap on the accelerator, I looked over as the jogging began. Walter had a little smirk on his face and the young man was now talking at feverish pace. He ran alongside the police car for a few seconds that, in his mind, must have seemed like an eternity. Walter finally got the right answer and let the guy go. We laughed about it as I drove him down to the office. I'm willing to bet that guy never shook hands with Walter again.

It was close to three o'clock in the morning and I had just turned off the Post Road and headed southbound on South Lexington Ave. It was a boring night and most of the bars in town had already closed and kicked the last drunk out. I was driving 12 car that night due to somebody on vacation and another guy who had called in sick. As I proceeded, a call came in over the radio. It really wasn't so much a call but information regarding something that had happened in another town about five miles away. There had been several cars in that town that had been vandalized; car stereos stolen, a few speakers taken and a lot of smashed windows. Somebody had gotten a partial license plate number and advised that there appeared to be three subjects in the car. As I continued up the road another 300 feet, I caught up to a vehicle just before the crest of the hill. I radioed in the plate number and told headquarters that I was behind that car. If they had given out that information five minutes later, I would have turned right and they would have turned left, never to be seen again. After pulling the car over, everything went according to plan. The three subjects had a hard time answering any questions and stolen merchandise was observed in plain view. They ranged in age from 15-17 and were all transported to headquarters where they were read their rights and separated. The youngest being a minor, we couldn't talk to him until he had his mommy and daddy with him or some legal guardian. He gave me a phone number for his parents, but there was no answer. I told him that I knew his father. His dad was a mason and it just so happened that he lived near my mother's home. At 15 years old, breaking into cars doesn't make you John Dillinger, but it's not what you want to put on your resume when you apply for a job at Burger King. After getting clearance from my sergeant, I drove up to his parents' home to advise them of what had transpired and that they would need to respond to headquarters. I rang the doorbell enough to make it sound annoying and end somebody's deep sleep cycle. The home was an old two-story that sat on a corner lot and was made from stone and mortar. From the other side of the door, a tired voice asked," Who is it?" I responded back, "White Plains Police Department." The door opened about six inches and the mother and father looked at me. After identifying myself, I informed them of what had happened and that their son was at the police station. "That's impossible," she said. I grabbed my black notebook from my back pocket and read off his name and date of birth and the bullshit phone number he had given me. "That's not your phone number, is it?" "No, and besides, my son is upstairs sleeping in his bed." Parents can really be funny even at 4:30 in the morning. The husband opened the door fully and stood there in his greyish robe trying to get a handle on the situation. He said very little and let his wife do most of the talking. Remember, always let your wife do the talking. You can be married or you can be right, it's your choice. She spun away from the doorway and started up the flight of stairs. Within seconds, she returned and uttered, "He's not there, and the window is wide open." That's what I just told you, woman, and you didn't believe me. I'll be at headquarters with your dopey kid, come on down when you're ready to pick the little thief up.

Trish was a rock star when I met her. If there was a party, alcohol, music or a hot guy, she was in. She worked at the parking garages that were scattered around the city, handling permits and dealing with people who got parking tickets. Her nickname quite simply was 'Trish the Dish'. She got reprimanded at her job one spring afternoon. Not for yelling at customers or showing up late for work - no, she did that enough, but that wasn't the reason today. Trish had gone out on her lunch break and bought a new yellow bikini and was now in the office modeling it for the world. That was Trish. Thing was, if anybody should have been modeling, it was her. She was in her early 20's when we first met, her long brown hair and outgoing personality made her even more attractive. Trish was a concert lover. It didn't matter if it was a school night or the weekend; she was always up for a road trip to New York City to catch a band play. She went to venues that included Webster Hall, Irving Plaza, Radio City Music Hall, Carnegie, The Beacon and, of course, the bigger arenas like the Nassau Coliseum and Madison Square Garden. So, it wasn't unusual when I saw her one Monday morning after she had been out the previous weekend with a glass in her hand and dancing in the aisles. She was leaving the concert when she almost tripped over somebody's small duffel bag that had been left behind. She picked it up and, being as curious as the next person, she looked inside. I guess the best way she could describe it to me was, "Holy shit." A bag full of money and a .38 snub nose revolver. There was nobody she felt comfortable with at the event to turn the bag over to, so she exited the venue onto the street and found two cops that were in the area. She explained the situation to them and they directed her to the precinct which was about a block away. Trish, being the person she was, turned the property in and left her name for the owner. Well, the owner of the cash and weapon turned out to be a cop. In fact, he oversaw the security detail there that night and the money was the payroll for all the cops he had employed to do security. He can't stop thanking Trish and said to her that if she ever wanted to go to a concert, he could get her in and he would be buying the drinks all night. Trish told him, "You know I go to a lot of concerts?" "Whatever I can do for ya." Trish never had to pay for another event or a red solo cup. She was afforded backstage passes like she was royalty. They became good friends and, in the long run, it would have probably been cheaper if he had let her keep the contents of the bag.

I've had to lock up people for a variety of offenses. There was a guy once who stole a tube of Krazy Glue from a store and the owner wanted to prosecute, $2.99. Guess what he wanted that for? I was working a detail at a local park one evening; moms, dads, kids, and some music playing as the burgers and dogs were being grilled up. I stood off to the side near an outcropping of trees when I observed an elderly gentleman walking over towards me. I was waiting for the stupid question he had to ask. Yes, there are stupid questions. Instead, he unzipped his fly and almost pissed all over my leg. He told me he was legally blind and I should give him a break. The local high school kids used to hang out on a golf course in town and throw keg parties late at night. How did we know where they were? Because when we were in high school, we used to do the same thing on the same golf course, probably on the same hole. A buddy of mine once got punched in the chest by his girlfriend one evening. Thing was, he retaliated by pushing her away, she fell, bumped her head, domestic violence. "Hey, man, I got no options here." It can escalate that quick and the next thing you know, you're in the back of a police car, saying, "That bitch."

I had a woman flag me down early one morning. The sun was just breaking over the horizon and I had the feeling that the bacon, egg and cheese sandwich for breakfast was not going to happen. "Officer, officer... I've just been raped." She appeared to be in her late 20's or early 30's. "Where did this happen?" One of the first things you learn when you're a cop is that people lie. She told me a tale of being out with a date and while he was walking her home, he forced her into a parking structure stairwell and forced himself on her. "What's his name?" I asked. There was an uncomfortable pause as she leaned through the car window and was talking a mile a minute. "You got to go catch him, you got to get him." "When did this happen?" When she told me it was a little over an hour ago, the bullshit meter went to 75%. I called for an ambulance, notified the supervisor and got a description of the assailant from her. She took me back to the scene where it supposedly occurred. It was your typical cold concrete form landing between the second and third floors. Did I mention the used condom on the ground? The meter just went to 100%. We located the other party and got his story. Boy meets girl and says let's have sex and then do some crack. When he didn't produce the rock after sex, she plays the rape card. She actually was full of delusional thoughts. I tried my best to explain it to her; the guy doesn't have to say I love you, walk you home, or go back to your house and have cheesy grits. The whole incident was cleared up in less than an hour.

My first robbery arrest happened on a day tour at about two in the afternoon. I was still a rookie and thought that I would be able to change the world, fight crime like Captain America and make a positive change in the community. Wrong. An elderly woman had just been knocked to the ground and her purse was taken. In order to commit a robbery you don't need a knife or a gun, all you need is force and the taking of property. Often somebody who commits a crime will have layers of clothes on. When you're given a description, they have already discarded the top layer and thrown them in the bushes or down the sewer. It's easy to spot the guy with three shirts on when it's 85 degrees out. On this day we were looking for a subject wearing a blue sweatshirt and blue sweatpants. We canvassed the area driving around in circles and with each passing minute expanded the perimeter where we were looking. It was almost 10 minutes from the initial call when I observed him walking on the sidewalk on Barker Avenue. He turned to head north on Broadway. He glanced a couple of times over his shoulder, but still had not seen me. I punched the accelerator and felt the old adrenaline rush throughout my body. I crossed over the double yellow line into oncoming traffic and was now within 30-40 feet of the subject. *Please run*, I thought. As I prepared to jump out of my car, a detective's vehicle came to an abrupt halt in front of mine. I thought for a second he was going to crash into me. Mike exited the unmarked vehicle and ran at the party grabbing him by the sweatshirt and sticking his revolver at the base of his neck. The subject was pushed head first into an oak tree and I saw pieces of bark fall to the ground. I grabbed for my cuffs and helped secure the party. The rule of thumb is that if they are your cuffs, it's your arrest. Mike had a few years on the job and had made detective very quickly. I looked at Mike and he said to me, "Don't worry, this is yours." The subject didn't run or resist and was patted down for weapons. Mike took the lead asking questions, we were able to find the purse and we convinced the victim that this was the party who robbed her. See most people want the right party to go to jail for the crime that was committed, but there's that doubt factor. He approached me from behind. I didn't get a good look at his face. I thought he was taller. I brought the subject in and he wrote out a full statement and signed it.

I had worked a double shift that day, getting up at the butt crack of dawn, driving the 25 miles to work and strapping on the duty rig that weighed close to 20 pounds. The weather reports had been for an ugly day. Snow, ice, that wintery mix of crap that was going to make for a long tour. After finishing up an overtime assignment about 3:30 p.m., the first couple of flakes started hitting the ground which was soon turning to ice. The temperature did a nose dive and I prayed the heater worked in the car. The police vehicle got chains about 6 p.m. and we did the bare minimum that night, answering the necessary calls but not going out of our way. There was an Irish cop on our job who still had the brogue from the old country. He called over the radio that there were a lot of black guys up on Ferris Ave. The dispatcher was aware of the area in question and knew the demographics. "10-4, what are they doing?" "What is who doing?" "The black guys up on Ferris Ave.?" "Not black guys, *black ice*; we need a salt truck up here." The snow and sleet kept coming down and I was waiting for the tap out. The car ride home was white knuckles the whole way and a 30 minute ride turned into an hour and a half. As I drove into my complex I could tell there had not been a plow there all night. Why the hell am I paying a monthly common charge? My car slid to a halt and I figured it would be better to park it then to wreck it attempting to get it into my garage. I had a 300-foot walk to my front door and could already hear the ice cubes hitting the bottom of the glass. I took one step out of the car and fell on my ass. 16 hours of work and two hours commuting to and from and I'm lying on my back like a turtle. I fell twice more as I skated to my home; crashing onto my left side once and a direct hit to the tailbone. It was at that time I vowed to never see ice or snow again if I could help it.

You just walked out of your house and see your car that you parked in the driveway last night has been vandalized. What a great way to start your day. Your tires are gone and the frame is up on blocks and as an added bonus, the headlights are missing. For a period of about six months, we would get about five of these calls each morning. The thieves were hitting mostly higher-end vehicles, Lexus, Infinities, and BMWs. The department set up extra patrols running from 10 p.m. till daybreak hoping to catch these guys. Nothing. The complaints poured in on a regular basis. Then one evening I'm working an overtime job patrolling one of the parking structures at a local mall in town. As I drove down the ramp I noticed three guys were outside a white panel van changing a flat tire. Does it really take three guys to change a tire? "Hey guys, what's up?" I got the typical blank stares and the trio was deciding who was going to talk first. Then, as the first guy began the tale of bullshit, they all wanted to talk. "Flat tire, we're just gonna change it out really quick." I looked in through the windshield and saw about four more tires and some tools in the rear of the van. "Who are the rest of those tires for?" "My mom, I'm working on her car tomorrow, yeah we just picked them up." And then came the easy question, "So, you have a receipt?" Dopey one looked at dopey two as dopey three began to dig into his pockets. "Maybe it's in the van." As he opened the sliding door to check for the receipt, I had all the proof I needed; burglary tool, headlights, cinder blocks, and jacks. When my supervisor saw me the next day, he asked, "How did you catch those guys?" "Sarge, I was just going to help them fix a flat tire, didn't look like they had a clue as to what they were doing."

CHAPTER 30

ROY & RICH

The second home I bought was right after my 28th birthday. I hate moving, but today felt pretty good. I was getting situated, unpacking boxes and figuring out where I wanted to put the coffee maker and where the peanut butter jar was going to go. It was a small condo, 1100 square feet, a two-bedroom, one-bath, and it was all mine. Well, 21% mine and the rest owned by some bank in the Bronx. Prior to purchasing it, I had inquired as to what the building was behind my unit towards the woods. There was a dramatic pause. Somebody has to live next to the septic plant. There were 84 units in the development, a small clubhouse and a pool that sat at the entrance, and then there was the maintenance man. He oversaw the property and fielded the majority of the phone calls from the residents. Many of them thought that they were living on Fifth Avenue. Roy handled water leaks, snow removal, maintaining the pool, landscaping, and anything else that they could throw his way. As I walked through the doorway into his office, there seated at his desk was Grizzly Adams. Here it was a raw April morning in Brewster, NY and there was Roy in his stained t-shirt and jeans smoking a Marlboro. He was on the phone trying to explain to the other party what was going on. He rolled his eyes and threw one hand up in the air. The full beard and chest hair kind of grew together and there was no definitive ending point of either. There was a tattoo on his forearm that showed a picture of a piston wrapped around itself and the inscription Rod

Bender. I introduced myself and told him I had just purchased a home and was still getting used to the area. Did he just tell me his name was Roy or Rod? I must have called him Rod for a week. Great porn star name, I thought. He confided in me he had done his share of street racing when he was younger and, according to him, had blown up a few motors in the process. Roy and I became friends very quickly and he trusted me enough to let down his guard a little and tell a few stories of his past. He did a couple of years in prison and told me if he had ratted on the others involved it would have shortened his sentence by a couple of years. His rule: don't be a rat. We drank a lot of coffee together and I had once asked him why he drinks it black. His response was simple, I don't want to drink burned milk and it was tough to get sugar in prison."

In the years to follow, I started working for Roy on a few odd jobs. He had started a company that managed water and septic facilities. Most were based in large condominiums and I would have to do daily inspections of all, testing well water for impurities, levels, and contaminates. A couple of times a year I would have to shovel human waste that had been cleansed into dumpsters. Yeah, complain about your job. Not as bad as it sounds. The waste water dried on top of large sand beds and dehydrated over time. It was three hours of raking chocolate corn flakes, but I would always tell Roy it took me at least six. It's unbelievable what people throw down their bathroom toilets. Where did you think that two cups of grease was going to wind up? Condoms have a place; on your junk or in the garbage can. I was at a plant one morning going through the various steps of testing the incoming water that was to be used by the residents. There was a small hut where we did the calculations with test tubes and beakers. About halfway through I noticed what I thought was a small snake coiled up in the corner. I hate snakes. I finished up quickly, signed the form on the clipboard and made a beeline to get out of there. I knew Roy was going to be there tomorrow so I left him a note on the door leading into the shed, 'Watch out for the snake!' When I saw him later that week he said, "Are you fucking crazy?" Roy was quick to tell me it was a copperhead and a little more information would have been nice. I tried to explain it was in the corner under some shelving and I didn't have time to do a police line-up with it. Roy was that guy that was the jack of all trades. He could fix anything from plumbing, electrical wiring, car repair, to carpentry. If you had a problem, Roy had the answer. There were few questions that he didn't have a solution to and if he showed you once how to do something, you better remember. At any given point, there were at least seven cars in various states of repair in his driveway and garage. I showed up one Saturday morning and there was a Komatsu road grader parked just outside his driveway. If the price was right, Roy would buy anything. I spent that weekend sanding and wire brushing the rust off it and painted it a few days later chrome yellow, just like a school bus. In 1989 he had gotten married to Sally and soon after had two kids, Cody and Jessie. I guess the theme they were going for was names from a Zane Grey novel. Roy was old school Italian. He would work and Sally would take care of the kids and home. Roy came to my wedding in the fall of 2002 and rented a car when he got to Hilton Head. We were all headed to the pool one morning to get the cocktail train in motion, Roy wanted no part of it. "I'm going to take a road trip." "Where are ya headed?" "I'm going to the Okefenokee Swamp." 400,000 acres of swamp in the middle of nowhere Georgia … that's what Roy wanted to see. He had rented a Corvette and, unlike most people, told the representative at the counter that he wanted full insurance on it. Who buys full insurance when renting a car? Roy does. When I saw the car later that night at dinner Roy had smoked the rubber off most of the tires.

It was springtime in 2003 and I think everybody and their brothers were borrowing money from banks and buying homes. Do a quick makeover with the minimum resources and sell it. This became Roy's latest passion, flipping houses. Buy something cheap, fix it up for cheap, and sell it for as much as you could get. His latest project was an old beat-up farmhouse that was built in 1850. This home needed everything from a roof to new electrical, paint and plumbing. After closing on the property, Roy discovered one morning that a mother deer had left a newborn on the doorstep of this old house. He picked it up and threw it into his truck and began the process of trying to care for it. It was only a couple of days old when he took it in. Pretty strange for a guy who hunted with a passion and wouldn't think twice about taking an eight-pointer on the first day of deer season. He assumed the mother may have had two fawns that year but was unable to care for both and left this one behind. A couple of months went by and Roy had his very own deer for a pet. He had nursed it with formula and drove the deer around in the front seat of his pickup. Can you have a deer for a pet? He named him John, John Deer. I came over to his home one afternoon to see the deer in the front yard with a red bandana around his neck and ID tags listing his home address and Roy as the owner. The deer would have the run of the house and would often be found in the kitchen looking for food, and on one occasion eating a tray of muffins that Sally had just baked - lemon poppy, if I remember right. As time passed, the cute little fawn with the spots was now the big deer spraying and urinating all over the house. Roy had finally had enough and John lost his inside privileges. About a year and a half later, Roy gets a call from an Environmental Police Officer. "Do you own a deer?" "Yeah, why?" The officer was calling from about 20 miles away and had been able to capture the deer (which wasn't that hard because he was so tame and would come up to anybody that had an apple or a Twizzler). He told him it was illegal to own a deer. Roy felt differently about it, "I raised him, I fed him, I saved his life; that pretty much makes him my deer." The econ officer then wrote Roy a handful of tickets and told him the rules and regulations of owning wildlife. He argued with the officer going back and forth, but it was useless. The real kick in the ass was that now he had to drive a half hour away to get the tickets he was issued. John Deer was gone, transported from the area and never to be seen again.

Roy's marriage was coming to an end. The year was 2007 and I was getting close to retirement. I think he knew in his heart that when I moved to Florida, he wanted to sever the relationship. Cut ties with me as well as his bride. Roy had done a lot for me over the course of 17 years; between the side jobs he set me up with, he also treated me to some fantastic meals at his home. I tried to call him a few times, but it was always met with an answering machine or voicemail. He never reached out to me once I left the area. We all have had friends like this, there one minute and gone the next. Out of sight, out of mind.

I was sitting in the auditorium of my junior high school, it was eighth or ninth grade. You're at the age where you think you can get away with a lot of stuff, but the truth is you're still a few years away. I imagine there were at least 250 of us crammed into the room that day getting ready to watch some boring video or hear the school principal talk about something. The lights went down and there was just a single spotlight that came from the projector in the balcony. From the right side of the stage, Rich emerged from the curtains pushing a four-foot janitor's mop. The place erupted with laughter. With his head down he moved forward sweeping the floor in his own methodical way. He gave a quick turn of his head as he hit his mark in the middle of the stage and I could see a little smirk as he looked out into the seats that were occupied by his classmates. By the time he reached the opposite side and disappeared behind the drapes, I said to myself, *That's the funniest thing I've ever seen, and not a word was spoken.* Everybody knows kids can be hard on kids, nobody wants to be the last one picked in gym class. We all know what happens to those kids, they spend their time in the library doing research on how to build pipe bombs. Rich was either going to be a superstar or called 'mop boy' for the remainder of the year. Our lives were changed from that point on.

I would always leave the house as early as possible. Another school day awaited and I would run about a half mile to get to Rich's home where his mother made me toast, a bagel or some eggs before we headed off to high school. His home was very simple and consisted of the bare necessities. It was like walking into an old farmhouse which reminded me of my grandmother's home. Rich told me one morning over breakfast that he was moving and in his very serious voice wanted me to know that we would stay in touch. "Where are ya movin' to?" He pointed across the street to a wooded lot. Who moves 20 yards away? His parents had bought a lot and groundbreaking was a couple of months away. We would make our way to the bus stop and hit up the neighborhood store for some candy or something to drink on the bus. There were the usual faces we saw every day, including the neighborhood bum. He was always dressed in his light blue denim shirt, navy jeans, and towered above us as he leaned against the facade of the store. His hair was white and buzzed like a military officer. Most people didn't know his name because it was easier to ignore him and go about your day. It didn't matter what you said to Bob, you were always greeted with the same response; "Mind your own damn business, you'll live longer." That was the routine five days a week. On the weekends we would travel to New York City and ride the subways all day talking about nothing and everything. We would travel to Manhattan then down to Coney Island, finally returning to the Bronx to get the bus home. We rode the train, riding between the cars, holding on for dear life. There was always a panhandler on the subway. Thieves looking for a handout and that guy playing a violin with three strings thinking he was Mozart. In high school Rich didn't play sports and was not accepted by the in-crowd. He didn't want to work on the school paper or participate in the French Club. At the same time, he wasn't a burnout either. We've all seen them, wearing a Black Sabbath t-shirt and smoking butts in the bathroom during third period English. Each year there was a vote for the class president and Rich was tired of seeing the same select few being nominated and crowned. He knew he couldn't run because he would never win. That's when he became the force and sought for a new school leader, somebody that was able to be a voice and leader for the school and the kids that went there. Next up on the ballot, please vote for your new high school president … Otis T. Johnstone the 3rd. He was a made-up kid, a ghost, a figment of the imagination. Rich was more than willing to support this candidate and posted billboards and signs throughout the hallways and talked him up whenever possible. "You got to vote for Otis, he's got some big things lined up this year if he gets elected." Rich was in politics and didn't even know it, he was promoting a guy for school president that never existed. No one had ever seen Otis or heard his views on school lunches or the prom, but Rich made him out to be a cross between Kennedy and George

Washington. A man for the people. The snowball continued because everybody that Rich knew was going to vote for Otis. He was the kid that was never in class. "Yo, you seen Otis today?" The excuses were endless. He got suspended, he's away looking at colleges, his car broke down, and the epic, 'he had to be with his grandmother today, she's not feeling very well'. Mr. Johnstone came in a distant second that year in the race for school czar, which when you think about it, shows the voting mentality of kids 16-18 years old. Otis would leave high school, never to graduate and never to get his picture in the school yearbook.

I sat on the living room floor with my back against the couch. My world as I knew it was coming to an end. The tears that ran down my face could not be controlled. I think at one point my mother came into the room and asked what was going on. She wouldn't understand. Rich and I had both found girlfriends while in high school and there was always enough drama and bullshit to make your head spin. On any typical weekend, there could have been 20-25 of us who were hanging out together. Whose parents are going away this week? That's where the party will be. My girlfriend had decided to go back to her old boyfriend and the tears just kept on coming. He was one of the gang and a pretty interesting guy; I couldn't even fault her. He was very involved in boxing in high school and would set up a regulation-sized boxing ring in his backyard a couple of times over the course of a summer. There were always two guys from the neighborhood who didn't get along and he would have them square off; three rounds, two minutes each round. It was like you were at the MGM in Vegas. He would charge $5 admission and that got you a cup and warm tap beer. The word about the fight would get out to the neighborhood and come fight night the place would be packed. He would act as referee in his black and white striped shirt inside the ring and the punches and jabs from the 12-ounce gloves would start flying. Here we were in a residential backyard at 10 p.m. watching two guys go at it under porch lights. If there was something illegal about it, the cops never found out and the gaming commission never got a cut.

Rich and I assembled a fort in the woods behind his new home shortly after it was completed. It sat up on a hillside and was camouflaged by the shrubs and evergreens around it. We had found some leftover wood the builder had left behind, or did we just take that, and made our very own Marriott that was about 6' x 4'. It kept out most of the bugs and let us build a bond and friendship. It was a good place to drink beer at 17 without the parents knowing and attempt to choke down a smoke every now and then. That was our place to get away and still be close enough to his fridge when we got hungry.

Each weekend there was always a salt and pepper game we would go to. If it was the fall it was football, spring softball. It was that simple. Our hangout was a school located about a mile away and nobody made a big deal about it. Black kids against the white kids. I'm sure today there would be a lot of news crews dispatched and the NAACP giving a speech at five o'clock. Rich and I made this a part of our lives during high school. I was already signed up to start the Air Force in the fall of 1980 and Rich wanted to do something in radio. We would have our last summer together and what better way to spend it than a trip out to California? We booked our flight to Los Angeles, said goodbye to friends, and pretended like we knew what we were doing. Our first night on the left coast we wound up sleeping in some park near the airport with one eye open. We bummed up and down the coast from San Luis Obispo to Huntington Beach. We camped out wherever we could and found the cheapest motels in the wrong part of town. It's lucky we didn't become a statistic out there; two 18-year-old kids with sleeping bags and New York accents. One night on Catalina Island we slept on a golf course and woke up to the sound of mowers and, "Get the fuck out of here before I have you locked up for trespass." After three weeks of California sunshine and beaches, Rich and I were ready to head back east. We had both put aside enough cash for the flight home, or did we? "What do you mean the cost of a flight back to New York went up?" We were so naïve. I looked at Rich and thought, *We are so screwed*. The travel agent suggested we check with Greyhound, which turned out to be our only option. Five days on a bus is five days too many. Having a friend like Rich around made life a little better. His humor was a little ahead of his time and you had to listen carefully to pick up on all the innuendos. He pretended he had a radio station in his bedroom during his high school years. Two turntables, a mixing board and a microphone where he would record his show and master his trade. He now heads up Cox Media Group as their operations manager for several radio stations in the Tampa area. We still keep in touch 40+ years later.

CHAPTER 31

OUCH

Welcome to Biloxi, Mississippi. After a bus ride from San Antonio, Texas that took about 10 hours, this 18-year-old kid was now spending the next six months in the land of the rednecks. We had heard a lot of stories about the South and how they were still fighting the war against the North and, on top of that, they hated the fact that the Air Force was in their backyard. Guys in the service always had money and a steady paycheck, and there were plenty of women in the area that were looking for a way out. We've all seen An Officer and a Gentleman. I had completed my six weeks of basic training being called every name in the book and learned from my drill instructor that the definition of a friend was somebody who went into town and got two blowjobs, then came back to the base and gave you one of them. It was now off to learn all about electronics. How does electricity flow through a piece of wire? Amplitude modulation, frequency modulation, generators, capacitors, diodes, watts, amps….how am I gonna learn all this crap in six months? It all came together after a while; you learn to settle in with a certain crowd, do the necessary homework and make sure you don't volunteer for anything. I made that mistake once and I got stuck with the laundry detail. Didn't sound too bad at first….until you find out you're at a hospital medical center sorting bloody sheets from the towels soaked in urine. Reds in that pile, yellows in the other. That was one long day. Away from home and missing friends from high school, I met up with a few guys I trusted and, before too long, had a regular partner that was always up for cocktails. After a long week in school and learning how to get a signal generator working properly, we made it a pact to find a new drinking hole in the middle-of-nowhere Mississippi. Most of the guys opted for the clubs in town with half-naked women looking for free drinks and a Perkins breakfast at 4 a.m. For me, a nice local bar with a pool table or dart board was all I needed. I'm not sure how we stumbled on the Tic Toc Bar, but it became our Friday night hang out. We would exit out the south gate from the base and walk about 15 minutes down a deserted railroad track. It was dark, quiet and tree-lined and was the best shortcut we knew of to get to our new watering hole. Outside the bar were a couple of dim lights and you had to look closely to even make out the name of the place. We got to know most of the locals there and never had a problem with any of them - or did we? It was about two in the morning as we headed back down the tracks after what you would call a normal night out. No drama to speak of. It was late January and cooler than usual. After exiting the tracks, we had a couple of blocks to go to get back on base when a guy approached me. "Hey, have you seen my dog?" We were now in a small residential area so I didn't think the request was that abnormal. We both shook our heads and I recall asking what kind of dog. It was at that moment when a second subject came up from behind me and I felt the baseball bat strike me in the back between the shoulder blades and waist. The air went out of my lungs. My friend was then struck and we both went down to the ground. We were defenseless. The first subject who had inquired about the dog also got a few licks in, though I do not recall what he was hitting us with. I barely remember what they were yelling as they continued to wail away at us. We were both curled up in balls lying on the cold asphalt trying to protect our heads. It probably only lasted 30 seconds, but it felt like forever. They ran off yelling, laughing, and proud of their accomplishment of beating up two guys who were in the service. We staggered to our feet and made it to the gate. Bloody and sore, the military police guard checked our ID and asked if we needed medical aid. We declined and made it to our dorm room. I crawled into bed and could barely get up in the morning to take a leak. I was sore for a few weeks and had to take some time off from school due to my injuries. The Tic Toc Bar was destroyed during Hurricane Katrina. Did I say sorting laundry was a long day? My mistake.

In the fall of 1986, the leaves do what they do every year in the Northeast; change color and look great. A friend of mine who was a landscaper always said they sure do look pretty...up there. Autumn means football and the guys from the airport where I was working put together a little game of two-hand touch one Saturday afternoon. Two-hand touch is the equivalent to a little roughness, but not enough to get anybody hurt. It was a battle between the morning shift and the afternoon crew. We had a field picked out and the girlfriends gathered on the sidelines to watch. The day was going great; a lot of good fun, the trash talk, and the weather was crisp but the sun was strong. As the second half began, I fielded the kickoff and started running up the field. I caught a couple of blocks and could see a little daylight ahead of me. That was the last thing I remembered until somebody said, "You okay, hey Coach you okay?" What the hell just happened? I felt a headache coming on and just wanted to stand up. There were people standing over me whose faces resembled that from a police sketch artist. This was two-hand touch, right? At some point, somebody said, "He doesn't look good," and moments later I was lifted onto a stretcher and driven by ambulance to the hospital. I failed a whole bunch of tests at the medical facility, but it wasn't enough to keep me. My girlfriend at the time, Cyndy, was told that I had sustained a concussion. They probably told me too, but I had forgotten what they said before they said it. After being released that evening, Cyndy brought me back to my apartment where I sucked down some more pain meds and anti-nausea pills like they were M & M's. She stayed with me all night, waking me up every hour on the hour to make sure I was still alive - I would have settled for the mirror under the nose. I was tired and all I wanted to do was sleep. She was a trooper though; 1 a.m., 2 a.m., 3 a.m., 4 a.m., 5 a.m. - enough already, put some coffee on. For some reason, your first concussion will always be the best because the ones that happen after that just seem to scramble the eggs a little more.

A friend of mine during the mid-90's was a drummer in a band called The Divide. He had hooked up with two brothers, one who played bass and the other lead guitar. Each weekend they did the local bar circuit from New York City to points north including Connecticut. Load up the van with instruments and amps, travel to the venue, then offload the crap and set up. Then repeat the process four hours later after the show. Anthony had been banging on the skins since he was a little kid and annoying the neighbors in the process. I showed up late one night to a small bar where he was performing. I had already missed the first set and arrived just in time to observe his brother dancing on one of the tables and exposing his junk to the flock of senoritas that were around him. He did that all the time when he was out getting hammered so I had already seen the act. There were new songs on the playlist that night and a new direction that the band was hoping to attain. Anthony was a very likable guy who came out of college with a business degree. Weeks prior to this gig, he had a friend who was the secretary for Tommy Mottola. We're talking Sony Music Entertainment and Casablanca Records. At the time Mottola was married to Mariah Carey and lived 15 minutes down the road on an estate that you could land a helicopter on. If there was a guy who could get you into the business, he was the guy. Anthony was able to get a meeting with him and presented him a CD filled with their own original songs. Mottola's response was, "Good, now go write me another 12 songs." So on this night they had added some new arrangements and were looking to get some feedback from their friends and family who had come to watch them play. Don't remember what I was drinking that night, but the music was good and after leaving the bar area I found a place near the front door to camp. This served two purposes, (1) getting some fresh air every time the door opened from all the smoking that was going on and (2) was the view of the stage. I took a look back in the direction of the bar and the hottest girl in the place was still sitting there with her friends. If a pink elephant walked into a bar, would you look at it? Of course. Same thing with a beautiful woman. I was tired before I even got there and knew that the night was going to be short. Yawning is never a good sign. I put my drink down on the table and felt the inside of my cheek explode. What the fuck was that? Why am I on the floor? As I started to get up I heard the sound of the bouncers. For some unknown reason, as three or four guys were exiting the place they decided to use me as their human piñata. It was only one punch but it felt like a car tire had just run over my face. I spun towards the front door and was stopped by two redwood trees that were hired by the club. "You don't want to go out there!" No, I *do* want to go out there. The bouncers looked at me and assured my ego that four against one is never good. Several guys I had known through Anthony came to my aid and we talked it over in front of the bouncers. They were doing their job and protecting both the establishment and me I guess. Another reason never to carry a gun in a bar.

It started as an idea and before long became a reality. Our police department had a yearly hockey game against the city's fire department. The cause was to benefit Muscular Dystrophy, but all that aside it was the Finest vs. the Bravest and who was better. Cops and fireman duking it out on the ice. Every year that I played in this annual event would start out the same. The first period would be calm and about feeling out the other side. If somebody ran into you, there was almost an apology. A couple of goals later, someone gets a little pushy in front of the net and the game would get chippy. By the third period, penalties were getting handed out, elbows were up and there was enough cross-checking in the corners to make your kidneys sore. This game is for charity, right? Each year, we would get in a few practice skates before the big game. There was an ice rink in town that let us skate pro bono. The ice time came with a price as we left our warm homes and beds to be at the rink at 5 a.m. We were about halfway through this one particular skate and I was feeling pretty good. Another 15 minutes on the ice, take a shower, get changed, a little breakfast at the deli, and start my tour just before 8 a.m. To this day I don't remember it happening but, at some point, I either hit the ice or maybe took a check into the glass. Whatever the case I was in a complete daze. Everything seemed like a dream sequence. After getting off the ice I had no recollection of anything until about an hour later when I found myself sitting in a police car behind the steering wheel. I sat there in the car in full uniform with my leather jacket on feeling like I was going to throw up. It was cold outside and the windows were down. How did I get here? Should I call over the radio for help? Is my gun in the holster? The headache was now coming across my forehead and hitting the temples above my eyes. That's it, I'm done. I drove the car back to headquarters, very slowly, and headed for the locker room. In the days to follow I would be seen by two different doctors that administered concussion tests. The first was reading colors and patterns. Another exam was shapes and lines. Then there was the ever-popular game called 'which way is the arrow pointed?' Sounds simple enough, but after a concussion it gets a little tricky. The doctors advised me to stay home for a few days, no heavy lifting, don't operate any machinery and stay out of direct sunlight. The darkness is your friend. No machinery - does that include blenders? He gave me some pills to take for the migraines that actually worked pretty well. Two weeks later, I was back on the ice 'feeling like 10,000 nickels' as my friend John used to say. We raised a lot of money that year for a good cause and got beat in the final minutes by the fire department.

There are some things in life that you will never forget. In the second grade, Walter Shaw became that person, that event, and a lesson you remember forever. As we sat in class, Walter's chair was beside mine on the right. It was early morning and we were just getting settled in for the day ahead. He wanted to show me a trick and asked me to put out my hand. With that, I placed my left hand on the desktop waiting to be amazed by his magical powers. It was nothing like that at all. He then jabbed a number 2 yellow pencil into the palm of my hand. Now I'm crying in pain and the tip of the pencil is lodged under the skin. Of course, at this point the teacher and about 25 other kids are all staring at me and the blood oozing down to my wrist. Walter got some time off after that and our friendship was nonexistent. The scar is still visible today and reminds me there are no tricks in life...and I still hate clowns.

Growing up there was only one daredevil that I knew of. If you were a kid with a bicycle and could find something to jump, you were Evil Knievel. Find a couple of pieces of plywood and you were jumping the fountains in Las Vegas, over buses in London, or in a rocket ship over the Snake River Canyon. Who could jump the furthest? I took on a new experiment one afternoon trying to jump off a masonry wall that was next to the bus ramp of my elementary school. It was a mere five feet tall, sometimes you have to start small and work your way up. It was a fall day and my take-off ramp was the greenest 30 feet of grass that would make for an unbelievable stunt. Once I got airborne the landing below would be the toughest to negotiate. It was simple; get up enough speed, pull back on the handlebars, stick the landing, and hit the brakes. There was nobody around that could laugh when I failed which made it that much more inviting. As I crashed to the ground seconds later I felt a pain on the left side of my jawline. Some part of my now bruised bicycle had torn open the flesh and I lied there in pain. I'm sure I made up some sort of excuse after getting home as to why the bike was damaged, and I wore turtlenecks for the next week waiting for the scar to heal. I never really thought about how close to my jugular the laceration was. That's the beauty of being a kid, rip a three-inch scar into your neck and be more worried about your bike and what your friends are going to think.

I played on a little league baseball team and got called in from centerfield one evening to catch when our starter went down with an injury. Our pitcher, Mike, was a big kid and the star of the team. At 13 this kid was shaving twice a day. We all looked up to him and thought he was amazing. He threw smoke and only lost one game in the two years I played with him. He went into his windup and there I was catching with an outfielder's glove. It hit the palm of my mitt and teardrops formed in the corners of both my eyes. Shouldn't I be wearing a cup also? I toughed it out for the half inning, wincing on each pitch. At 6' 4" and 220 Mike had the chance to be something special, but after several ailments in high school, the colleges stopped calling. I used to see him around town after I became a cop; dejected, using drugs, and wasting his life away. Sad.

CHAPTER 32

NEVER SAW THAT COMING

My wife was feeling very ill the other day and, being the great husband that I am, I did what every man would do. "Honey, can you get me some wonton soup?" "Of course I can." I drove the few miles down the road to The Happy Dragon. I had never been in the restaurant before and it seemed like it was lacking furniture. Off to the right were three tables for dining, two of them being occupied by small children maybe six and eight years of age. Why is it when you walk into some restaurants they seem overcrowded and you wind up listening to the conversation at the next table over? Not so with Chinese takeout - it's almost like they don't want you to hang around. As I entered the restaurant the woman at the desk asked, "Yes sir, what can I get you?" She looked to be in her late 20's and a little over-anxious. I took another step into the establishment and was still too far away to start a conversation. I looked over the menu and ordered up a quart of chicken fried rice and the soup. She yelled to the rear of the kitchen, "Jirou chaofan, huntun tang, shiying." I paid the bill and she told me it would be about 12 minutes; not the number you often hear when ordering food. The two children were still coloring or drawing and I didn't pay much attention as I made a quick phone call and answered a text. "All ready sir." I picked up the bag and thanked her and just as I was leaving the store heard her yell over to the children with her best Italian accent, "Aaaaay Anthony, have ya finished your homework yet?" "Yes, mom." Was that Barzini or Fredo?

In high school, Glen was one of the quiet guys. He could have been on the debate team but in order to take a stand on the day's given topic, you have to say more than two words. He was a shy guy and that person who would have been voted most likely to get sand kicked on him at the beach. I never saw him play sports or take any interest in girls. His parents lived in the south end of town and I always felt that he came from wealth and would one day be a lawyer or an accountant. So it came as a little bit of a shock when he was appointed to the police department where I already had five years on the job. I thought to myself, *Why is Glen a cop?* He would put in 22 years with the department and retired in January of 2015. The psychological test I took prior to becoming a police officer was called the Minnesota Multiphasic Personality Inventory Test; 567 questions, all of which are answered true or false. I took the test at a doctor's office which was located on the grounds of a mental hospital, check the irony in that. There were about 20 of us there that day all looking to become cops and start a new career. The booklets were handed out and the doctor gave a brief description of what the exam would tell. If you are depressed, have paranoia, or a psychopathic deviant... probably being a cop is not for you. The doctor asked, "Any questions? Last one done, turn out the lights and lock the door." With that, he grabbed his briefcase and exited the office. I looked around for the camera but couldn't find one. I started looking over the questions and trying to calculate how long it was going to take to finish this. Some of my favorite questions were, 'I used to play drop the handkerchief?', 'I have diarrhea at least once a month?', and 'I like to smash things?' It was the most bizarre test I have ever taken. The questions went on forever and those of us in the room were laughing and making fun of the entire quiz. On February 21, 2015, Glen killed himself in his garage with a .40 caliber Glock. Somebody from the press was able to get a picture of him lying on the concrete floor with his stomach exposed; it's burned into my mind. Prior to that, he killed two of his children, ages 13 and 17, as they slept in bed. He also executed the three family dogs. His wife and oldest daughter were out of town. They had an argument a day earlier regarding an $80 cell phone bill. I still think there's more to it that I may never know. It is believed that he left an extensive suicide note that can never be explained.

It's March 3, 1991 and Rodney King is driving his 1988 white Hyundai down Foothill Freeway in the northern section of Los Angeles. So what does that have to do with me? One would think nothing. It's 3000 miles away and I don't own stock in Hyundai. King had just been released from prison in December after serving six months on a robbery charge. We watched the video that was recorded that night by George Holliday and I thought to myself, *This is not going to be good*. The whole world saw what was happening but had no idea what the future held. Four white cops from the Los Angeles Police Department being recorded as they struck a black man 56 times in 81 seconds. It's just over a year later when the criminal trial concluded for the four LAPD officers involved in the incident. There were two things that I recall from the trial; Officer Powell, one of the officers on trial, had just failed a baton training exercise that day. How the hell do you fail that class? The other thing I thought was a little unusual was that King never took the stand to testify. On April 29, 1992 I was working a 4-12 tour. When the decision was read it was 6:15 p.m. east coast time. All four officers involved were found not guilty and the rioting began. Not just in LA, but a block away from our headquarters in an area called the Windbrook Housing Facility. It consisted of five buildings, nine stories tall and about 450 apartments. If you take an average of two idiots per apartment plus their friends it brought the total to well over 2000 assholes throwing rocks and lighting fires that night. The decision was made by the brass in the department to basically contain the area of destruction within that zone. The streets were flooded that night with people yelling and screaming. Our command center was set up just a block away. As the sun set tempers flared even more. The order from our chief and captains was not to enter what they call the 'hot zone'. Streets were blocked off, but don't ever tell somebody who drives the same way every day they can't go down a particular road. "But that's how I go home." There are 2000 animals throwing bricks in front of you and that's where you want to go. It never slowed down the entire evening, plus we were also handling calls for the rest of the city. I was assigned a line car that evening and had all the necessary tools of the trade with me in my vehicle; helmet, riot gear including shield, my usual bulletproof vest and a couple of guns that weren't issued or approved of by the department. It's always better to be judged by 12 than carried by six. I had two other cops with me in the car that evening and there was nothing but constant noise on the police radio. Yak, yak, yak. A lot of it was useless garble by guys who just wanted to be heard. It was almost midnight and I knew that nobody was going home for a long time. I figured if we were released by 4 a.m. it would be a miracle. As I turned the vehicle from the Post Road onto Martin Luther King Jr Blvd., I saw about 10-15 youths running towards my car. Within seconds a 4-iron golf club came smashing down on the windshield of the police car. I've been playing golf for a long time, definitely a 4-iron. The group ran back towards the projects trying to get us to follow. On any other day, it would not even have been a thought. The windshield was destroyed and the spider web stretched from one side to the other. I thought about it for a second, opening the car door and chasing down some kids that smoked Kools that I knew I could outrun. I drove back to headquarters trying to see the roadway through a kaleidoscope of glass. The city was letting the patients run the asylum and I had to go along with it. After about six days of bullshit, it became a non-factor and there was another headline in the paper. Out in LA, there were over 50 dead, 2000 injured and about a billion dollars in damages. We had a few broken windows, a couple of small fires, and a little pride hurt.

McSorley's Old Ale House sits in lower Manhattan on 7th Street. One of the signs on the front glass reads, 'We were here before you were born'. The bar was established in 1854 or thereabouts, depending on what historical books you read. It's an old Irish bar that didn't allow women in the front door till 1970. Above the bar is a four-story apartment building whose residents must not get a lot of sleep. The first time I walked through the front door it was a throwback in time. The sawdust on the floor, the old pot belly stove off to my left and a couple of cats lounging around liked they owned the place. It was just after 11 a.m. and we had about an hour to kill. You order beers there two at a time and the selection is very simple, light or dark, both with the McSorley's name on the draft barrels. The menu is simple and we got a cheese plate with some crackers and the hottest mustard in the world. Above the bar area and hanging from the ceiling there was a triangular metal fixture supporting two gas lamps. The lower arm of this apparatus had what appeared to be wishbones placed on them. I asked about the wishbones from the bartender and he told the story about how young men would have their last meal here with their families before going off to war. The turkey or chicken wishbone would then be placed over the bar between the lights. On the day I saw them they were covered in about an inch of dust, but nobody was complaining. Those who made it back from serving their country could remove a wishbone. There were still many there on the day I visited. I made it back to McSorley's a few months later with a friend and had to wait in line to get in; it was close to 8 p.m. on a weekend night. After being seated and ordering up beers four at a time it was time to go see a man about a dog. The bathroom was at the back of the establishment and the old porcelain was calling my name. As I walked past a mob of patrons one of the servers was carrying 20 beers in his hands to a nearby table. We had already ordered burgers and another round should be waiting by the time I get back. As I stood there staring at the wall and looking down at the pink hockey puck I was aiming at, a female voice from behind me said, "Hello" and proceeded over to the sink. I thought to myself, *If that is a guy in drag, he looks really good.* I glanced behind me and saw another woman closing the door to one of the toilets. "I think you're in the wrong bathroom." She looked at me and said, "There's only one bathroom, we have to share." "Excellent, see ya in about three beers."

I had sold my first home, a beat-up old trailer, for a motorcycle. It happened in 48 hours. I owned 10 acres of land once that I thought would never be sold...gone. I had helped my wife sell a couple of properties, including a co-op and a 55 and over townhome that her mother had lived in. My condo sold in less than a week for the full asking price. So, I felt fairly comfortable going down to Home Depot and getting a 'FOR SALE BY OWNER' sign to place in the front lawn of our home in Sunset Beach, NC. We were trying to sell it during a brief stay there over the 4th of July holiday. We had the property for about seven years, but it was time to move on. Within two weeks we had several hits and finally agreed on a price. We sent all the info off to the lawyers and closed in 30 days without ever getting an agent involved. It's now more than three years later when I open my mailbox and find that I owe back taxes to the State of North Carolina. I file my taxes every year just like everyone else, wink wink. Besides, how much could it be? $5,077.12. This can't be right, I'll make one phone call to my accountant and it will be fixed. So my accountant calls me back after doing a review of my taxes for 2006. "Well, everything looks in order except the fact that I should have paid those taxes to North Carolina and I paid them to New York State." He then explained that because it had been over three years we would have to petition the courts to look at the situation and get them to release the funds so they could be applied in the correct state. Ken had been my accountant for more than 15 years and I never had a problem with him. Now we're trying to chase down five large that you know deep down in your heart the State of New York will never part with. A couple of weeks later, I get the phone call and Ken tells me, "There's nothing they can do about it, you'll have to pay the audit." As we spoke on the phone, I'm sure Ken didn't see the bulging veins and arteries protruding from my neck and forehead. "Ken, this is your error, why don't you feel that you should be paying it?" The tap dance began. The letter that I received also had stipulations in it that additional interest and penalties would accumulate if the debt was not paid. The phone call left on a sour note and he said he would think about it, but I felt that this was his way of saying, 'Leave me alone.' A few days had passed when my wife decided she was going to call him. "Ken, we have been paying customers for 15 years and this is your error, you're the professional, figure it out." You can buy insurance for anything, your hands if you're a pianist, your arm if you're a quarterback, and an, 'Oh shit!' policy if you screw up as an accountant. In a few weeks Ken had done the right thing and got North Carolina to drop one of the penalties on the bill and he paid the remainder, just under 4K. Well, he didn't quite pay it all. I received another notice in the mail from North Carolina with all the amendments and a final payment due. $1.33. I'll just hit the easy button on that one.

As we approached the bar, he was standing there with a glass in both hands, laughing and joking with an attractive female. She was about 5' 3" with olive skin and dark brown hair that was almost black. That's the guy that I want to party with. My first wife and I had just been married a day earlier in Palm Beach, Florida, and here we were at The Sandals Resort in Antigua. We had traveled all day and it was time for a cocktail and some much-needed rest. We became friends almost immediately and with all of us being from New York we had a lot of the same interests, not to mention the same accent. The following day while the girls were hitting the beach and talking about manicures, we decided to rent a catamaran from some of the locals for an hour or so. The guy with the Rastafarian hair looked at us and asked if we knew how to operate it. I was clueless, but my new running partner convinced me he had been on them before and he was experienced. We jumped in and left the sandy white shores behind. Things were going well until we were about a quarter mile off the shoreline. I felt the wind shift and as we tried to adjust the sails the craft tipped over onto its side. There was no way for us to upright the boat. We hung onto the hull thinking, *This is not good*, but the beach was loaded with people and somebody must have seen us go over. I think there is a story every year where some tourist dies while vacationing in the islands. Its 10 minutes later and nobody is coming to our rescue. I asked myself if there were sharks in these waters. Finally, two guys from where we rented the catamaran came out on a jet ski laughing and giggling like school girls. We got up-righted and towed in and felt like the two biggest losers on the island. That's when the guy with the dreads looked at us and said to my buddy, "I thought you knew how to operate the craft, mon?" With that, he held out his hand and showed us the drain plug from the aft end of the boat that he had removed. "You always have to check your ship, mon." We were pissed to say the least, but getting into a fight with the local militia would not have been good. We laughed it off and headed to the bar.

CHAPTER 33

SHIT HAPPENS

Have you ever met a person for the first time and everything just clicks? There are no dramatic pauses in the conversation and you can tell right away this is a good guy. Meeting Kurt for the first time proved to be this exact recipe. He worked as a funeral director and actually lived in the apartment above the funeral home. I know, a little creepy. The basement consisted of the embalming room and it also housed the limos and flower cars. The casket room was just inside the back door and had about 15 boxes there for viewing. This gave families a chance to see what was going to be covered in dirt or burned in 48 hours. One of the caskets was engraved with a depiction from The Last Supper on the side of the box. Kurt would say, "That's an easy sale when ya get a devoted Catholic family in here." The main floor was where the offices and two large rooms for services were. There was always the smell of flowers in the air from the wreaths and all the bouquets that were being dropped off. With me being a cop on a motorcycle we were assigned to almost every ceremony. We would go over the details and what church or cemetery the funeral procession was heading to. It became very routine after a while; get there 15 minutes prior to the start, block traffic so all the cars could get in line, and get everybody to their destination. While services were going on we would get coffee and shoot the shit. Then it was a possible drive past the family's home and off to the cemetery. Kurt always had a story to tell with different things that occurred in the business. There was the time I met him downstairs in the prep room and he was working on a subject on the table. The bottles of embalming fluid stood on a shelf a few feet away. The young man being worked on had been involved in a car accident and his severed leg at the hip was lying a few feet away in the sink. Kurt had a stomach for the job and as far as I knew laughed more than he cried. There were a few perks that went with the job, how many of your friends have had sex in a casket? He once had a burial out on Long Island and jumped into the HOV lane with the hearse. You need at least two persons in the car to use this lane, nobody said they had to be alive. He told me of a family who after the burial now wanted items placed in the coffin. It's six months later. Dig up the remains, pop the seal and drop some worthless crap in the box. Not pretty. Fly larva does not help preserve the body.

Services at the funeral home were usually scheduled from 2-4 in the afternoon and again from 7-9 p.m. for anybody wanting to stop by and pay their respects to the family. So it was just after four when the husband of the deceased came to speak with Kurt and complained about the blouse his wife was wearing in the casket. Kurt had dressed her earlier with a dark navy skirt and an off-white shirt that had pearl buttons in the front. The only problem was that the pearls were supposed to be in the back. So, now Kurt had the dilemma of what to do. His first instinct was to start shopping and get a replacement. He went to several of the big stores in town looking for the exact shirt. Sax's, J.C Penny's, Nordstrom, Sears…. nothing. He knew that if he took it off there would be some rips in the fabric and of course the inevitable staining. See, no matter what you think you're not as flexible when you're dead. It's like dressing a store mannequin and the arms keep falling off. Kurt had exhausted all possibilities, he was even going to go into his own pocket for a new shirt. When he came to me and asked what his next move should be. It was getting close to 7 p.m. and families would start arriving. "Tell him the truth." Kurt pulled the husband aside and explained very tactfully that it would not be in the best interest and apologized for the mistake. It all worked out for the best in the end and the husband told Kurt not to worry about it.

Kurt was like the local mayor of the area; working at the funeral home and then crossing the street to the local gin mill called Dunne's where he would hold court. At one time, he was dating two girls at the same time - both named Chrissy. One was black and the other white. The running joke was, "Are you having white or brown rice for dinner tonight?" I was talking with Kurt once as he was doing an embalming on an older woman who was laid out on the table. She was 90 if she was a day and weighed in at 95 lbs. "Let's have one last smoke together. " He reached for the pack and lit up two nails. One for me and one for you.

Working on Halloween sucks. Being a cop and working on Halloween really sucks. There was always a need for additional guys to combat the teenage kids who walked the streets in packs and dressed so they couldn't be recognized. Half of them wearing hockey masks like Jason and the other half all dressed in black hoodies. Anybody carrying a backpack was up to no good, it's that easy. The Fourth Amendment covers search and seizure of property and has to do with probable cause. So how do you get into that pack that has eggs, fireworks, laser pointers and who knows what else? I took a gun off a kid one Halloween night that was concealed in his backpack. He was about 14 and thought that watching Law & Order mad him a Yale law professor. You're trick or treating, put some face paint on and hold out a pillowcase. It was getting late in the tour and I felt about an hour or so of overtime coming. The call was about a group of kids in the woods possibly having a bonfire. People panic and exaggerate sometimes and a lit cigarette can sometimes look like the Kuwaiti oil fields during the Gulf War. I was sent on the call along with a couple of other units including the street sergeant. As we rolled up on the scene you could hear the voices coming from an area that was on the border between our city and a neighboring village. We turned our radios down and started the journey into the wooded area. We walked about 50 yards, trying to stay quiet and at the same time not wanting to trip over any fallen trees or rocks. The noise got louder and the smell of weed got stronger. There were probably 15-20 kids there and we walked them out of the darkness with their beer, pipes, and backpacks. As we started to go through their stuff under the streetlights, one of the lawyers in the group felt we were invading his privacy. Really? Stop me! We confiscated everything and that's when the first egg was launched. Not by the kids, by the cops. It was time to release a little stress. At first it was underhand softball tosses, but in time grew to 80 mph fastballs. I ducked down behind my Harley, which didn't give me a lot of protection, and took the first one on the shoulder off my leather jacket. The kids looked at us like we were crazy. Six cops having an egg fight at 11 p.m. The high school kids looked on from the sidelines watching the event unfold. You can go through a lot of eggs very quickly. The battle was over in five minutes and we left the area leaving behind egg slime all over the street and a crowd of teenagers that must have been saying, 'What the fuck just happened?'

White Plains had two railroad stations, the downtown location was designed by an engineer that for all intents and purposes had no clue. I might have had more respect for him if he told me he drew up the plans while he was stoned. There was always congestion with traffic trying to figure out where to park and a barrage of signs that would confuse an MIT grad. Arrows, one ways, taxi only, short-term parking, do not enter, permits only, and my favorite… clearance 6' 6". Everybody complained about it. Have you ever taken a test where one of the answers is "always" or "never" and you can rule that one out? Not so with the railroad parking design, EVERYBODY thought it sucked. Inside the lobby was your basic newsstand, a box about 10' by 6' where Gary would sell you some ink for your fingers, gum, candy, and grape soda for breakfast. Just beyond his storefront was the Dunkin Donuts. You could miss your train waiting in line for a regular. When I learned of the larceny from the donut shop I didn't give it much thought. Our detectives would give it the once over, but there wasn't a lot to go on. Maybe some video, but half the time those cameras weren't working or they were very grainy. Well, Dunkin Donuts Corporation wasn't going to let somebody steal their sign and get away with it. The sign was probably 6-8 feet long and a couple of feet wide with their pink and orange logo and a tasty old fashion and Bavarian cream on it. The company hired a private investigator to look into the matter. Weeks went by and a lot of videos were analyzed, and then several vehicles considered. One car was traced to a college two and a half hours away in Albany, NY. The investigator was able to obtain a search warrant through the local courts. As they knocked on the dorm door a young man answered who must have been in complete shock. Hanging on the wall behind him, over his bed, a sign which read... DUNKIN DONUTS.

During my years in middle school, grades 7-9, there was a gym teacher by the name of Coach Forsythe. He was loud and funny and looked like he just stepped out of Muscle Magazine. Each September was a new beginning, a new school year, and a new team. The years were 1974-1977 and the school was Eastview. There was very little political correctness back then. There was a black kid in one of my classes and the teacher called him 'Midnight'. Another teacher left his Playboy Magazines in the desk drawer only to find out some went missing when he left the room. One teacher, fascinated with horses, would have the Daily Racing Form on his desk. On more than one occasion, I had chalk or an eraser thrown in my direction. In gym class, everybody got picked onto a squad, you were either the red team or the blue team and it stayed this way till the end of the school year. Points were accumulated during class and a record kept as to which team was leading. We played everything from kickball, flag football, and dodgeball. We even climbed ropes to see who could do it faster. It was competition long before Survivor or The Amazing Race. Coach Forsythe would call his gym, 'The Valley.' I often wondered if he had been a Marine or served in Vietnam and brought back the term from some hellhole he was stationed at overseas. It didn't matter, it was the red team against the blue team and you don't want to lose. Losing meant you were now up against the SWAT. It hung in the back of our minds all year; push harder and don't let the other team beat you. When the calendar turned to June, the competition was over. The SWAT consisted of a small burlap or canvas sack about 15 inches long and a few inches wide. I think it was filled with dried corn. If you held it in your hand, you could make a knob at one end like a baseball bat. Each player from the winning team would now get to pick a player from the losing team and the SWAT was on. The losing team member would stand in front of the winning team member and the whistle would blow. It was one lap around the gym and if you were on the losing end and a poor runner, your ass was getting smacked. It was like getting hit with a stale loaf of bread. We had a front-row seat where kids would get beaten by other kids under the supervision of adults. Try and picture that today. Your son just came home from school and his ass looks like a stop sign. Every parent must have known about it, mine did. "What did you do in school today?" Ran as fast as I could.

Jimmy and I went to the academy together. He was smarter than me and a little more serious than I was. Okay, a lot more serious. He had gotten into the detective division about the same time I got into the traffic unit. He confided in me with the following story one morning in the garage after I had just finished up a couple of court cases. "You remember that homeless guy they found dead about a year and a half ago in that lot on Mamaroneck Avenue?" "Yeah, across from the diner?" See it doesn't matter who you are or what you did for a living, a homicide is a homicide and a case folder gets opened up. The investigation got turned over to a few of the senior detectives who passed it back and forth to each other from shift to shift. A year had gone by and they weren't any closer than the day they started, and nobody cared. There was no family calling, and the media went away months ago. That's when they gave it to the rookie detective. "Here, kid, good luck." Jimmy started developing characters and going over different variables. At one point, he thought he had a pretty good lead and traveled five hours north to Vermont to interview somebody. This was the turning point in the case and, through this contact, Jimmy now had the name of the man who had committed the crime and where he was living. Jim approached his supervisor from the detective division and relayed his findings. He then needed to go to Arkansas and extradite this guy back to New York. This is where the bad news took over. Jimmy was told to go sit on the sidelines and take his helmet off while the three senior detectives originally assigned got to travel to the Ozarks. As he continued to tell me more of the details, he just became more enraged. "This is bullshit." He did all the work and got none of the credit. Jimmy knew at that moment he wasn't long for being a cop and getting treated like a second-class citizen. In the months to follow, he quit and started working with the DA's office. He wound up doing security and chauffeuring around Jeanine Pirro, who was the first female district attorney in Westchester County. She held that position for twelve years. On the few occasions that I got to see him after leaving our job, he looked happy and knew he was in a better place. Oh, and with the overtime he racked up, he tripled his earnings. Sometimes that little push is all you need.

I've seen a lot of wacky crap in my life and thought it was just going to be another hot summer evening with the usual cast of characters loitering about the projects. See the guy over there with a little Old English 800 protruding from out of the top of the paper bag? What about that 12-year-old kid on the bicycle that, for some reason, has a best friend who is 22 years old? It's easy to tell what's going on when the same car has now gone around the block three times. Ferris Avenue was one block east of the railroad tracks and was, at one time, a mostly Italian neighborhood. A friend of mine who has since passed used to take action on the block. That's right, gambling. This was long before the Lotto and Mega Millions. Powerball is bullshit, everybody who wins loses almost half paying taxes on it. Not back then, it was totally different. There was a new three-digit number every day that came from either the racetracks handle or the stock exchange. The block was mostly Italian in the 1950's and 60's, but soon became affordable housing to an increased number of African Americans who had moved into the area. It wasn't long before the Columbians and Mexicans would become the majority in the neighborhood and nightly fights would occur around the bodegas. See, anybody who has come into the country illegally has a unique problem. I don't have a social security number, so I can't get a bank account. The majority of them work for cash, so now it was the problem of safeguarding it. So, what's the best way to protect your money? Very simple. Go down to the post office and get a money order for 75 cents and send it back to the other side of the border. I parked my police car across from the eight-story apartment building as the beginning of my shift was uneventful. I learned from a veteran cop, when I first came on the job, that it's always good to make yourself visible. It can always flip on a dime as the saying goes. Two members from the street crime unit pulled up across from me and I didn't really give it much thought at first. They could have been looking for somebody or had some informant call in with information about the area. Communication within the police department as a whole pretty much sucks. Each unit doesn't want to tell the others what they're doing. The old 'secret squirrel' BS. This is especially true for the vice squads and crime units. Then the shit hits the fan blade and the screaming starts on the radio. As I glanced across the street, I noticed Dennis getting into it with some kid and the crowd starting to gather. Fuck. I was out of the car now and walking across the street trying to figure out what was going on. Dennis had probably 15 years on the job at that time and, for some reason, decided this was the afternoon he wanted to go toe-to-toe for a brief instance talking shit about nothing. Then I heard the youth call Dennis out. "Shit, I ain't gonna throw down wit you as long as you got that badge and gun on yo hip." Without missing a beat, the detective removed his holster with the weapon and took his shield that was around his neck and tossed them all on a concrete table that was just off the sidewalk. I looked over the landscape and thought to myself, *If I get hurt over this cop being a total dick, I'm gonna fucking kill him.* Three cops against 20+. "Well, my shit ain't on now, so what are ya gonna do?" The staring contest began. I thought he must have seen this in a movie because what cop is stupid enough to give up his gun? The weapon was a good 10 feet away as the two approached each other. There were a lot of wandering eyes from the crowd also taking in the weapon's location and peered in its direction. In three years of working that area, it was never this quiet. "Man, fuck you!" Those were the best words I had heard all day as he turned and walked away, leaving the crowd behind him a little shocked. Dennis yelled back, "Yeah, that's what I heard about you - all talk." The situation was diffused and we all went to neutral corners. I never spoke to Dennis about what that was all about; I don't think I would have gotten a straight answer anyway.

Nobody likes being sick and I'm the biggest crybaby around when it comes to a head cold, the flu or a rash on my ass I can't get rid of. How do I deal with it? The couch, the remote and don't talk to me because I'm miserable. When my wife got ill on vacation, it was a trip to the walk-in clinic in a nearby town of Calabash, NC. We got to the waiting room mid-morning and signed in with the receptionist. When your insurance is from 800 miles away, you always get that blank stare like they have to decode the missile sequence and take on Ali in the ring all at the same time. We got the usual, "Have a seat, we will call you shortly" routine and we proceeded to a couple of chairs covered in pastel flowers. I gave the room a once over because that's what cops do. To my right were two guys dressed in their best fishing gear, they were probably in their late 60's or early 70's. The conversation was about lures, trucks and whether or not the spots were running. A spot is a small fish and if you catch 12 of them, you almost have enough for a meal. Across from me, and on the other side of the coffee table, were two ladies about the same age; one reading and the other with a pair of crochet needles in her hands. Whatever she was making, it wasn't her first time. Her thin fingers and ligaments appeared purple in the room where the air conditioning was blowing ice cold air. Off to my left was a grandmother in her early 50's who was with her granddaughter. She was probably about 10 years old and had one too many Cheerios or Lucky Charms for breakfast. We sat and listened to the conversations which made for some pretty good people watching. This little girl off to my left was up and down and her guardian finally told her to sit on the chair and behave. A couple of minutes passed and this kid put her shoes on the fabric of the chair she was sitting on. "Put your feet down, I'm not going to tell you again." I glanced over less than a minute later and knew it wouldn't be long before it occurred for a second time. When the shoes hit the chair, I thought to myself, *Here comes more yelling and idle threats from grandma.* With that, the grandmother smacked the girl's inner thigh just below the cuff of her shorts with the back of her hand. I felt the sting and I was 10 feet away. Her eyes swelled up in pain and her lips started to quiver. A noticeable red mark appeared. I waited for the cell phones to come out and the 911 calls to report child abuse. Nothing… the boys went back to talking about jig lines and the ladies about proper stitching on lace dresses. I just sat there and remembered all the times I got wacked by mom, dad and my grandmother. To this day, I bet that kid has never put her shoes on another piece of furniture.

CHAPTER 34

STRANGE

There are certain things in life that are just a little more unusual than the everyday mundane crap. I'm not talking about the first time that you shared a beer with your dad at the ballgame or when I walked into Nordstrom's today and the sales lady wanted me to model men's watches for a female customer. She was trying to get an idea of how it would look on her boyfriend. Let me get this right; he's 27 years old, a Marine, 6′ 8″, serving overseas, and you haven't had sex in months? It's gonna look totally different on his wrist, but I played along. No, these are the little things in life that if you were to tell your best friends, they would shake their heads and say, "Can't make that up."

It was about seven degrees out that night and I had a rookie cop with me in the car. It was getting close to 3 a.m. The wind was still howling and it blew what little snow there was on the ground into those funnels and then they would disappear. As I made my way down the street, there was one lost soul off to my right who still hadn't made it home. As I got closer, I was able to tell who it was and pulled over to the side of the road. We spoke briefly and she told me she had no place to go. I asked her if she needed a ride to the diner or someplace else, but all she wanted to do was to get warmed up. "Get in." She jumped into the rear of the squad car and we talked about a couple of girls whom she had been fighting with and some new guy on the block that tried to rip her off. She didn't divulge any big secrets or hand me the map to where Hoffa was buried. We drove around for the better part of 30 minutes with the heat blasting from the vents. "You want to look into getting into a shelter tonight?" From the rearview mirror, I could see the expression on her face. She would never go to a shelter. I bought her a cup of coffee and drove her back to her block where she felt most comfortable and told her I would see her around. My partner looked over at me as we pulled away from the curb and I was waiting for him to say something. I figured I would beat him to the punch and let him know that she was a working girl. We were all rookies once.

Before I got on the job, there had been a cop who was suspected of doing a few illegal things and eventually got caught for it. If you dangle that string with enough drugs or cash, it's just a matter of time. I'm not sure how my name came up in the barrel this week, but I was on somebody's watch list. Or as it's sometimes called, the shit list. Our department required each officer to do an inspection of the car prior to taking it out for the tour. There was a checklist for each car in the fleet. We checked everything from lights and sirens to how much oxygen was in the medical bag in the trunk. If you ever have a hangover, suck down some 100% pure oxygen and you'll feel like a new man. Then you would remove the rear bench seat and determine if any prisoners who had been there from the previous shift had left any souvenirs behind; crack, weed, a syringe. This was also referred to as the integrity test. Well, it was my turn. It was just after four o'clock when I separated the cushion and found the brand new crisp $50 bill. I think at one point Grant was the most interesting man in the world doing ads for Dos Equis. It couldn't have been placed there more perfectly. I just shook my head and thought, *Who is filming me right now?* I walked back into headquarters and notified communications that I would be out of service as I needed to start an incident report. I made my feelings known and said to the lieutenant on the desk, "50 bucks, you gotta do better than that." I was fucking pissed. "Buy me an island in the Caribbean and we can start talking." I let out a few more F-bombs and was waiting for him to say something. He never did, which means he knew about it. I was thinking about going home sick. No, I'll just stay here all night and do as little as possible. How fast does the word spread in your job? 200 cops could have been mistaken for 200 washwomen. I told everybody about it and gave them the heads up. It took me three hours to do the paperwork; I even made a copy of the bill, front and back. The following day, I called in sick just for the hell of it.

When I showed up at the ice rink that night, I had no idea what was about to hit me smack in the face. The rink had closed up an hour ago and I was doing the last mandatory check. It was just after 11 p.m., closing time. On a typical Friday or Saturday night, there would have been kids everywhere, but this was the middle of the week and even the parking lot was empty except for a couple of cars. I walked in through a rear door where the Zamboni was kept and saw the skating guard closing up shop. I had known her for a few years, she was cute; blond hair, spectacular ass, but a little naïve. Kind of the glass is always full and the sun will come out tomorrow personality. I asked if she was heading out soon and needed an escort out to her car. "Can I tell you something?" She fiddled around with some papers on the desk and then stated to me that she had almost been raped about 20 minutes ago. "He came in here and pushed me into the locker room and got on top of me. I kept yelling no, no." I let her run with the story, not wanting to cut her off or make her hit reverse. He finally got off of her and left the building. "I think he got scared." That's when she dropped the atom bomb and told me who it was. He was a cop on our job and driving 17 car that night. She didn't want to pursue anything or go to the hospital. "Can you tell him to stay away from me?" I've been in awkward positions before, but this ranks up at the top of the list. I confronted him later that night, he denied it ever happening.

Okay, so picture this: It's my first week working a new part-time job for a furrier. Today was going to be a little different. We had to travel down to New York City and stop at a few places to have some coats altered and there were a few that needed new embroidery and monograms done. We had a very plain white panel van that was modified with interior racks so one could hang the furs instead of throwing them on the floor of the vehicle. Yeah, that was never done. My partner for the day showed me the route he liked to take to get to the city, avoiding a lot of the traffic and tolls. When we pulled over on 7th Avenue at 27th Street, we had arrived. We were now parked directly in front of the Fashion Institute. I knew we were parked illegally, but I figured my partner had this step figured out. Serving dirty water dogs and salty pretzels 25 feet away was Charlie. He stepped out from behind the metal box and I was introduced to him for the first time. My partner and I both grabbed a handful of furs and proceeded to our destinations. There was no telling how long it would take. Was the service elevator to the building working? Was there an operator working? See, in New York City it's all union jobs, and you have to use the service elevator. You're not even allowed to press the button for the 21st floor. Once you got into the showroom, you had to wait your turn behind sales persons, clients, models, and that annoying lady at the desk that pretended she was on the phone and kept flipping her hair backwards. But it didn't matter, Charlie was downstairs watching the van out on the street with about a half a million dollars in pelts in the back. After we finished our rounds, I would sometimes grab a knish for the ride home with extra mustard. For years, it was always the same; park in front of the blue and yellow Sabrett umbrella and throw the guy with the apron on the keys to the van. There were other times before we even made it to Charlie's that we would head a few blocks west, just south of the Javits Convention Center. That's where all the hookers hung out early in the morning. The place was especially busy on Fridays when everybody got paid. On this one particular morning, it was bone-chilling cold and here's this girl wearing a green bra and Daisy Dukes strutting down the avenue. No jacket, no hat, not even a pair of gloves. We drove around for a few minutes then parked in what I would assume was one of her usual spots. This next procedure was called checking the oil. I exited the vehicle and would pretend like there was a problem with the engine. I put the hood up and thought to myself, *I'm freezing my ass off out here, he better hurry up*. I located the dipstick to kill some time and waited for the all-clear. Some poor lady's fox stole in the rear of the van was soon going to look like a glazed doughnut. I would continue this charade until I saw the girl exit the van and shove the $20 bill inside her bra.

Having been a cop for over five years, it was still a little bit of a surprise when I was asked by supervisors to become an FTO (Field Training Officer). In layman's terms, it was a fancy title that meant you were going to be in charge of training rookie cops straight out of the academy. In this world, it's nice to be thought about and get that little pat on the back... but what's in it for me? The first rookie I had the chance to supervise turned out to be a friend's wife; he and I played golf a few times a month and got along great together. Somebody call The Flamingo and check the odds on that. It was difficult from the word go. She wasn't the sharpest knife in the drawer and had seen more ceilings than Michelangelo. One of our first calls that we handled together came in from a business in town that was the management company overseeing a mall. The complaint was that somebody had spray painted a little graffiti on a portion of the building. While attempting to write up the report on the incident, she asked me my opinion on how it should be worded. Who, what, where, when, how. "Make it simple," I told her, "don't overthink it. Address of the building, where the tag had occurred, color of paint used and what was written; everything else is just speculation." She started out the narrative in good order until she got to the point where she was describing the color of the spray paint used. "Blue... How do you spell that?" I looked at her in disbelief, "Really?" She looked down at the form in front of her and her mind was blank. "Well, I know it's not like the cheese," she answered.

At the south end of Westmoreland Ave. stands a two-family home that was built just before the depression in 1929. If you threw a rock, you could hit the train tracks. The school for misfit toys was right across the street, where kids who couldn't make it in high school got a second chance. When a friend of mine moved in there, he must have gotten a pretty sweet deal on a one bedroom apartment because in 20 years I don't ever recall anything good happening on that block. Kevin had worked a day tour that day, 8 a.m. to 4 p.m., and then followed that up with a side job, driving for a local taxi company. After a 16 hour day, he was just looking to go home and crash into the most comfortable bed he owned. As a cop it didn't matter what shift you worked, somebody was always up to grab a beer with you at the end of the day. Not everybody has a wife and kids they have to go home to, that's why pubs were created. There were cops on our job that would play practical jokes and those that would start rumors just to see how far they would spread. Yes, we are still living in a frat house off campus. This evening started out with a few rounds at the bar and then the encounter with a female party who had no place to go when the bar closed. With no place to sleep that night, my buddy decided he would play the Red Cross and give her a ride over to Kevin's apartment. She was tired, drunk and passed out almost immediately. Imagine coming home after a long day and finding a woman sleeping in your bed. He was pissed, and the following day wanted to know, "Who put the fucking one-legged lady in my bed." It must have been pretty funny watching him yell at this woman while she hopped over to the dresser to get her prosthetic. We thought she just had a bad limp.

Everybody tries to save money in their own way. It could be coupons, waiting for an item to go on sale and hit the clearance rack, or carpooling. I worked with a guy who had his own method and got caught because of two reasons; he did it in broad daylight where everybody and his brother could see him, and he did it in front of security cameras that were located at headquarters. Brilliant. He was studying to become a sergeant on our job which meant that you had to pass the civil service test. The kick was even if you came out number one on the list they could take number two or three and leave you in the dust. He was confronted one day by the commissioner and asked if he was still living upstate about 40 miles away from work. He replied that he was and doing the daily commute. The next question asked was, "What do you have up there as far as garbage pickup, is it a private company that you pay for or is it done by the town?" "No, it's a private company, you have to pay for it." And that's when the conversation ended. It was a nice way of telling him to stop bringing your garbage to work. This guy was loading up his car a few times a week and transporting his garbage to the police station where he would throw it out in the dumpster. Things that I never want in the back of my car: dead body, dead animal carcass, and last night's dinner of chicken wings with rancid beer bottles and those annoying gnats that show up.

In the fall of 2000, Heineken USA was moving its headquarters from White Plains, NY to White Plains, NY. The four-block move was going to take place during a period where the local union for movers was walking the picket line against the trucking companies. Teamsters looking for better wages, less work, and do I really have to pick up that mahogany desk? Heineken was concerned that, during this move, there may be some problems since they had hired non-union people for the trek that was to begin after 9 p.m. I got hired to do security that night and had this bad feeling that there should have been two of us assigned to the detail - well, maybe three. The offices were located on the 16th floor and I took a quick tour of the boardroom that had an impressive rug under the massive table and leather chairs. It was a light charcoal grey with the green Heineken logo in the center and the red star. I walked into the next office and it was the bar. A wall to wall mirror 25 feet in length engraved with the company's seal decorated the rear area behind the stick. There were also several taps ready to pour. I almost wanted to jump into one of the stools that lined the dark oak counter. Several trucks started lining up in the loading zone and the business at hand began. These guys were efficient and never stopped for a break. They were so honest that not one of them even offered me a case. I was waiting for the other shoe to drop, but it never did. The offices were cleared by 4 a.m. and nobody was bothered in the process. I got one of the managers to sign my overtime slip and my one-day job working at Heineken was over.

It was that time of the year; a bunch of guys invading Myrtle Beach for some golf and beach time. Spring break. My buddy Peter said his parents had an older home a few blocks from the beach. We were all invited to crash there for the week with no price tag attached. It was a little bit run-down but had enough hot water for showers and the roof didn't leak. A step above the trailer park. If it's free, it's for me. It was early March, and the spring breakers were attempting to consume all the alcohol in every bar and hotel. The golf courses were perfect, we would hit an early round in the morning, grab some lunch, and then hit this little tiki bar a few blocks from the house. On the second day we were there, the eight of us sat on the sand watching the waves roll in off the Atlantic. It couldn't have been better. We were all cops and spoke the same language. At 27, we were on top of the world. When my friend pulled out his camcorder, the day got kicked into overdrive. Within minutes, the filming began and we met two girls from the University of North Carolina at Charlotte. They wanted to become rock stars or porn stars as soon as possible. One of them claimed to be the bartender from hell and insisted on making drinks at all times. Need a beer opened? She was there. Vodka cranberry margarita? "I'll do that." Okay, and make me a sandwich also. We spent a few days together and, to this day, I can't remember her saying 'no' to anything the whole week. Her friend was a space cadet and if I was going to put money on it, she had no chance of graduating college. After playing some drinking games back at the house that evening, one of my buddies - a cop from New York City - asks the space alien if she wants to take a walk along the beach. How romantic, bare feet and a bottle of champagne. The rest of us had decided to stay in for the night with a few more cocktails and find some clothes for golf in the morning. It was a couple of hours later when he got back and I could tell right away it was not good. He said, "Everything was going great, we were just hanging out on the beach when she starts to take her clothes off and goes running into the water, yelling at the top of her lungs." There are people all over the beach that heard her screams. "You know what she was yelling? RAPE!" We all looked at him like he was making up the story. "What the fuck am I gonna do?" His mind started to run faster than his thoughts could process them. "We were just sitting there and the next thing I knew she was waist deep in the water." He continued with the story saying he tried to go out and get her, but she swam out further and continued to yell, "Stay away from me!" There was a small group of people who had gathered when he came out of the water looking at him. He said he grabbed the bottle and glasses and just started to run for the house. I looked over at the bartender from hell, but she was passed out. "She knows where we're staying, you think the local cops are going to care that we're cops? Hell no." The next thing I knew, he was on the phone to his sergeant back in New York. It was brief and the verdict was "get the hell out of there." He packed up his clothes and said his goodbyes and was gone before the sun came up. Nobody ever saw her again and the bartender from hell crawled out of my bed the next morning and headed back to Charlotte.

SMARTS was a local company that was started by a woman from Iran. With about 200 employees, they were a software company that could get your business up and running twice as fast as the next guy should your company's computer system fail or become infected. Their offices were diagonally across the street from our headquarters at 1 North Lexington Ave. There had been a rash of robberies in the area as of late, and people walking to their cars at night were getting knocked over the head and having their purses taken. The CEO hired us to walk their employees out to their vehicles after work to make sure they were safe. It was perfect after a day tour; get there at 4 p.m. and stay till 11 p.m. We would sit in the lobby and re-read the newspaper or finish up the crossword puzzle. On a busy day, I might take five trips to the parking structure a couple of blocks away. Then there were the benefits of the job: getting paid in cash, sitting on your keister the majority of the evening and the company of Mary, the office secretary. She was a natural beauty that never wore make-up and never needed any. A 25-year-old Barbie with brown hair. She usually stayed till 6 p.m. and if you felt like talking, you could bend her ear. Early on, we were bullshitting as she sat around answering the late phone calls and waiting to punch out. The most amazing thing about her was that she never watched TV or went on the computer unless it was work related. She couldn't care less who the president was, what was happening in the Middle East or the rising national debt crisis. I asked her about her typical day and got this: "I get up in the morning, run three miles on the treadmill, drive an hour to work; when I'm done, I drive home, make dinner for my boyfriend, fuck him, listen to some music and go to sleep." "Do you know who the president is?" There was a pause, but I got Bush as the response. I didn't want to press the issue and ask which one. "So, what are the weekends like?" It was pretty much the same answer: "Running, some boating, drinks, restaurant for dinner, fuck my boyfriend and go to bed."

CHAPTER 35

OSWEGO

When I first met my stepdaughter, Amanda, she had just turned 16 and was busy with her social life, talking on the phone, hanging with friends and going to school….most of the time. She began her search for colleges a year or so later and had sent out a few letters to various universities. When she got accepted to University of Hawaii, I figured it was a no-brainer. Easiest job in the world is to be a weatherman in Honolulu, "It's going to be 82 degrees today with light variable winds and a chance of darkness after sunset." No, she decided on SUNY Oswego in Upstate New York. When her father decided he was not going to co-sign the student loan, I stepped up and scribbled my name on the documents. I wasn't even her stepfather yet. It was 1998.

Oswego sits on the shoreline of Lake Ontario. Just saying Lake Ontario makes me want to put on a sweatshirt. We had heard the rumors of the winds that howled off the lake, the ropes that were installed so students could navigate from building to building during blizzards and that there were only two seasons there: winter and the 4th of July. My first visit to Oswego was nothing short of an eye-opener. Amanda was living in the dorms like all first-year students and had a roommate with a whiny voice who was quickly putting on the freshman 15, drinking and eating mac and cheese. I was all set to grab a hotel in town but Amanda insisted her mother and I sleep in her bed and she would crash down the hall in a friend's room. After a short night of bar hopping, we returned to the dorm and tried to fall asleep. Moments later, I heard the door open and some guy creeping into Whiny's bed. They threw a good one for about five minutes as we tried not to laugh from under the covers a few feet away. The next morning, I sat on the couch in the dayroom trying not to stick to anything and stared out the double-hung picture window. Sure enough, walking across the quad was a girl doing the walk of shame and coming home in the same clothes she went out in last night.

Having played rugby for a couple of seasons in Japan, it didn't faze me when I learned that Amanda was going to be a hooker. Her mother, on the other hand, took two steps back and reached for the vodka in the freezer. A hooker is a position on the team that supports the props, but as long as the NFL is around nobody in America cares. The girl's team at college was called the Black Widows and they sported green and black jerseys. There were about 30 girls on the squad of all shapes and sizes and everybody had a nickname. There was Smelly, Roofie, Corn, Gizmo and, of course, Punani. My daughter was Jabber. They funded themselves and played against other schools in the region. Of course, there is always an initiation process you have to go through to officially make the team. Sometimes it's being locked in a hall closet, other times it's having your hair painted with actual house paint. It takes a long time to get that shit out.

It was her third year at college and we came up to watch her play in a game and spend the weekend together. She had moved into an off-campus house with about eight other girls and was now living at 13 Liberty Street across from the hydro-electrical power plant. A charming little street with that refinery look and smokestacks just outside your front door. We called the house 1313 Mockingbird Lane, home of Herman, Eddie, Lily and Grandpa. It was an old off-white saltbox home that hadn't seen paint in years. The stairs leading to the second floor leaned to one side and you had to brace yourself against the wall to make it to the top. There was no point locking the front door; even if it did work, nobody would venture inside. The bong on the coffee table actually added to the décor of the place. The following morning was game time and we made our way over to a place called the Hidden Fields. It was situated on the far side of campus and required about a 15-minute walk through the woods to get there. There were no bleachers or benches and the best seat in the house was on a cooler. We had packed up some beers and started throwing them back at 10 a.m. There were a lot of friends, family, and even some rugby fans there that had come out to watch both the girl's and men's' teams play. Everything was going along well until I noticed the two campus cops walking up the sidelines about an hour later. There were open containers everywhere and enough underage drinking to complete the exacta. They wanted to open the coolers and start taking down names for their report. I became the spokesman for the group and asked one of the cops if I could speak with him privately. We stepped off to the side and I told him that I was also on the job. I gave him the assurance we would move the party to another place and that when we left, the place would look like a Better Homes and Garden shoot. We shook hands and he and his partner left the field. Damn, I'm good.

After every rugby game, there is a little thing known as the 'drink-up'. It's not complicated. Drink, get wasted, sing songs and tell stories. Well, at least that's the way it was when I played. In Oswego, it has a slightly different flavor to it. The town is full of neighborhood bars that spring up in the middle of residential areas. Is that a house I just walked by or a bar? Maybe it was both. Today we were headed to The Patch where the bartender knew we were coming. From the outside, it reminded me of a Holstein cow with that familiar black and white nondescript pattern. Inside, the floor was stained and there was enough stale cigarette smoke to make you want to break a window. The drinks started flowing and the senior members of the men's rugby team let everybody know that a 'landshark' was about to come through. See, when a rookie gets to play in his first game, the landshark is the right of passage. The rookie stripped down naked in front of everybody in the bar and was then hoisted up in the air with four of his teammates taking his arms and legs. This kid is now horizontal to the floor with his white ass sticking up in the air.

But that's only half the fun. The next part of the show was when a paper plate was brought out, folded in half, and stuck in the crack of his ass. The yelling and hollering continued in the bar and I thought for a minute I was back in The Philippines. The rookie was then marched around the bar like a landshark and we were all laughing our asses off. But again, that's only part of the fun. It was now time for some audience participation. The next thing I know, somebody pulled out a lighter and lit his dorsal fin on fire. Here's this kid, 19 years old, butt naked, six feet off the ground, in a bar with patrons, with a paper plate in his ass that's on fire. As he's being paraded around the bar, the chants of, "Put it out, put it out," were being yelled by both the girl's and men's teams. With that, everybody in the bar started throwing their beers at him, hoping to extinguish the flames. It didn't matter where you were standing, you got a few suds on ya. The fire department was never called.

We made the five-hour drive north to see Amanda every year while she was in school. I was 40 years old and felt like I was Rodney Dangerfield in Back to School. Hanging out with kids half my age and getting the college education I never had. I remember one spring morning after an all-nighter, a few of her girlfriends had decided to head down to the lake to go swimming. I had just stumbled down the Munster steps and was looking for a little breakfast. Her roommates were in swimsuits and bikinis already and passed along the invite. "Where are you going?" They were headed to Lake Ontario. "Wanna go swimming with us?" I figured the water temperature was about 45 degrees and the last thing I needed was a cold shower that morning.

A year later, Amanda had moved eight blocks away and was still hanging with the same group of girls - well, most of them. A few moved on when they graduated, but there was always a new rookie to join the clan. The house she was living in was a lot nicer...from the outside. From the inside, it was still beer cans, pizza boxes and dirty dishes in the sink. Her friends were down to earth and didn't need to impress anybody with the latest fashion or a new set of nails. Her calls home to her mother were always filled with the same question, "What the fuck happened?" There was the time she broke her breastplate in a rugby game and was having problems breathing. A few months later, she was stopped by the cops at a nuclear power plant about 15 minutes away for trespassing. It all got worked out in the end. I always had the feeling that she didn't want us to worry but enjoyed telling the story anyway. While she was living there, she did what every college kid should do; she got a six-week-old puppy while extremely intoxicated. The way Amanda tells it put it all into perspective, "Well, I could've gotten pregnant......would that have been better?"

I remember bars with simple names there, nothing cute or fancy. The Brick, The Sting, and a bar my daughter worked at called Potters Pub. A real townie bar where you could get Pabst Blue Ribbon or Natty in a can for a buck. Who the hell drinks that crap? I looked down at the end of the bar and I had found the guy. We drank there one afternoon for a few hours with her working behind the stick and still got change from my twenty. There were two guys who came in soon after us that were regulars. I thought to myself, *There's a pair that beats a full house*.

After five years, it was graduation time and our last trip to the great white north was in May of 2003. School always came easy for my stepdaughter and if I was laying odds, she stayed around the last year just to party. The commencement was at the hockey arena and the celebration was just down the road at a bar called The Shed. The bar sat on the main thoroughfare and intersected three different roads. It was the first bar you came to leaving campus, so it had that attraction, and a McDonald's across the street didn't hurt. Inside were old cracked grey tiles on the floor and a semi-rectangular bar that was set up 'Cheers' style. There was a small porch out front and a few tables that probably never got used between November and March. On graduation day, the place was mobbed and the bartenders were staring at three-deep in line for cocktails. Everything was good for the most part until my wife and some of Amanda's friends went to the bathroom. When there is only one bathroom and there are 200+ people in the bar, the rule is to get in and get out quickly. Don't put on makeup, comb your hair, or spend 10 minutes doing a bump. With the line growing outside the ladies room, the girls started pounding on the door and were met with, "I'm almost done." A couple of minutes later, after more pounding, the girl that was inside finally came to the door and cracked it open and tells the whole bar that she's not done yet and everybody is going to have to wait. That was her first mistake. The pushing began from both sides of the door, F-bombs were flying and the tug-of-war continued. The struggle didn't last very long because the idiot inside the bathroom decided she was going to take on two of my daughter's friends and my wife. That was her second mistake. As they pushed their way into the bathroom the girl who was inside had one of her fingers smashed between the door and the interior bathroom wall. More screaming and cries of, "You broke my fucking finger, you broke my fucking finger!" As my wife entered the bathroom she was met with a rum and coke being tossed all over her. Game on. Not a lot of people win 3 on 1 fights. My wife dragged her over to the toilet as the hair pulling continued and my wife sat her down on the throne and explained to her the errors of her ways. I'm sure there were some claws displayed during the altercation; a cat fight I didn't get to see. Like most bar fights they are usually over in five minutes or less, just as the police are pulling up. As everybody involved told their side of the story to the local police I remember seeing this girl's finger, my wife in her soaked shirt, and waiting for somebody to get locked up. It was almost time to call my attorney and the law offices of Dewey, Cheatham, and Howe. We all got kicked out of the place. Another brawl in the bathroom, hysterical isn't it?

After college, Amanda went on to work at an event planning firm working with Magic Johnson, Jack Nicklaus, and Joe Namath. She currently works for The Leukemia & Lymphoma Society. And I thought she was just there to party.

CHAPTER 36

GOLFING AGAIN

I have seen a lot of really stupid things in my life, but on this particular day I just couldn't understand why anybody would even think about attempting this. There used to be a golf course in Sunset Beach, NC that I could walk to from my vacation home. It was only about a half mile away down an old dirt road that was seldom used. The place was called Angels Trace and had two solid tracks there, the North and South courses. By the time I had reached the 6th hole on the North side that morning, things had started to slow down and our foursome had to wait off to the side as the group in front of us teed off. If you're a golfer, there is nothing worse than waiting - well, maybe rain. The hole was a par 3, with a little aqua in front of the tee box that stretched out to about 170 yards. There was a ranger up in front by the green trying to keep the pace of play moving as he sat in his cart and stared back towards us. As the last member hit, we watched him top the ball; it took two skips off the water and was snatched out of the air on the far side of the pond by an eight-foot alligator who was catching some rays a few feet off the water's edge. We all looked at each other and said, "Did you see that?" Just then, the ranger pulled up with his golf cart and wanted to know if the guy who had hit the shot wanted his ball back. There was a quick nod and, with that, the ranger asked for a golf club from out of his bag. So, there we were, eight guys standing around as we watched in awe as the ranger began walking towards the gator and pounding the club on the ground like a caveman. I thought to myself, *Nothing good can come from this.* He kept getting closer, tapping the club on the ground with every step. Has he done this before? When he got to about five feet from the gator, I thought there were only two things that could happen. We were all mesmerized. It was like watching a car crash. You want to look away, but everybody takes a peak. The alligator spat out the golf ball and made a quick exit into the water. Now the ranger bends over and picks up the ball and tosses it back to the guy. I think that's one you can display on the mantle above the fireplace. After the round was over, I saw the guy back at the 19th hole having a couple of cocktails. We spoke briefly and I asked him if that ball was going into a frame on his desk? He told me, "You'll never believe what happened. I teed up that ball on the next hole and, without thinking, duck-hooked it into the marsh." What an idiot.

It was the eve before Christmas in 2008 and we were having our usual friends over for the holidays. We would exchange some gifts and eat like we were going to the electric chair. The menu that night consisted of some pasta and chicken parmesan, a spiral ham and the usual sides of string bean casserole and a broccoli soufflé and, of course, some adult beverages. There is never a shortage of food when my wife is cooking and we wind up looking at each other the next day and asking why we made so much food. When you run out of Tupperware containers, you have a problem. That night, my buddy handed me a gift and I opened the small bag to reveal a single golf ball. With a closer look, I see it has a logo on it from The Masters. Mike has this big grin on his face, "That's right, you're going." Anybody who has ever played the game dreams about a trip to the sacred course in Augusta, Georgia. The second weekend in April couldn't come fast enough. Mike had been to The Masters a few times and had the details laid out well in advance of us leaving. So, on April 10, 2009, we set out on the trip of a lifetime. Mike's co-worker, Bo, was going to be doing all the driving and we hooked up with him about nine that morning. Just picture a good ol' boy from the South, 6' 4" and can chew dip with the best of them. He told us on the ride up that he used to work one of the scoreboards at The

Masters when he was younger. There would be a roar on the course because somebody had made a birdie or eagle and Bo would get the word on his headset. He said he used to take his time changing the board, keeping the crowd on edge. The fourth in our party was a guy named Tyler that worked with both Mike and Bo. He had a pretty good stick and was playing golf out of TPC Tampa at the time. So, there we were in Bo's driveway, loading up his white SUV with our clubs and bags for the weekend when the first Budweiser was cracked. The plan was to drive up to Macon, Georgia and spend the night, head over to Augusta on Saturday morning, play golf that afternoon at a nearby course, then catch Sunday at The Masters. About two hours and four beers into the trip, things started going bad. We were stuck in a severe traffic jam on Interstate 75 that runs north/south in the middle-of-nowhere Florida. Nature was also calling also and I exited the vehicle and started walking toward the nearest woods. The guys were really concerned about my departure from the car, but my bladder wins every time. By the time I got back into the car, we had moved three car lengths. We finally got to our first destination where the wind and rain had picked up. I thought to myself, *This ain't good*. After checking into the hotel, we found a local roadhouse for dinner where we caught up on the golf action that day and threw down some steaks at the bar.

The wind continued to howl that night and the lights flickered a few times. We sat in the room that evening and the weather forecasters had the watch boxes up where tornados were possible. We went to sleep early knowing we had to travel in the morning and the bus was leaving at seven. That night, starting at about 9 p.m., the area around Augusta got hammered. Maximum winds were 120 mph and a reported EF3 had touched down in the area. One section had 30 homes and 10 businesses damaged. A mobile home overturned in another part of town. Trees were twisted everywhere and power lines were down all over the area, knocking out power. It must be holy ground because The Masters Golf Course escaped without a scratch.

We ate a quick breakfast that morning and were off taking the back roads over to our destination. The sun was up and the weekend was supposed to be gorgeous. There is nothing worse than planning a vacation and the weather turns out to be shit. Jim, our host, had gone over the top in all he did for us that weekend. When we showed up at the two houses he had rented for the week, the pantry was full and a shelf of anything you wanted awaited us in the kitchen. *Johnnie Blue will be fine,* I thought; *I just walked into a liquor store.* We sat and bullshitted for a while, then he told us he had set up golf for us that afternoon at a course just over the border in South Carolina called The Reserve Club at Woodside Plantation. We were also being treated to lunch prior to the round. We made our way over to the course passing through areas that had been damaged by the storm from the night before. Cop cars and saw horses were blocking roads and getting around the area took longer than expected. Prior to leaving we had grabbed a bottle of Ketel One knowing there may not be a cart girl working. Like a Boy Scout, always be prepared. The track was in great shape and the day was filled with a lot of laughs. The Ketel was gone by the 14th hole. I thought about how fortunate I was and wondered what the chances were of waking up from this dream. The drive back to the house was a little rough. Bo had tweaked his back playing and was unable to drive and let Mike take the wheel. Traffic was a mess on the ride home with people leaving from the event. I had given Bo some pain relief medicine for his back that was causing his stomach to become upset. We attempted to hit some side roads through a residential neighborhood and that's when Bo said he needed to throw up and I needed to relieve myself... again. We were all laughing so hard we were crying. At this point, both doors on the right side of the car are open, Bo was yakking behind me and I'm pissing in front of him. As all this is happening, a cop drove past us without even slowing down. He gave a quick glance over and since we weren't wrapped around a tree, it was all good. At dinner that night, Tyler was putting the moves on our server. He was trying to get her to come back to the house where we were staying, but she was more interested in getting a ticket for The Masters.

The first time I walked onto the grounds of Augusta that Sunday morning, I felt a thrill like no other. We had already spent a mortgage payment in the gift shop and were now walking on the green grass of the first hole. We got a full tour of the place from Jim's son and walked the course prior to the first pairing going off. We set up our chairs behind the sixth hole green in the second row next to the walkway where the players would exit for the next hole. Breakfast was egg salad and pimento sandwiches, and with a soda it was under five bucks. Sunday at The Masters, awesome. Tyler had played some golf with Ryuji Imada in Florida and when he and his playing partner that day, Trevor Immelman, came to number six that afternoon, Tyler couldn't resist. We were seated a few yards from the back of the green in your typical golf setting with everybody being quiet while Immelman was looking over his putt. "Ryuji... Ryuji... Ryuji." The place was silent except for Tyler acting like the annoying person in every movie theater I've ever been to. The two finally made eye contact and Ryuji walked over to where we were sitting. He and Tyler made some small talk, then he walked off to hit his tee shot on number seven. The majority of the day was centered on the Tiger and Phil Mickelson show who were paired together and both finished in the top 10. When the last group came through, we moved down to the 16th hole and were now ordering beers two at a time. When you're with people who have been there before, it makes it a lot easier to navigate the terrain. That year, there was a three-way playoff between Chad Campbell, Kenny Perry and the eventual winner, Angel Cabrera, being crowned on #10. Trip of a lifetime.

Working in the golf field for the past 10 years, I've seen and heard just about everything. I've witnessed golf carts being driven into lakes, sand traps, and into five-foot-deep culverts. This one nut actually drove across the green hitting the flagstick with a cart once. He was boxed. I played in an outing once and my partner was in a playoff after the 18 holes. This other guy he was going to be playing against was drunk off his ass and hit reverse instead of drive. He backed into our cart, ejecting both of us from the vehicle. He then told the staff it was our fault and tried to get us to be responsible for the $1200 in damages.

I was playing one afternoon and had hit it left off the tee into a small grouping of old oaks. It was fairly open so I thought I might have a shot out. As I walked towards where I thought my ball had landed, I almost jumped out of my Footjoys when I saw an eight-foot alligator a couple of feet away. You want to talk about scared shitless. Needless to say, I couldn't hit the ball for the rest of the day.

My most painful day on the course had nothing to do with losing money or getting hit by another cart. I was playing in our usual Tuesday afternoon foursome on the Lakes Course at Palm Aire Country Club when one of my partners hit his first shot out of bounds. The guy I was riding with was good enough to take a look for it and found it just on the other side of the stakes. I had exited the cart to hit my second shot and was standing just off the fairway. Jimmy, who had retrieved the ball, could only see out of one eye due to a little medical mishap years ago. As he threw the ball back to the rightful owner, he never saw me standing just a few feet away and launched a fastball hitting me in the cheek. My whole face felt like it was on fire and an instant headache was born. Two inches to the right and it would have missed me completely, two inches to the left and I would have owned Jimmy's house.

I worked on a golf course with a very attractive beverage cart girl for a year or so. Misty looked just like a Misty and could have danced at any strip club and cleaned up. She asked one day who I was working with. After I told her, she said, "He's kind of anal, isn't he? And not in a good way."

Anybody who has ever played golf has been nervous at one time or another. Whether it's for a $2 Nassau or a serious match with serious coin. If they tell you differently, they're lying. I was speaking with a guy once who had a pretty good game and had made his way onto a Florida senior event. He was about 55 at the time and was playing at the Trump National Blue Monster Course in Miami. He told me he got up to the 15th hole on that Friday afternoon and had a great chance of making the cut. He was two strokes inside the cutline and stood on the tee at the par 3. With that in mind, thoughts and ideas started to race through his head. His main concern was the fact that if he made the cut, he didn't have clothes to wear for the weekend. He stood on the tee with an 8-iron and that's all he could think about. The next shot went into the trap on the right. He took two to get out and recorded a smooth six on the hole. When he reached the next tee, he realized he wouldn't be needing clothes for the weekend.

If you have been fortunate enough to get a hole-in-one playing golf, you know about the thrill. There's also a price tag that goes along with it because you're buying drinks. My only one to date came on March 27, 1987. The course, now closed, was called Locke Ledge Country Club and was in Yorktown, NY. I can count on one hand the number of times I played golf with my father, so when I dragged him out that Friday morning, it was pretty special. The day was overcast and in the upper 50's. When we reached #14, I knew my tee shot was long, but it had just enough spin to suck it back into the cup. I haven't been able to do that since. My dad's eyes lit up and there was a quick high five. Good feeling.

During a yearly golf outing at the Canyon Country Club in Armonk, NY, I was paired up with a buddy of mine who worked in base operations at the airport. Pete was a solid partner and no stranger to the bottom of a glass. The day was going along pretty well, we had made a few putts, but knew we were nowhere close to being in the money. The beverage cart girl for the event, Liz, was also employed at the airport with us and had decided that a miniskirt with no panties was the attire of the day. Pete and I stood on the 11th hole tee box and we both figured we could cut the corner of the dogleg left over the tree line. After we both hit awful shots, it was time to go and find them in the timber. It was a popular decision by a lot of golfers and there was an actual path that went through the woods. Just then, we both noticed a brown leather wallet lying there. We were at least 20 yards deep into the brush and opened the bi-fold to see what Santa had left. When we got done counting, it was $1100 in cash and the typical credit cards and ID. Pete said he knew the guy and told me he was probably out here playing in this outing. At the dinner afterward, they gave out the awards, some golf balls, towels and the usual crap that is donated for the event. Pete and I went up onto the makeshift stage and told the audience that there was still one more award to be given. One of the promoters looked at us like we were crazy and motioned that there was nothing left to give out. Pete called out the man's name and he walked to the podium. "What did I win?" We then thought we would have some fun and asked to see his driver's license to ensure it was him. He reached for his back pocket and the sign of fear and 'OH SHIT!' lit up his face. "I think it's in my golf bag." He knew it wasn't in his golf bag. We tossed the wallet to him and a calm came over his face. He ripped off a C-note and passed it over to us. It was a nice gesture but that's like leaving a 9% tip if you were going out to dinner. My new rule of thumb is that if you find money, take your finder's fee of 20%. There are too many cheap people in this world which is almost in direct proportion to the amount of assholes in the world. When you return the item and they question you as to why there is money missing, you have an easy out. "First, if you think I took money, why wouldn't I take it all?" Then tell them, "I found your wallet, I returned it, that's all I know."

CHAPTER 37

THAT WAS SCARY

When the door slammed, I felt my heart try to connect with my brain that this was the right thing to do. The steel around me was nothing more than high-grade chicken wire. I took a deep breath and surveyed the interior of the cage. Yeah, I'm afraid of heights. Moments earlier, I was just standing around making a little extra cash, doing overtime on a job site. The building that was being constructed was going to be about 45 floors and was being erected in downtown White Plains, NY. The crew had finished up for the day and I was ready to get out of there. One of the construction workers I knew asked me if I wanted a free tour of the building which was still a shell with only concrete and iron girders. I should have told a lie or fabricated a story that I had something else to do or needed to get a manicure before I started my 4-12 shift. He urged me over to the service elevator which was attached to the exterior of the building. I had seen people use it often and thought to myself, *I'm never getting in that thing*, but that's where I was. The interior area was small and maybe could have fit six people. As we got in, I realized there was no backing out now. The elevator shook as we went to the highest floor possible. The ground below me disappearing and the continued rattling of the steel parts and mechanical hoist made for an interesting trip to the top. Bang! There was no gradual slowing or that familiar sound like in most elevators, you know that little ding... ninth floor. We hit so hard I thought we broke it. I was now feeling a little better as I walked off the lift and onto solid ground. The sky was clear and from where I stood, there was a great view to the south of New York City. The next two flights up required us to take steps which were only partially completed. Slabs of concrete with no handrails and open on either side. Finally, we took a wooden ladder that looked like it came out of your grandfather's garage to the top floor. We hoisted ourselves up through a small opening. There were no walls, no safety ropes and no way I was getting anywhere near the edge. We were on the roof over 500 feet up. The view was amazing, so was the lump still in my throat. We talked for a few minutes and I watched as my tour guide walked within a few feet of the perimeter. It didn't bother him a bit. I thanked him for the opportunity and couldn't wait to get down. 60 degrees out and my palms are sweating, it's only fear if you don't do it.

As a rookie cop, everything is new. And on this Sunday morning, it proved to be just that. I was walking a foot post in the downtown area and learning the ins and outs. You walk around enough and you can discover things that most people don't know. Hidden alleys, doorways and tunnels that were concealed below street level, and how many rats there are. I received the call about 10 in the morning and was about a five-minute walk away from the building where a burglar alarm had just been received. I checked the exterior of the premises, making my way around to the rear of the building which backed up to a parking garage and a recording studio. I pried on one of the doors and found it to be unlocked. After calling back to headquarters to inform them, I was advised there was nobody available to assist so I proceeded inside. I announced who I was with no response. The place was dark with only a few rays of sunshine coming through the front windows. My weapon was out of the holster and my heart rate was on full throttle. I had never been in this store before and, from first glance, it appeared to be a women's dress store or a tailor's shop. I yelled out a few more times with no response. I thought to myself, *Where the hell is the light switch in this place?* And that's why you carry a flashlight in the daytime. There were plenty of bolts of fabric and enough places where someone could hide. As I cautiously moved forward, out of the corner of my eye, I saw a suspect standing near the counter. My adrenaline was pouring out of my skin. My gun came up and my flashlight beam hit the subject square in the chest. As I started to give orders to the subject, I knew it was a waste of time. I was giving commands to a mannequin. I was really glad nobody was with me at that point because the jokes and pranks in the locker room would have gone on for weeks. I remember an incident when our street crime unit was trying to apprehend a suspect who was stealing bicycles from the downtown area. They brought out an $800 bike and set up surveillance waiting on the thief. Moments later, the guy shows up, takes the bike and rides off. They gave chase but he was gone before they knew what happened. That evening, pictures of bicycles were posted all over headquarters, everywhere you went there was a photo from a magazine of a Schwinn or Huffy just to remind the two cops who were involved. Over the urinal, a 10-speed, in the break room, a kid's bike with the banana seat, next to the water fountain, a tandem. Cops are ruthless, ya better have thick skin.

I've been on rollercoasters and have come to accept my fate should Space Mountain, the Aerosmith ride or Expedition Everest one day fall off the track and plummet to earth at a Disney Park. Did I already tell you I'm afraid of heights? This past spring, while on vacation in Saint-Martin in the Caribbean, I decided to throw all my chips in the middle and take on the extreme zip line course at a place called Lotterie Farm. It's located on the French side of the island and the mountain is called Pic Paradis. It's a little oasis off the beaten track that has a pool, restaurant and a couple of bars. An old sugar plantation about 300 years old that has seen a great makeover. My wife and I proceeded to the sign in counter where she was soon rejected after telling them that she has some heart issues. See what happens when you tell the truth? It's like going to the doctor's office and they ask how often you drink. The correct answer is 'Just socially'. It's not a couple of beers a week so why even begin to make up stories. The form was two pages long and stated the usual stuff that they were not responsible for anything should my harness break, I crash into a tree, or the native monkeys piss on you while you're in their jungle. I had never been on a zip line course before and thought that this was a good test. My wife, very disappointed, headed off to the pool and started drowning her sorrows in vodka and Diet Sprite. After meeting our guide we jumped into the rear of an old pickup and started heading up the road to the highest point on the island. There were three of us there that day with a guide that looked as if he had just sparked up with his buddies back at the shack. The instructions were very simple and in less than two minutes he had finished his dissertation. Always have your "D" rings attached to the lower line and use the one Michael Jackson glove you were given to break if necessary. This place doesn't give you a helmet; guess they figure the fall will probably kill ya. "Okay, who wants to be first?" Guess who didn't volunteer? After the first zip, it was a short climb down from the tree and then onto a series of ladder walkways that were unstable and made my heart race even more. Another zip atop a blanket of trees and the jungle that was below us. The course was exhausting and the climbing down from trees burned my calves and thighs. After about the 10th zip line, I had that feeling that I may be able to finish this. I was keeping up for the most part, but that would soon change. We were about halfway through the course when I hit reverse. The next task was to walk on a single guide wire about 40 yards through the jungle. I looked down and, due to all the foliage, couldn't see the ground below me. Scared shitless. There were two cables at shoulder height; one to latch onto and the other for your left hand. I froze. The guide came back and I told him I was done, "Where's the path to walk down?" "No path, you have to do this." I would have thrown up right there if I had been hydrated. I crept out onto the wire and took the baby steps I needed. The guide was urging me on and showing what happens if you should slip. He intentionally falls off the wire and the D-ring held him up. "Strong wires, man, you can do this." By him falling off the wire, it now caused a rippling effect and reverberation where my feet were. That didn't help. Inching across like a snail I made it to the other side. After about three more zip lines I'll be in the pool drinking a cold one. The adventure lasted about two and a half hours, and after climbing down from the last tree the rush was still there. Next time we just hit the bar.

With only a couple of years on the job, I got asked to be a part of an operation called "Clean Sweep." The roadwork had started months ago with an undercover cop from another jurisdiction who was buying cocaine, crack, weed and whatever else the dealers in our town would sell him. He would then identify the subject and, through the courts, get a sealed indictment for a warrant. This went on for some time as crack became the drug of choice in the late 1980's. After putting together all the names and addresses of these fine outstanding people it was finally time to go out and affect the arrests. With over 75 names on the list, we broke up into small teams and started knocking and ringing doorbells at 4 a.m. The first apartment we hit had all the makings of, "This is not good!" The guy refused to answer the door then proceeded to uncrate his pit bulls so they could bark and wake up the neighborhood. We finally made entry and told him for the fifth time what was happening. He still wasn't satisfied and backed into the kitchen with his two dogs on leashes between him and me. He didn't want to go to jail and I didn't want to start shooting animals. "If you let your dogs go they will be shot." The standoff went on for a couple of minutes until he finally realized we weren't there to sell him a timeshare in Cabo. He couldn't fathom that he was being locked up for something he did almost a year ago. With the dogs secured and the bracelets on the subject, we moved on to the next address.

I hate flying, and it only got worse after September 11, 2001. While I was working at the airport in the mid-80's, there was a pilot there who had started his own charter service called Westchester Air. He had a couple of planes and was running the wealthy to Martha's Vineyard, Nantucket, The Berkshires and wherever else their wallets wanted to go. David was a very likable guy and would often bring his aircraft close to the terminal to facilitate the loading and unloading of his passengers. He was never a douchebag about it either. He would always get with base ops or tap me on the shoulder and ask if there was room for about 10 minutes to get his passengers and cargo on the aircraft. He often told me that if I ever wanted a ride cheap, he would take care of me. Millie worked inside at the airport as a supervisor and she and I coordinated the daily grind of flights, ticketing, passengers, and all the problems that go with it. She asked me one day who the guy was I was talking to earlier out on the ramp. I gave her a brief background check and told her as far as I knew he wasn't wanted by the FBI. "Can you introduce me to him?" A few weeks later they were already on their third date and we all know what that means. Marriage followed and I figured my matchmaking days were complete, batting a thousand. On August 5, 1994, I finished up a round of golf mid-afternoon and headed over to a friend's bar called Tom & Jerry's. I ordered a pint and sat alone at a table reading through the morning paper. A small article listed a fatal plane crash of a Beech A100 King Air in North Adams, Massachusetts. David was listed as the only one on board. He had crashed just after takeoff at 4:05 in the afternoon.

While working at Palm Aire Country Club I met Nancy who was in charge of human resources and was an all-around good egg. Her husband, David, had been a juggler, clown, and worked with Ringling Brothers going through the school in Sarasota, Florida. He was an interesting guy who had unicycled across the United States at 22 and had done over 1100 skydive jumps. He had settled down and was now working for UPS delivering packages to the pro shop daily. We would bullshit for a few minutes each day then he would hurry down the hallway to see his bride. He took pride in the aircraft he had built and was always willing to take new people up and show off his aircraft. On November 29, 2009, the airplane he was flying crashed just east of Tampa, FL. There were no survivors. Two Davids, two planes, and I could have been on either one of them.

At an early age, my mother thought it was important for me to learn how to swim. I have never been a big fan of the water and hated going to these classes on a weekly basis at the YWCA. At some point during the learning process, the class had to dive into the deep end of the pool and swim to the far side. I was reassured by one of the teachers that it would be fine and she allowed me to take a position near the wall. She even went as far as to hold an eight-foot bamboo pole out that I could grab onto if I needed to. She told me it was going to be fine, "I'll be right here, you can do it." I dove into the pool knowing my safety net was there. When I came up for air there it was, two feet in front of me. She held that pole in front of my nose knowing it was just out of reach. Running out of breath and watching her walk with that pole away from me enraged me enough to swim to the side of the pool. There were some words exchanged and my career as an Olympic swimmer ended that day.

CHAPTER 38

WRAP IT UP

My mother told me a story when I was a small boy about her father who walked into the kitchen and told the family that they were down to their last $1.29. The choice going forward was whether to put food on the table that night or buy a harness for the oxen. Hey, ya gotta plow the fields. My grandmother kneaded a loaf of bread and went down to the cellar and got a couple of Ball jars of potato soup that she had canned six months ago. I try not to complain very much. My grandfather was like that, a man of few words. He had 13 children and a home that was only big enough for eight. It was another one of those mornings as he walked into the kitchen and told the family about the tragic news from the prior night. Four kids were walking home from a high school basketball game when a milk truck lost control on a snowy road. As the rig slid down the hill, three kids ran in one direction and Arthur in another. That's all it takes. The vehicle overturned and my uncle was gone before his 18th birthday. My grandfather relayed the information like he was giving a weather report; clouds giving way to partial sunshine in the afternoon. The day went on.

I met Frank through some friends after being on the police department for about five years. He owned a small liquor store in town where there was a card table in the back where we could sit down and write out reports, have lunch, or just bullshit for a while.

The poker game usually started about 1 p.m. or so with the usual players. He would always take care of me, vodka and bourbon at his cost, and never asked for anything in return. Frank got married in September of 1985 and had planned a honeymoon to Mexico. They were going to spend a night in Mexico City then fly to Acapulco the next day to enjoy a week at a resort on the Pacific Coast. At the reception, Frank was talking to one of his distant cousins who told him, "Why do you want to spend a night in Mexico City? That place is a shit hole." He told Frank he would cover the charge, getting them to change tickets and see if the resort had a room for the extra day. It all worked out well and a few days later, Frank and his wife boarded a plane out of New York City. They made their connection, and after eight hours of travel, they relaxed in the hot tub at the hotel. The following morning, September 19, 1985, an earthquake registering 8.0 hit Mexico City killing 10,000 as well as injuring thousands, destroying buildings, and knocking out the power for most of the city. Over 400 buildings collapsed in the quake and Frank and his wife were supposed to be in one of the hotels that was destroyed. Since the new plans between him and his cousin came along at the last minute, Frank never got around to telling his parents, family or friends about the new itinerary. Phone lines were out in Acapulco also, so Frank did what anybody else would do; ride horses along the beach with his new wife, have honeymoon sex, then cocktails back in the hot tub. They were able to make plans later in the week and with a little navigating and some help from the locals, they made it safely back home. His parents had feared the worst. With no phone calls and very little information being provided by the Mexican Government, they believed the two had been killed in the collapse of the hotel. Frank now walks into his parent's home and thinks it's a party for him returning home. He noticed all the cars on the block and thought, *What a nice gesture.* No, he walked in on his own wake. Family and friends dressed in black, pictures of him and his wife throughout the home, everybody eating Italian food and crying.

Have you ever been so tired that you have to stop and actually talk to yourself to figure out what you were supposed to do next? I'm not talking about where did I leave my car keys or what aisle did I park the car in at Walmart. You're so physically tired that you shake your head trying to remember the simple things you do every day. I recall driving to work one morning and drove right past the exit. 5 a.m. and I'm exhausted. Working two and sometimes three jobs during the week led to a lot of problems. I was wiped out, but then the caffeine from a Red Bull (which really doesn't give you wings… # lawsuit) or adrenaline from a late call at work would kick in, and I would drive home wide awake and couldn't fall asleep. A couple of drinks later and I could finally think about the mattress, set the alarm, get a four-hour nap, and do it all over again. This went on for a while and then I started sleepwalking, not remembering a thing and shaking it off like it was normal. My wife asked me once what the smell coming from the living room wall was. It was easy to blame the cat, but it was really me taking a leak in a Mikasa glass serving tray that was on top of a Bose 901 speaker. Who peed in the washing machine? I'll take the blame for that one too. Our friends invited us down to Long Beach Island in New Jersey for a long weekend and after a day working, we hit the road for the town of Beach Haven. After dinner, I can only recall the walk up a flight of stairs and then everything else is a mystery. At some point, while sleeping, I got up and decided to walk the streets of the island and somehow made it back home, naked and bleeding. I'm not sure when or where I got cut up or where my clothes are. Last year, some family and friends were staying at our home. The rule of thumb is whoever is putting you up for a week, you take them out to dinner once. I was told one morning that I was doing sit-ups in the living room at 3 a.m. after we had all gone to bed. My brother-in-law's friend came out to get some water in the middle of the night, saw what I was doing, and decided he was going back to bed. His words to me were, "I didn't want any part of that."

I trained for a solid three months biking almost every day. The plan was to ride from Plattsburgh, NY, where I was living, to my parents' home just over 300 miles away in White Plains, NY. I figured it would take about two and a half days if all went well. My bicycle was nothing special, 18 speeds with the old "U" shaped handlebars, and I had put a racing sprocket on the rear so there were only two speeds: fast and stopped. When I get something in my head, it becomes an obsession to a point and I try to do everything in my power so I don't look like a total asshole telling friends, "Nope, it didn't work out." Training started slow and worked up to me riding about 60 miles a day, three times a week. I used to ride up to the Canadian border after work, give a quick wave to the guard on duty, and then ride home. There were plenty of days with the sun setting and the wind out of the north that life was simple. It was just me, the bike, another cornfield, and another 20 miles to go. As I left work one day, just after 4 p.m., I was struck by a car making a left turn in front of me. The guy was barely apologetic, but who knew in the early 1980's you could sue anybody for anything. I should have laid on the street and called a lawyer. I sat on the curb looking at the bike and trying to figure out which part of my neck felt worse. I fixed the bike with a little help, and I was back riding a week or so later. It was now July 4th weekend in 1982, and I was going to hit the road at dawn Friday morning for the first leg of the trip. I was able to ride about 110 miles the first day with only one small tire problem that I was able to repair with some tools I had brought along. The bicycle was stripped down, no reflectors or kickstand and I had removed the rear brake. I even took the playing card out of the spokes. After a night in the hot tub at the motel, some serious painkillers and a cheeseburger, I was ready for day two. The following morning, after getting a fast 10 miles in, I stopped for breakfast in the small hamlet of Salem, NY. I ordered the two-egg special with bacon, home fries, rye toast, and the bottomless cup of coffee which came to $2.99. What's the punch-line? 'Ya get locked up for stealing as soon as you leave the place.' Everybody there knew everybody, I was such an outsider and felt the stares as I ate at the counter. The whole place is in flannel and denim and I'm wearing lycra bike shorts. My ride continued south on Route 22, passing the towns of Cambridge and Hoosick Falls where I saw the best name I have ever seen for a bar. It was called, "Third Base"... Last stop before home. By noon that day, I felt as if I had hit the proverbial wall. I was wiped out, the sun was blazing, and I pulled off the road in the town of Berlin, NY. I laid down on the grass in front of the high school and fell asleep in minutes. When I woke up and looked at my watch, my 15-minute cat nap had turned into almost an hour. I got back on the bike and had to make up for some lost time. I put in about 125 miles the second day and started losing some feeling in the palms of my hands and fingers from the amount of pressure holding onto the handlebars. The final day, I woke up to some guy called pain and it hurt just to get out of bed. I was in some dive motel in Amenia, NY. I told myself that if I didn't get up, the bed bugs were going to need liposuction. The last 60 miles were fairly easy with the gentle rolling hills and the anticipation of seeing the family. I rode the bike into the front yard early that Sunday afternoon and propped it up against the maple tree where the American flag stood in its usual place. My parents had no idea I was coming home. They were watching the men's final at Wimbledon on TV. Jimmy Connors against John McEnroe. I fell asleep on the living room floor and never saw the last set. I had already gotten my orders from the Air Force that I was being deployed to Japan that fall. I left the bike at my parents' home and hitchhiked my way back a week later.

It was just after lunch and whatever I had just choked down gave me that nauseous feeling in the pit of my stomach. It was just going to get worse. After years on the police force, I had heard just about every call which each dispatcher described in their own way. Boring call equals boring voice. Husband beating his wife and you can hear the anxiety as they try and describe the circumstances, weapons involved, children in the home and extent of injuries. The blood starts pumping. "Respond to the seventh floor of the Galleria parking garage, east side, report of a woman down and bleeding." The incident occurred across the street from our police headquarters. A woman walking to her car after lunch and maybe a little shopping in the mall. Today, it was more than that. Connie had been stabbed multiple times by an unknown assailant and would never make it home. Cops flooded the area. You try and set up a perimeter and stop anybody on the street who looks dirty and fuck their civil rights. Fuck the ACLU and I will lie on the stand if necessary to get some piece of shit off the street. Connie lived in town. Her kids went to school and played with my kids growing up. She was 56. A few blocks

266

away, a subject was stopped with no shirt on and sweating like he had just run a marathon. He was a registered Level 3 sex offender, homeless, and had recently been released from prison after serving 20 years for raping three women. He showed us where the knife was he used to end her life. In his statement, he said he wanted to kill a white woman that day with blonde hair and blue eyes.

We've all had those friends and acquaintances that seem to come into and out of our lives. Most friends from high school disappear when you get to college. It's like that when you move from job to job or change addresses. This guy I used to know would introduce himself to new faces as a retired director of adult films and his wife being a retired porn star. This was all done with a straight face and a full profile of some of his location shoots, people in the industry he had worked with, and movies he had done. Kinda creepy, you can judge for yourself. We were out one night and I introduced them to some friends of ours. The same old story was told, leaving our friends to believe all that was said. When the night came to an end, my friend Cindy - who thought she had just met porn king of South Florida - made it a point to give a wave and not have to reach in for that uncomfortable goodnight handshake. She later found out the real truth, he was just a regular guy with a boring job.

After the third cocktail on a hot afternoon, my bride was in no condition to drive, and after another dip in the pool was feeling the need for some nourishment. She was trying to talk me into some Chinese food, but I'm lucky if I can eat that mystery meat twice a year. She placed her order for delivery and got ready for some boneless spareribs, a little chicken and broccoli and a couple of spring rolls. So far, so good. After a quick exchange at the front door a half hour later, my wife walks back into the kitchen and opens the brown bag in the kitchen sink with the usual oil stains that have already eaten through the plastic containers. She starts pulling out a few fortune cookies, the mini packets of duck and soy sauce and the main portions of food. "Where are the spring rolls?" She yelled from the other room, expecting me to know and put out an all-points bulletin alert for them. Now she's in a bad mood and calls back to the restaurant where she got no resolution. The lady who answered the phone said they were packed in the bag. Then there was some confusion as to who packed the spring rolls. The conversation on the phone continued and she was told that if she wanted them, she would have to come back to the store to pick them up. Now my wife is going to drive there blowing a .16 and possibly catch a DWI for $2.50 worth of spring rolls. I was able to talk her down off the ledge for a minute and things started to calm down. It's hard to enjoy a meal when you're fuming inside. Five minutes later, my wife got back on the phone and as soon as the lady answered, she yelled, "ASSHOLE!" With that said, I figured this will be the last meal we ever eat from there. I poured myself another drink and sat down in my office as my wife began to clean up the food and put some dishes into the washer. Out of the corner of my eye, she was throwing away the brown paper bag and had some interesting news to tell me. "Honey, you'll never guess what's in the sink?" Spring rolls.

THE END

When I first met Jacques, he was larger than life. His body and presence would capture a room. He had a fantastic laugh and if he was telling a story, you listened for more. He did imitations from cartoon shows that were spot on. My favorite being, "Oh Magoo, you've done it again." It was November of 1987, and we were going through the police academy together. About six years later, when I was getting assigned to the wheel, Jacques had been appointed to the mounted unit; that means you ride a pony for a living and take care of it. He was one of only three guys assigned to the unit and would ride his horse around the downtown business area. Our job didn't have dogs at the time, but we had horses. When the chief was asked about this once, his reply was, "I would need a drug dog, a bomb dog, and a dog trained for searching residences and buildings. Who's going to supply the funds, training, and work with these animals on a 24-hour basis?" About 10 hands went up in the classroom. Everybody liked Jacques, he was just that kind of a guy. Before he could retire and get his pension, a strange thing happened. He had an affair with somebody, and before long the wife found out about it. She was so pissed she notified our department that Jacques was using drugs. The loveable guy who sat on the horse each day resigned soon after that.

Cops have parties and sometimes they get out of control. With a room full of guns, alcohol, and a few big egos, anything can happen. When the wives and girlfriends are around, the ratio goes up. There was a lieutenant on our job, married with kids, who stepped out from a party one night with a new recruit. She was hotter than your average cop with a couple of years on the job. Everybody saw them leave together and saw her return 45 minutes later. She walked back into Patrick's Pub and all she could say was, "He had whiskey dick, useless." The whole bar knew about it and that's where it stayed. During a retirement party at a bar called Dooley Macs, we were at the downstairs bar that felt like you were standing at a train station in India. The place was packed and a trip to the bathroom meant you lost your standing room only pass. I was lucky enough to be at the bar with a sergeant from the detective squad we called Iggy and his wife. I ordered another Guinness and was listening to the heated words that were now being passed between them. As the foam settled on top of the pint, she reached over with her left hand and slapped him as hard as she could across the face. There was no dramatic pause, he returned her blow with a backhand of his own that brought redness to her face and those little tears you get as the eyes start to swell. The whole bar witnessed the event. She left, and everybody went back to drinking.

20 years of being a cop, you work with a variety of personalities. Every day was like watching Guiding Light except you were the show. Nicknames were handed out like candy on Halloween. The oldest guy on the job was Pops, of course. We had the Admiral and the Colonel and Fighting Mike who also was the Shooter after being involved in two incidents, missing on both attempts. There was Jimmy Two Asses who should have gone on the Atkins Diet, and Desi, his biological twin. I worked with a cop we called Stylish Stevie. He wore a lot of silver and turquoise and thought he was performing on the strip. Late in his career, he walked around with the use of a cane after he stated he was struck by a vehicle while doing traffic control. I would see him walk to his vehicle on a Friday night, toss the cane into the trunk of the car, and never see it again till Monday morning. We had Buzz Lightyear, Deadeye, and a friend who was losing pigmentation in his hands that Shecky would call Two-Tone Cerone or The Gooch. Eric got his nickname from playing goalie on the police hockey team; Red Light. There was a cop called Rocky, not because he looked like Stallone but because he resembled Cher's son in the movie Mask. There was Big "E", the Wacky Packi, and a captain called Skeletor. It didn't matter if you were B.N. or J.R., once you put

the uniform on, we were all blue. They don't make movies and TV shows about dental hygienists. Everybody got made fun of at some point, and if you couldn't take it in the locker room, you wouldn't be able to take it on the street.

I drove 17 straight hours from New York to my new home in Florida. After 20 years, I no longer had to put on the uniform, wear the bulletproof vest or remember where my gun was. When I started to see unicorns on the highway, I was hoping the trip was almost over. A week or so later and still unpacking boxes, I met my next-door neighbor Frank and his wife, Vicky. They had both retired from the United States Air Force. He had been a pilot and she was a nurse. The couple were well into their 50's and had children from previous marriages. So, when I learned they had adopted a son, I thought to myself, *Why the fuck would you want to do that?* Alan was about seven when I first met him. He was a shy little nerdy kid with new glasses that he was getting used to. As the years passed, he became a martial arts fan and rode his bike around the neighborhood. The good times didn't last long. Soon, it would become a habit for him to jump out of his bedroom window on the second floor, make his way down the ridge line of the roof and jump onto the small patch of grass that separated our homes. The momentum from the jump would cause him to brace himself against my home, we would hear the bang at all hours of the night. Whenever I discussed it with Frank, it was like talking to a statue. Frank looked like Bill Belichick and spoke as little as possible. He would light up a cigarette from the one he just inhaled and throw the butts in the direction of my home. The kid grew up to be a real piece of shit. He got kicked out of high school in his first year and did about nine months in a drug rehab program. He would hang out with his drug friends in front of my home with his pants halfway down to his knees and tats covering his upper torso. He was leading the thug life and I had a front-row seat. It became a common occurrence to see a couple of police vehicles parked in front of the house. I kept a record of various cars that frequented the area and passed them along to the sheriffs who knew the kid all too well. One morning, at 5:30, some 16-year-old kid is standing in my driveway in the pitch black looking for Alan. It was not uncommon to smell weed out the back door or find liquor bottles in my side yard. In February of 2017, it all changed. I punched the middle button on the Keurig and looked into my backyard, a preserve just beyond my pool and lanai cage. I had an 8:30 tee time that morning and needed a trip to the library before the first hole. The two cops I saw out the back window with long rifles were nothing compared to what I saw in front of my home. At least 10 squad cars and unmarked vehicles parked on both sides of the street. After checking the home for Alan, a detective sergeant walked up my driveway and I met him in front of the house. The usual questions were asked, he handed me his card and appreciated all the information I had. About three weeks later, Alan, age 17, was picked up on armed robbery charges and murder. He and another genius are accused of killing a party about a half mile from here in a park late at night. It was the best news when I learned Frank was moving and the house was up for sale. Alan is still awaiting trial. When I looked at the house photos on Zillow, a strange irony came to mind. The last few pictures posted of the home also include photos of the nearby park where Alan was that night of the murder.

The sky was perfect that morning. That vivid blue which should be a Crayola color. Not a cloud around. The bride was off to work, and I laid on the living room floor with the PlayStation controller and Howard Stern talking off in the distance on his radio show. Hockey season was a few weeks away and I was warming up my thumbs. X, O, triangle, square. It was our generation and you remembered the day as it passed in slow motion. September 11, 2001. It was Pearl Harbor, it was Kennedy. When I went into work that afternoon, there was anger, fear, and a little 'We just got our asses kicked and what do we do now?' I spent that evening, a 4-12 tour, parked in an elementary school lot with all the guns and ammo I could get my hands on. The police radio was unusually quiet and the streets were empty. Stores in the area had closed and the sidewalks had been rolled up. I walked around the schoolyard a few times, not a kid around playing hoops or skateboarding. It was eerie. In the days to follow, a few guys from our job who had days off volunteered and went down to Ground Zero. There was so much help down there that they were turning people away who wanted to assist. So, was 9/11 a bunch of terrorists from the Middle East or was it our own government? Listening to the experts, I wonder. I wonder how a commercial aircraft flies at low altitude and at the speeds of 550 mph doesn't break up. I wonder how cell phone calls in 2001 could have been made from 30,000 feet. I look at the pictures from Shanksville, Pennsylvania, and can't believe that is the wreckage from a 757 that just crashed. No wings or tail section, not even a toilet. Two of my favorite movies with Robert Redford are 3 Days of the Condor and Spy Game. Both flicks about the CIA and what you will never know.

The lights flickered a few times, but the power was still on. I sat on the couch after dinner and listened to that first driving rain of the year. Another bolt of lightning and a crash of thunder. Dishes were going into the sink to be rinsed and there was nothing that was going to get me out of the house tonight. Then the phone rang. The trembling voice of my mom was on the other line. My dad had just collapsed in the living room. In the prior weeks, he had been diagnosed with cancer and been put into a medical coma. He was now back home and had suffered an apparent heart attack. My mom asked for my advice on what to do, which I thought was kind of strange coming from a registered nurse with over 40 years of experience. By the time I hydroplaned my way to her home, it was 30 minutes later. The ambulance was there and a fellow officer, Ernie Geraldez, was doing chest compressions on my father. I felt my father's hands and knew he was gone. I looked at Ernie and told him he could stop, "It's okay."

On November 6, 2014, my mother passed. The events leading up to this and those that took place afterwards still amaze me. I had sisters at the time. We weren't really close but we would make the three necessary phone calls a year for birthdays, Thanksgiving and Christmas. My older sister and I were both working two jobs, and my younger sister had not been employed for 10 years. She lived in Michigan with her husband and had no children. In the spring of 2014, I sat with my mom and older sister in the cancer treatment center. After several rounds of chemo, the doctor told my mother there was nothing more they could do. Instead of the tumor shrinking, it was growing. My mom leaned forward from the examining chair and told the doctor, "I will give you a million dollars if you can make me better." My mother never smoked or drank, but cancer doesn't care. She was now fighting the tumor that was attacking her mouth and cheekbone. Since my mother was going to need homecare, we asked our younger sister if she could take the lead. She seemed a little reluctant to do this, so my older sister and I agreed to give her money for being away from home and things she would need while caring for my mom. When I spoke to the doctor, she told me she had about six months to live. I flew up a couple of more times from Florida and my older sister would make the drive from Upstate New York to my mother's home. I felt we were all involved and, for the most part, communicating. My mother's twin sister also flew in from Montana to lend a hand. We were all there in her bedroom the night she took her last breath. The following day, my older sister suggested that a trip to the lawyer's office should be made concerning the estate. My younger sister and I went there and they were shocked that we were in their office less than 24 hours after her passing. Don't I feel like a real jackass? My older sister looked at the drafted letter from the law firm and couldn't believe the $20,000 price tag they wanted in order to settle all the accounts. My older sister knew a vast majority of what mom's financial status was and began working on it right away. There was no way she was going to pay 20 grand. See, my mom didn't just have one account, she had over 20 spread out with various banks and agencies. First thing Monday morning, my older sister was on the phone calling each one to get transfer paperwork set up. This is when it started to get ugly. I was still mourning the loss of my mother and she was yelling on the phone to some kid who was still working on his series 7 license. Most people get buried after they die. Not when it comes to my sisters. After my mother was cremated, they wanted to wait till the following summer to take her ashes back to a family cemetery in Pennsylvania. I was later informed that my oldest sister's husband was going to dig the grave. When it came to selling my mother's home, it was another debacle. The oil burner was rotting out, the radon levels were unacceptable, and the main water valve needed to be replaced. I was ready to bring in a 30-yard dumpster and start throwing stuff away. My sisters, on the other hand, needed four months so they "could go through everything." I was outvoted: girls 2, me 1. Between the two of them, they would overthink each issue that came up. There were interviews with contractors and spreadsheets that littered my inbox. I had a friend on the police force who had sold my last home and didn't take the usual sales commission. Trying to convince the two of them that 4.5% is better than 6% was like teaching them Chinese algorithms. The frustration continued for months and I began to hate each one of them more and more. Let's talk money. We were all in the black. I had no idea how two civil servants could have put away and invested that much money over the course of a lifetime. I guess those egg salad sandwiches and meatloaf again for dinner was all part of the master plan. When I left my parents' home for the last time, I took my dad's Billy clubs from when he was a cop, a Korean War helmet, two blankets my mom had made for me and the American flag that was on my father's casket. I left my sisters thousands of dollars in jewelry, furniture, you name it, for them to fight over. It still wasn't good enough for them. My anger came to a pinnacle when I received letters from both demanding additional monies for things they had done. It included driving expenses, tolls, 49 cent stamps and even wanting reimbursement for vet bills. We had a three-way call one night and I was about four deep at the time. I offered to give them five grand each, more than what they were asking for, if they promised to never to talk to me again. Here's the best news: We haven't spoken since and I'm fine with that.

I hope you weren't expecting a Stephen King novel or something by Patterson. Nope, just a few stories from my life. My wife often wonders why I watch the same movies over and over again. You know, Goodfellas, Jason Bourne series, Pulp Fiction, and The French Connection. The endings are predictable, but at least I don't have to sit through two hours of garbage. So, how long does it take to write a book? Just over four years. In that time, I've lost my mom, a brother-in-law, and had to put down two beloved animals. Nobody gets out alive. My final thoughts in today's world: Stand for your flag, have eyes in the back of your head, and the toilet paper always goes over the top.

Edited by my beautiful daughter, Amanda Leah Sturino.
If there are any mistakes, you can call her to complain; I believe she
gets a flat rate of $400 an hour.

Cover photography by Matthew Henry

Toronto, Ontario

Made in the USA
Middletown, DE
20 December 2018